Black Obses

Also by Gregor Paul:
Hard Men Fight Back (Exisle 2006)
The Reign of King Henry (Exisle 2007)

BLACK OBSESSION

The All Blacks' Quest for World Cup Success

GREGOR PAUL

EXISLE
PUBLISHING

First published 2009
Exisle Publishing Limited,
P.O. Box 60-490, Titirangi, Auckland 0642, New Zealand.
'Moonrising', Narone Creek Road, Wollombi, NSW 2325, Australia.
www.exislepublishing.com

National Library of New Zealand Cataloguing-in-Publication Data

Paul, Gregor, 1972-
Black obsession : the All Blacks' quest for World Cup success /
Gregor Paul.
ISBN 978-1-877437-31-1
1. All Blacks (Rugby team) 2. World Cup (Rugby football)
3. Rugby Union football—Tournaments. 4. Rugby
Union football—New Zealand. I. Title.
796.33365 —dc 22

Text and cover design by Sarah Theodosiou
Printed in China through Colorcraft Limited, Hong Kong

Contents

Introduction

THE IDEA OF writing this book was hatched about 10 seconds after the All Blacks crashed out of the 2007 World Cup. In the higher reaches of the Millennium Stadium, two Kiwi girls had climbed onto their seats, their faces painted black, their optimism so strong it shone in their eyes. Fate had stuck them next to two Frenchmen of similar age and with a comparable passion for their country; the red, white and blue was starting to streak a little on their cheeks in the wake of what was no doubt a hefty pre-match indulgence. The atmosphere crackled with tension and yet, for all the previous failures, there was almost zero expectation among those clad in black that something could go horribly wrong.

Not this time. 1999 was a freak. 2003 was a case of being a little complacent and then coming up against the full cunning of the Wallabies. 2007 would be different and, 20 minutes into the quarter-final, the two Kiwi girls certainly let their new French friends know that was the case. By half-time, there was just a hint of some of the confidence drifting. With 20 minutes remaining, the Kiwi girls watched in abject silence and when the whistle blew on 80 minutes, there were tears – made worse by the opportunistic inquiry from the Frenchmen as to whether there was any possibility the two New Zealanders had tickets for the final.

The unthinkable had become the thinkable once again. The All Blacks had crashed out of the World Cup, just as they had done in 1991, 1995, 1999 and 2003. How could this be? This wasn't a bunch of schmucks drawn from the local pub and chucked out to play without a single world of advice. This was the All Blacks – the world's undisputed best team. A team crammed with supremely talented players, a team that had lost, prior to the quarter-final, just three games in three years; a team that hadn't lost at home for four years; a team that had been setting the highest standards since 1905; and a team that had, by some distance, the greatest winning ratio in the history of the sport. The All Blacks were rated so strongly by most bookmakers that they really weren't worth a punt.

It hadn't been so different in any of the previous World Cups. The All Blacks were the side no one really thought could be beaten. That belief wasn't flimsy; it had grown out of the fact that for most of the period between World Cups, the All Blacks were rarely beaten. And that's why the story of their continued failure at World Cups became truly fascinating in 2007.

This was the most vexing phenomenon. The All Blacks had developed rugby's version of the yips. Like a quality golfer who's prone to missing the easiest putts when under pressure, the All Blacks had become masters at blowing up in World Cups. They could win in any stadium, but when it came to the World Cup, they just couldn't do it. The undisputed best team in the world, the standard bearer for the last century, had one measly World Cup victory to its credit. That simply didn't add up. That would be like Tiger Woods ending his career with one US PGA title, or Roger Federer calling it quits with the French Open his only Grand Slam success.

There really couldn't be an easy answer to this ongoing disappointment. It couldn't be explained by saying the All Blacks' opponents had simply risen above themselves on the night. The All Blacks had encountered the same opponents at their peak on previous occasions and dealt with them.

And the pattern was too entrenched. If the All Blacks had lost once unexpectedly, that would be understandable. The beauty of sport is its unpredictability, its endless capacity to spring surprises. But the defeat in 2007 was the third time the All Blacks had entered a knockout game strongly fancied, only to succumb rather meekly. It was also the third time in succession the All Blacks had fallen to an opponent they'd crushed only months before the tournament. It was also the third time in succession that their decision-making had disintegrated when they started to trail on the scoreboard. The similarities in the way the All Blacks lost couldn't really be a coincidence.

Two things became apparent. First, there was clearly a systemic fault in the development programme of New Zealand's élite players – a fault that only really showed up at World Cups when the pressure applied was at its most intense. The World Cup was like an ultraviolet light at a crime scene, exposing evidence undetectable in a less harsh glare.

The second inescapable conclusion was that New Zealanders are obsessed with this vexed issue of World Cup failure. The inconsolable Kiwi girls shed tears as much out of bewilderment and frustration as they did because they were hurting. How could this keep happening? So they, like every other New Zealander, were left wondering in the days and months after the World Cup.

This book is essentially an attempt to deal with that very question – it is a search for answers, an exploration of how the strands of the rugby development package tie together. The All Blacks have always been a finishing school, a place for the very best to gather after they've proven their worth. So much goes into making each individual All Black; so much impacts upon them way before they get anywhere near the national team.

It may seem a little simplistic, but this book began with the premise that the development system has warped in the professional age. The pattern of World Cup failure has been consistent since money came into the game, while the only time the All Blacks have lifted the William Webb Ellis trophy was back in the amateur period. Everything points to New Zealand having lost something in the transition. The secrets of the amateur age were not all taken to the other side.

It's stating the obvious to say that since David Kirk held the World Cup aloft in 1987, New Zealand has undergone massive changes. Of course it has, on every front. The idea behind what follows is to try to determine how new societal values, how the softened education system, and how the very existence of professionalism – where players no longer work as well as play – have contributed to the All Blacks' World Cup failures.

Although there's an element of comparing and contrasting the development packages of the professional and amateur eras, more central to the narrative are the voices of many of the 1987 All Blacks. These are the only men to have been successful at a World Cup, and their testimony as to what worked for them should not be dismissed. It is by understanding the pathway followed by the men of 1987 that we can start to see how things have drifted in the professional age, how educational and societal standards have been eroded by a modern world determined to find instant gratification and the easy fix.

The aim of this book is to provide some clarity, and also to give Kiwis everywhere a greater understanding of why their heroes have fallen when the eyes of the world have been on them. The fixation with World Cup failure is one that needs to be broken. It can't be much fun living with so many questions, with the memory of disaster looming but without being able to exorcise the ghosts of World Cup humiliation.

If this book can serve as a self-help guide, it will have fulfilled its goals.

1
Simple times

IT WASN'T SO very long ago that New Zealand really did come to a standstill when the All Blacks played a test. Back in the 1950s and 1960s it was true that rugby in New Zealand was religion. An All Black test was a big event for the country – as big as a visit by the Queen, or maybe even bigger. Even now, more than 50 years on, there are thousands of New Zealand men who could name the starting line-ups and scorers from every test played in the never-to-be-forgotten 1956 series against the Springboks. The opening test in Dunedin had the country in such a fever that people were filing into Carisbrook from 8 am in the hope of securing a prime spot on the terraces.

It meant everything to be there, to be able to recount years later from personal experience the story of that day. And it meant everything because All Black tests were one of the few occasions when New Zealanders were united in a common cause. It was an opportunity for a young nation to express itself on the international stage. And it was hugely important for the nation's collective esteem that the All Blacks won, or at least conducted themselves in a way of which the nation could be proud.

Rugby was in so many ways the ideal sport for New Zealand. This was a nation of pioneers, of men and women who had arrived here with a commitment to build a better life. Just surviving the voyage from Britain required enormous mental and physical reserves. And once the new settlers came ashore their commitment to that better life was severely tested. The new arrivals had to do it the hard way. Trees had to be felled, land ploughed, houses built and food grown – all with their own fair hands. There was no one to whom they could turn; every problem had to be solved through hard work, ingenuity and perseverance.

It just so happened that these qualities were imperative for rugby. There was a rugged side to the sport that appealed to New Zealanders. Most settlers had endured tough times and working the land was physically demanding. It was a battle just to stay alive and much of New Zealand's early history was dominated by conflict.

All of that made rugby the perfect vehicle for New Zealanders. The sport embodied so many of the values and traits they held close to their hearts. To be good at rugby was tantamount to being a good New Zealander. That's why All Black tests were a big deal. When the best 15 players in the country were gathered and wearing their black jerseys, they were charged with not only winning a game of rugby – they were also effectively being asked to demonstrate a way of life, to play in a way that highlighted the positive values to which New Zealand society adhered.

Here was this country, terribly isolated from the rest of the world and from the motherland in particular, and it needed a way of saying, 'Look how we're thriving! The better life everyone came here for is a reality, and to prove it here's our national rugby team epitomising all that we believe in.'

It's also true that New Zealand was a simpler society during most of the twentieth century. Everything was underpinned by honesty, hard work and self-reliance. People didn't lock their doors. They didn't have to because there was trust. Neighbours looked out for one another and everyone had a feeling of being in it together. Where else in the world would you have found honesty boxes the way you did here? This was a country with soul, with integrity at its core, and generation after generation of New Zealanders grew up in a society where the best of human values shaped day-to-day life.

Self-reliance was a big theme. It wasn't only the farming fraternity who provided for most of their own needs. Even in the towns and cities there were plenty of families making their own jams and chutneys in summer and relying on their vegetable gardens through the winter. New Zealand was not a country that took convenience for granted. It wasn't the sort of place where people ate out because the fancy took them.

A make-do-and-mend attitude prevailed, and it was a fend-for-yourself kind of place – but never in the sense that you only looked after your own. This attitude was born out of the knowledge that there were few support structures in place for families to lean on. To get ahead, mums and dads had to sweat, but that didn't breed selfishness when it came to enjoying the fruits of hard work. Sharing was a big part of life. Neighbours popped in to offer a jar of homemade this or that. If it had been a good day on the water, no one stuck the fish they couldn't eat in the freezer. Friends would come round and before anyone knew it, there would be plates of salad, a pavlova and some cold ones – everyone chipped in and did what they could because that was the New Zealand way of life.

It might seem too long a bow to draw, but that really was what the All Blacks represented – that way of life, and those core values. That's why the nation stopped for rugby tests. The All Blacks were almost a measure of how New Zealand was progressing as a society. To see the side play with perseverance, with courage, with individual flair backed by team-work, was to believe that all was well with the New Zealand way of life. For those values to have been so prominently displayed, it followed that they had to have been learned and absorbed away from the field. The All Blacks were a product of their environment.

At another level, excitement was generated by the novelty of All Black tests. In those days there was definitely an appreciation that less was more. Anticipation was everything back then. Such was their rarity that All Black tests were collectors' items.

Logistics, and the fact rugby was an amateur sport, played their part. Not until the late 1900s was it possible to jump on a plane in Auckland and be in London 24 hours later. To get to the UK was a major. To get to South Africa was a major. Even getting to Australia was a mini-ordeal. Nor was it possible for players who had jobs to down tools for a few months every year and head off yonder to play rugby. As much as every-one loved a series against the Springboks, or to follow the fortunes of the All Blacks touring the motherland, the number of tests had to be limited.

Rugby was organised on an ad hoc basis until the 1980s, when more regular commitments were built into the calendar. Up until then it had been a case of making a little go a long way. The All Black programme between 1950 and 1980 was built more around tour games than tests when the team was offshore. And when the All Blacks were in New Zealand it was the same principle – the touring team would be subjected to an arduous schedule against provincial and select sides ahead of a test series.

This was a slow-burning strategy – a way for interest in both the tourists and the potential make-up of the All Black team to gradually intensify. The provincial and select sides were stacked with aspiring All Blacks and they were on trial as much as the touring international side. Likewise, when the All Blacks were on tour, the interest would build in the make-up of their first test selection. By the time the first test of any tour came around there was familiarity with the hosts, usually a fair bit of respect if they'd performed well in the provincial encounters, and a raging excitement about the prospect of New Zealand putting forward its best side.

For most of the period between 1950 and 1980 the All Blacks generally played just one opponent in each season, except when they travelled to the UK where they were likely to play all or most of the home nations. In any given year the All Blacks tended not to play more than four tests, which was the preferred number of games per series. The administrators of the day wouldn't want to take any credit for a policy that was driven more by restrictions than design, but they could legitimately be termed marketing geniuses. They stumbled upon a formula – it doesn't matter how – that engaged the public and kept interest at peak levels throughout a season. And they did it year after year.

Their cause was helped by the simplicity of the times and the lack of those alternative entertainment options that make it so hard now for rugby bosses to gain their share of the limelight. This was an age when sport, both playing it and watching it, was what most New Zealanders did. The rugby club was the focal point of the community. There were no PlayStations or iPods to distract the youth. Television was in its infancy and the notion of watching the box hour after hour was foreign to a population that yearned for the great outdoors. Shops weren't open on Saturdays, other sports had less traction and really, for young blokes, it was expected – almost compulsory – that come the weekend they'd stick on a pair of boots and play rugby.

It was through playing and being part of a club that interest flowed naturally to the top of the heap. There was something quintessentially Kiwi about watching the All Blacks. It was almost a patriotic duty to go to the game. At the very least it was expected a family would huddle round the radio or pile into the neighbour's lounge to watch their TV. It wouldn't matter where the All Blacks were playing. Generations of young men dragged their weary bones out of bed in the middle of the night to huddle round the radio with Dad to listen to games being played in South Africa and the UK. In fact, for many young men it was those sessions in the wee small hours that were the best part of following the All Blacks. The imagination would run wild, the dream of becoming an All Black was fortified, and stronger bonds were forged with Dad.

By the time they had played 50 tests – between 1903 and 1935 – they had amassed a win ratio of almost 75 per cent.

One other critical factor played a major part in elevating interest in All Black tests – the team enjoyed an exceptional win record. By winning so many of their early tests they established a precedent that created both interest and a need to see the tradition preserved. As time rolled on, winning became more and more important and the desire to maintain such a proud record never abated. All these factors combined to make New Zealand resemble the scene portrayed by WH Auden in his poem *Stop all the Clocks*. It wasn't death bringing the nation to a standstill though – it was the All Blacks.

NEW ZEALANDERS are not renowned for getting ahead of themselves. That probably comes from their pioneering instincts that warn against counting chickens before they're hatched. The early settlers knew there were threats lurking everywhere and it was only when the last of the crop had been safely harvested that a sigh of relief could be heaved. That attitude lived on for most of the twentieth century. New Zealand was a country that lived in the now, and that was absolutely the case when it came to the All Blacks.

A legacy could only be built one game at a time. There were no short-cuts. Those were the attitudes that served New Zealanders well in life so it was only to be expected they were the values that would be adopted by the All Blacks. They only lost three of their first 21 tests. By the time they had played 50 tests – between 1903 and 1935 – they had amassed a win ratio of almost 75 per cent. South Africa were the hardest nut to crack, particularly over there. If tests against the Boks were set aside, the

All Black win record would have been more than 80 per cent for that period. The nation had a rugby team of which they could feel enormously proud. If the All Blacks were an extension of New Zealand society, if they were indeed a team that embodied the noblest values of a way of life, then the fledgling nation was doing plenty right. The All Blacks were a team to make New Zealand proud.

There were some blips, however. In 1938 the All Blacks played three tests and lost them all. There was also that infamous year, 1949, when they lost all six tests played. And every tour to South Africa ended with a higher number of tests lost than won. But blips are only blips because they run against the norm – which in the case of the All Blacks was an extended period of excellence.

What helped sustain that excellence was a certainty that winning was all that mattered. Test matches weren't about coming second. Victory was the only thing that counted – such was the culture that developed among the All Blacks. Everyone coming into the side inherited this obligation to win. There was no ambiguity. It was not a case of play well and everything will be okay. It was a case of win and everything will be okay. Settling for anything else would leave an individual in grave danger of losing his spot in the side. To help maintain that culture, no one ever looked beyond the test in which they were playing.

That did two things. First, it heightened the anticipation and drama of every test. There was no sense of a test against the Wallabies being any less worthy than a test against the British Lions or Springboks. Really, there are no degrees of murder and that was the attitude to tests. Losing to the Wallabies was no easier to take than losing to the Lions. That was the inescapable truth – every test was of equal importance because each time the All Blacks played they were carrying the hopes and aspirations of the nation. The All Blacks were the international face of New Zealand, ambassadors in black carrying the flag for a nation too easily overlooked given its size and location.

The second factor born of taking each game as it came was the development of a culture that had every All Black feeling he was potentially playing his last game. The only way to win a second cap was to play exceptionally in the first. And the way to do that was to treat it as the most important 80 minutes of your life. That was the All Black way and it was why the team believed you should never give a sucker an even break. It was madness to believe that being injured wasn't potentially disastrous for a test career. If the bloke replacing you did well, that could be it – you might never get another look-in. It was not an environment where sentiment and sympathy were in evidence.

The All Blacks phenomenon was day-to-day, week-to-week, and it sustained interest. It brewed passion among the people, drew them to the team and meant that when they played, the nation stopped. This was their team and it was a team that they held close to their collective heart. It was as much the responsibility of the wider populace as it was of the 15 men on the field to do their part in securing victory.

To outsiders, this devotion to the All Blacks might have looked extreme; the fact that whole communities became ghost towns every time the All Blacks played might have seemed a bit over the top. But the passion, commitment and belief were not done for effect. It was all for real; this was a much simpler age. Rugby was the lifeblood of the community – it was the sport that made young men, defined New Zealand and marked it out as different from much of the rest of the Commonwealth. New Zealand was a nation of battlers, of innovators, of hard workers. Children grew up outdoors with only their imaginations and basic toys, and mostly they grew up with Mum at home.

Saturday wasn't a day for decadence, not a day for the wheels of capitalism to spin ever faster. It was a day for sport and that meant rugby. No one needed fast cars or electronic gadgets to feel good about themselves. No one needed a flash suit to feel fulfilled. New Zealanders lived in a world where fulfilment came from playing rugby and watching the All Blacks win. That was enough between 1903 and 1986. All the nation needed was an All Black victory and they could find reason to be chipper at work on Monday morning. But in 1987, the year of the inaugural World Cup, everything changed. From that point on, just winning tests was no longer enough.

2
Unhealthy obsession

ON THE FACE of it, having a Rugby World Cup was a grand idea. Even if it was just to prise loose the fingers of those quaint old public school-boy duffers who were clinging desperately to their control of the code. By 1987 rugby was barely amateur – much to the disgust of the home unions. The French were up to all sorts, renting apartments for players, finding them fictitious jobs and providing fast cars to get them to training. The South Africans had much the same view about how they could operate professionally under the façade of amateurism and in New Zealand there were ways and means to make sure those who could play a bit were able to get by.

The administration of the sport was split. There were those in the original rugby nations – England, Scotland, Ireland and Wales – who had deeply ingrained Corinthian values. For the administrators in those countries, the challenge was to preserve and maintain the code just as it was. They didn't want to see money change hands. They didn't want professionalism and they didn't want a World Cup.

In direct contrast, there were driven administrators in the southern hemisphere and in France who felt it was all too reminiscent of King Canute to believe the tide of professionalism could be resisted. The sport had become a joke. Clubs everywhere were stuffing cash – in the form of free apartments, transport, or the folding stuff itself – into players' pockets. It was ridiculous to pretend they weren't and just as futile to believe the sport was not going to have to embrace professionalism.

Organising a World Cup would accelerate the conversion to

professionalism. There was no way the world's best players could, every four years, take six to eight weeks off work to play in the tournament. There was no way – even if the best players in the world did have generous employers who would sanction that much time off – they were going to think it was a fair deal generating millions of dollars for per diems in return. A World Cup would force those old boys swigging brandy in the smoking lounges of their gentlemen's clubs to confront the issue of professionalism.

But the World Cup would also do something else – it would create an official and globally recognised mechanism for judging the world's best teams. The All Blacks' winning record may have pointed to them being the world's premier team, but the eclectic pattern of touring made for an imprecise assessment of just who was the best.

The northern hemisphere had an annual Five Nations tournament to establish their hierarchy. But however good the winning side might have looked, however much they gave the impression they knew what they were doing, the All Blacks would invariably come along and burst their bubble.

Scotland and Ireland to this day have never beaten the All Blacks. Wales have managed it three times and England six. France have the best record against the All Blacks of any European side, having claimed the most treasured scalp 11 times. Even with 11 wins though, France can only claim a 27 per cent success rate against the All Blacks. England can only claim 23 per cent and prior to the 1987 World Cup the English had only managed three wins against the All Blacks.

There was no real dispute among the Five Nations – they were unanimous the All Blacks were the best side in the world. The Australians would, maybe, have grudgingly admitted as much on the eve of the 1987 World Cup. They had regular exposure to the All Blacks through the Bledisloe Cup. It was an intense rivalry and one where the All Blacks just managed to retain the whip hand. The Wallabies were good enough to usually secure at least one test win per series and the occasional series. They were good enough to win the All Blacks' respect and good enough to always believe they were in with a chance every time they met. But isolate any decade and the Wallabies could never win more than 40 per cent of the Bledisloe encounters.

The only nation disputing the All Blacks' right to be crowned world champions were the South Africans. The All Blacks had never won a series in South Africa prior to the 1987 World Cup. In fact, prior to 1987, the Springboks had beaten the All Blacks 20 times and had only lost 15 tests with two drawn. Strangely though, while the Boks might have seen themselves as the best team in the world, no one else agreed.

The All Blacks had an aura – a more defined chemistry – that gave rise to the perception of invincibility. The All Blacks carried a mystique in a way the Boks never did. It was the All Blacks that captured the imagination of the rugby world, not the Boks. And it was the All Blacks that every other nation saw as the team to emulate in terms of training standards. Young players in the UK grew up believing there was no greater achievement in the game than defeating the All Blacks. Sure, it would be great to beat the Springboks, but that would never fill the soul in the same way as felling the mighty All Blacks. Some of that had to do with the Springboks' isolation.

Following their turbulent and divisive tour of New Zealand in 1981, the Boks were forced into the wilderness as a consequence of South Africa's oppressive apartheid regime. That lack of exposure to international audiences made it hard for them to win hearts and minds offshore. And also it's probably true that many saw the Springboks as a symbol of all that was wrong with South Africa. It was hard to love or respect a team that appeared to stand for the values so many non-South Africans found abhorrent.

The Springboks were not invited to participate in the 1987 World Cup. And even if they had been there, it still would have been the All Blacks that started the tournament as favourites. The World Cup was, as far as most rugby followers could tell, a vehicle that could be used by the All Blacks to ratify their status. Everyone knew they were the best team in the world. Everyone knew they'd been upholding the highest standards for almost 100 years, and everyone knew that in their own backyard they would be just about impossible to beat.

WHILE THE rest of the world was certain about the likely outcome of the 1987 World Cup, neither New Zealanders in general nor the All Blacks themselves felt so sure.

The previous year had been a turbulent one. The rebel Cavalier Tour to South Africa had stirred the emotions and caused tension. It was a tour that incurred the wrath of administrators and fans on many levels. There was the obvious point of concern that the tour broke the international boycott intended to pressure the South African Government into dropping apartheid. There were also strong suspicions that players on both sides were well paid for their endeavours and the International Rugby Board was not happy.

From an All Black playing perspective, the tour had two major consequences. It forced the New Zealand Rugby Union to select the so-called 'Baby Blacks' for two tests in 1986, as all those who travelled with the Cavaliers were banned for two internationals. That tested the depth of talent in New Zealand, which proved to be considerable. Into the side came Sean Fitzpatrick and Joe Stanley – two men who would go on to enjoy long and memorable All Black careers. It also saw David Kirk assume the captaincy and John Kirwan establish himself as a wing of enormous potential.

That was the positive side to the enforced selection of the 'Baby Blacks'.

There was also a downside: the established test players, the men who went away as Cavaliers, had to be melded into the team after they had served their ban. That was difficult on an emotional level. There was potential for resentment towards those who had gone on tour, filled their pockets with loot and broken international agreements.

The 'Baby Blacks' beat France in the opening test of the year in Christchurch, but then lost to the same opponent in the final test of the year in Nantes. That left a bad taste in the mouth. It was one of those old-fashioned brutal games where the French were up to no good, testing the boundaries and mixing their aggression with breathtaking flair. The All Blacks never looked comfortable with the intensity and lost 16-3.

That defeat capped a bad year – one in which the All Blacks had lost four tests.

But if there was one thing history had shown, it was that the All Blacks always bounced back. They had blips in form, not slumps. That was what the players, and coach Brian Lochore, had to convince themselves of at the beginning of 1987. The rest of the world saw the All Blacks as the team to beat, as the most likely, indeed only, winners of the inaugural World Cup. The All Blacks had to buy into some of that belief.

The other thing the players had to do, as Lochore made clear, was to bury the past. Any resentment or bitterness around the Cavalier tour had to be let go.

And so it was that an emotionally focused, harmonious All Black team kicked off the 1987 World Cup. And they did indeed kick it off in dramatic fashion, pounding Italy 70-6. The Fijians got much the same treatment when they faced the All Blacks five days later at Lancaster Park in Christchurch. The All Blacks won their second pool game 74-13 and then toasted Argentina 46-15. The tournament was supposed to get serious in the knockout rounds but the truth was that the All Blacks were just far too good. Scotland, whom they met in Christchurch at the quarter-final stage, had played some impressive rugby to draw with France and hammer Zimbabwe and Romania. But as hard as the Scots tried, as much as they gave, they couldn't even get close to the All Blacks. In a performance that oozed control, aggression and exemplary basic skills, the All Blacks cruised to a 30-3 victory to set up a semi-final encounter with the Welsh in Brisbane.

Australia had co-hosted and the Welsh had been based over there, possibly giving them a slight advantage. Or possibly not. The All Blacks clicked into fifth gear and destroyed Wales. Really destroyed them. It looked like a team of professionals playing a team of amateurs. The All Blacks were supremely fit. Their physiques were entirely different from those of the Welsh. The All Blacks played a ruthless, relentless game where they charged around at 100 miles an hour, yet every player in black knew exactly what he was doing.

Confirmation of the All Blacks' status came at Eden Park on 20 June when they beat France 29-9. The result had never been in doubt. John Drake, the late All Black tight-head, speaking shortly before his sudden death in December 2008, said that by the final even the All Black players had started to see it that way.

'I remember on the morning of the game talking to [hooker] Sean Fitzpatrick, and we both agreed we were going to win the game and we both wished that we could hurry up and get it over and done with. That was it. It was very matter of fact,' Drake recalled. 'It was a great relief and for a lot of us, because of the game against France the year before, it was certainly the monkey off the back. We were a bit disappointed that we thought we could probably have played a bit better, but we won it. We probably didn't appreciate what it was because it wasn't such great stakes in those days. We had a bloody good night with the French and went back to work on the Monday.'

There was no street parade. No great emotional outpouring. There was no bunting. People didn't jump in their cars waving New Zealand flags while driving endlessly round fountains. There were some beers with friends, a bit of a sing-song and a kebab on the way home. Some of the players even turned out for their clubs the next day, albeit with fuzzy heads. And the reason the nation didn't dance itself into a frenzy was that, really, all the All Blacks had done was ratify their position as the best side in the world.

Everyone – the Scots, the English, the French, the Irish, the Fijians, the Italians, the Zimbabweans, the Romanians, the Canadians and the Argentineans – knew the All Blacks were going to win the 1987 World Cup. And if the truth be told, despite the turbulence of 1986, New Zealanders knew too. But it wasn't just the inevitability of the victory that subdued celebrations. No one knew how big the World Cup would become in later years. In 1987 it felt like it was important without necessarily being worth going nuts over.

More important for New Zealanders, it also felt like it might be best to pace the celebrations. There was no point going mad in 1987 because there would be plenty more celebrating down the track. If there was one bet for which bookmakers would not have offered odds on 20 June, it was that the All Blacks would win another World Cup. To think they wouldn't win another would have been insane. It was probably more likely that on 20 June 1987, bookies would have offered odds on New Zealand winning every World Cup.

ASSUMPTION, AS every army officer knows, is the mother of all cock-ups. New Zealanders have learned this the hard way. To be fair, the assumptions New Zealanders made were those made by most of the other rugby nations. It was hardly pushing the boundaries of credibility to look at the All Blacks' winning record and assume they would win the World Cup when the time came.

The exception was 1991. The period between 1987 and 1990 had been a remarkable one for the All Blacks. On the back of their World Cup victory they swept through the rest of the year unbeaten, as they did again in 1988, and it wasn't until 18 August 1990 that their run came to an end. Australia managed to win at Athletic Park 21-9 and when they won again in Sydney the following year, there was a sense that a vintage

All Black era had come to an end. Not only that, but also the mantle of greatness had been assumed by the Wallabies.

Too many once-great All Blacks had stayed on for a year too long and, by 1991, the All Blacks were an ageing team whose powers were in decline. They were also affected by the selection of John Hart and Alex Wyllie as co-coaches – the two men were not exactly bosom buddies. When the All Blacks arrived in the UK to defend the World Cup in 1991 they were still widely fancied to succeed, especially as South Africa had not yet been invited back into the international fold. But those backing the All Blacks were doing so on sentiment and history rather than on an assessment of the fundamentals.

Most New Zealanders could see the All Black team of 1991 was vulnerable. It lacked potency and the dynamic edge required to produce something that little bit different. Because they were the All Blacks and because they still had a number of quality players, they were going to progress and with a bit of luck they might, somehow, sneak through to the final where they could possibly muster one major performance and retain the title. But there was no conviction, as there had been in 1987, and what belief there was soon began to seep.

Following a solid if unspectacular opening victory against England, the All Blacks spluttered to patchy wins against the USA and Italy. They didn't look like potential champions in those games and it became more and more of a long shot that the William Webb Ellis trophy would end up back in the mitts of All Black captain Gary Whetton. Confidence was further eroded when the All Blacks splashed around and made hard work of defeating a gallant Canada side in rain-soaked Lille.

That set up a semi-final clash with Australia in Dublin. It was hard to guess what might happen. Australia, like the All Blacks, had been mixed in the pool rounds and they had come within a whisker of losing to Ireland in the quarter-final. Came the semi-final however, and the Wallabies found something special. They were inspired, no one more so than mercurial wing David Campese, who pulled off two pieces of brilliance to enable Australia to score two tries and knock over the champions.

Out went the All Blacks. It was a shock. Not of the magnitude of seeing your granny naked – more like seeing a terminally ill patient die. You know it's going to happen but it's still tough to accept.

It wasn't altogether a bad thing, though. To have won the first two World Cups might have created complacency, a sense of ownership that would eventually have seen the All Blacks come unstuck further down the line. What defeat in 1991 did was make the All Blacks of 1995 that little bit more determined. It made them that little bit more aware that the World Cup was a different beast. It didn't matter how good a side's form was in the years leading into the tournament. That counted for nothing. All that mattered was delivering in the appropriate six-week window – stringing together six big performances. 1995 was an opportunity to put into practice some of the key lessons learned in 1991.

But 1995 had to wait. When the All Blacks of 1991 returned home, there was no public inquest into their failure. There was no prolonged grief or disappointment. The 1992 season was upon everyone soon enough and it was back to the serious business of preserving the All Black legacy – of taking each test as it came and winning, winning, winning.

It was also the New Zealand Rugby Union's centenary year. Neither the All Blacks nor the public deviated from their default stance of holding test football in the highest esteem and seeing it as non-negotiable that the All Black machine continue to collect the victories. The ethos of winning every test, of treasuring every test, had not been lost in Dublin and that attitude prevailed as strongly as ever right through to the 1995 World Cup.

Once the All Blacks got to South Africa for the third global get-together there was, as the world expected, a fierce determination among the men in black to win. Strangely 1992, 1993 and 1994 had been mediocre seasons for the All Blacks. They weren't troubled in the way they'd been in 1986, but neither were they vintage. There had been a one-off win against the Springboks in 1992 and a series victory against the Lions the following year. But against that were a series loss at home to France in 1994 and a painful defeat at Twickenham in 1993. By 1995 there was a sense the team had gelled, that some young players were about to come of age and that the World Cup was the ideal place to hit peak form.

When the All Blacks reached the quarter-finals there was no doubt they'd come to the boil at precisely the right time. Ireland, Wales and Japan were obliterated, then Scotland were carved up in the first knock-out round before England were destroyed in Cape Town in one of the greatest World Cup games ever played. The All Blacks were awesome

– none more impressive than 20-year-old Jonah Lomu, whose four tries against England astonished the world.

The All Blacks, as they had in 1987, were playing a different game to everyone else. It was a game certain to deliver their second World Cup when they met South Africa in the final. Lomu had been unstoppable in the semi-final. The All Black forwards had been rampant, the team's vision light years ahead.

In the final though, the All Blacks couldn't reproduce the intensity they'd shown in Cape Town. The forwards were competitive rather than dominant, and every time Lomu received the ball at least four Boks would jump on him and cling on for dear life. The contest went into extra time when the All Blacks had their chance to nail the winning points through a dropped goal – but they couldn't do it. South Africa had no such problem and their first five, Joel Stransky, like the proverbial cucumber, kept his head down and sent the ball sailing through the sticks to win the World Cup for South Africa.

New Zealand was stunned. They had been the team of the tournament. They had taken rugby to a new level with their skills, speed, power and creativity. They had come up one game short though, and that was perplexing. As the nation tried to take it all in during the days following the final, stories began to emerge about the All Blacks having been poisoned the day before the final. Players began to tell of seeing their team-mates vomit at the ground and throughout the day before. Coach Laurie Mains was adamant there'd been sabotage – and he spent his own money trying to discover the truth.

Conclusive proof and hard evidence never really emerged to solve the mystery. But there was enough of a stain placed on the Springbok victory to convince most New Zealanders they'd been denied their second World Cup title by outside influences. The prospect of foul play off the field couldn't be ruled out, and that gave New Zealanders legitimacy in their belief the All Blacks had been the better team and were denied the opportunity to do their best in the final. That made it easier to believe things would come right in 1999, and the World Cup title that should have been delivered in 1995 would be won in Wales four years later.

There was angst in the wake of the loss, concern that the All Blacks had failed in a tournament they looked so capable of winning. It wasn't the same navel-gazing exercise in blame that was to come in subsequent campaigns – more a sense of disbelief, driven partly by the failure to close out the tournament and partly by the hovering suspicion of sabotage.

Fortunately, the gloom was swept away as there was much to distract. The World Cup in 1995 had been a catalyst for professionalism and the code was suddenly awash with money, new teams and new competitions.

It was also particularly helpful that the All Blacks were scheduled to tour South Africa in 1996. That was an opportunity to exact revenge and, given that a series win in the Republic had never been claimed, for many New Zealanders that remained a bigger achievement than winning the World Cup. When that series victory was secured in Pretoria on 24 August, whatever pain had been lingering since the defeat in Johannesburg a year earlier vanished. The All Blacks in 1996 achieved what none of their predecessors had managed in close to 100 years of trying.

Winning a World Cup would have been nice, but a test series in South Africa – that was everything. Plenty of former All Blacks cried on 24 August. It meant so much to finally defeat the Boks on their home soil. Rugby had undergone some massive changes in the last 12 months – it was a professional game now – but in some ways it had remained the same. Winning tests was all that mattered for the All Blacks. Preservation and enhancement of the legacy was what everyone believed in.

It was the events of 1999 that began to push New Zealand towards an obsession with the World Cup. Having been denied victory in 1995, possibly by devious means, New Zealanders were convinced that 1999 would be the All Blacks' year. They were owed. They'd lost only one game in 1996 – the dead rubber in the South African series – and were undefeated in 1997.

The darkest year of course had been 1998, losing five on the trot, but the results prior to the World Cup suggested all was thriving again in the All Black garden. Samoa and France were hammered in the pre-Tri-Nations tests, and then South Africa and Australia were belted in New Zealand with the Boks also being floored in Pretoria. Even a record defeat in Sydney, 28-7, couldn't do much to persuade New Zealanders or the rest of the world that 1999 wasn't all about the All Blacks.

As usual the pool rounds only confirmed the superiority of the All Blacks. Scotland were defeated – in what felt like a customary quarter-final meeting – leaving no sense of fear about playing France in the semi-final. The All Blacks were in good shape; the French weren't. In truth, they should never have been there as their passage to the knockout rounds had been fraudulently secured by an appalling refereeing performance that saw Fiji denied legitimate tries in their pool encounter. The Tricolours picked their game up against the Pumas in the quarter-final, but they never found much flow or authority.

Also helping New Zealanders feel confident was the 54-7 pummelling they'd given the French four months previously in Wellington. The All Blacks were in a relaxed mood, relaxed enough to spend some of the week prior to the test frolicking in the Mediterranean. They had taken some downtime to recharge the batteries, and shortly after half-time at Twickenham it appeared to have been a smart call.

The French had risen to the occasion and were playing better than they had. Nowhere near well enough, however, to be a genuine threat and with Lomu close to the rampant form he'd been in four years earlier, the All Blacks were just about home and hosed when they went 24-10 ahead a few minutes after the break.

That was the point when they should have located France's jugular. That was when they should have announced the seriousness of their intent to win the World Cup and left their final opponent – either South Africa or Australia – quaking in their boots. Instead, it turned out to be the beginning of the end for the All Blacks. It became a defining point in All Black history. 31 October 1999 became the day winning tests ceased to be the overriding goal. France, without having given an inkling of their potential, unleashed the most phenomenal 35 minutes of rugby. They scored 26 unanswered points in a whirlwind of brilliance that left the All Blacks, and the rest of the world, stunned. The unthinkable had happened – the All Blacks had been dumped from yet another World Cup and this time by an opponent who really had no business beating them.

In the same way that the French found something deep within themselves in the second half, something rotten had gripped the All Blacks. As their defence melted and their structure all but disappeared, certain questions jumped out of dark recesses. Had the All Blacks really been poisoned four years earlier, or were they simply guilty of failing to respond to the pressure of the big occasion? That was clearly what happened at Twickenham – the All Blacks, to use the modern sporting parlance, 'choked'. They contrived to lose a game that was theirs for the taking, and they lost it by making poor decisions under pressure.

There was no player willing to sort things out. It was so very unlike the All Blacks – a team whose legacy had been built on their priceless ability to manage their own affairs. Instead of using classic Kiwi ingenuity to solve a tricky problem, the All Blacks that day stood back and expected someone else to be their saviour – perhaps the referee, or coach John Hart. This flew in the face of the ethic that had built New Zealand, which had seen a nation grow out of the bush into a world agricultural leader in less than 50 years. The greatest weapon a New Zealander had was self-reliance, a positive attitude and the utter conviction he wasn't owed a lucky break – no white knight was ever going to save the day.

Here was the class of 1999 left standing, mouths agape, looking hopefully to the stands in the hope the management team had some magic up their sleeves.

That belief was fundamental to the All Black mentality, the central building block of their success, and here was the class of 1999 left standing, mouths agape, looking hopefully to the stands in the hope the management team had some magic up their sleeves. They hadn't, of course. Hart and his coaching team could only watch, their hearts in their shoes, wondering like everyone else why the scoreboard was showing New Zealand 31-43 France.

The most alarming thought that couldn't be kept at bay when the final whistle blew was whether the All Blacks had developed a psychological fault line that was prone to slipping when subjected to unusually high bouts of pressure. And were they destined to never win another World Cup? Was 1987 going to be their only footprint? As these thoughts bubbled away it became harder and harder to see them as disconnected.

By 1999 the World Cup was huge, both commercially and in terms of prestige. The growth on both fronts was inevitable, particularly the latter. The dual hemisphere structure of rugby had created a problem that the World Cup had, paradoxically, both fixed and exacerbated.

The introduction of professionalism had extended the season. More money was needed so more games had to be played. That left players exhausted by the end of their domestic endeavour and fans feeling a little over-exposed as well. Turn the telly on and there was rugby – in February, in November, in July … it didn't matter when. The traditional end-of-season tours began to lose their lustre. When the northern hemisphere sides came south in June, they found it increasingly difficult to muster enthusiasm. Plenty of big names declared themselves in desperate need of long-awaited surgery. It wasn't too dissimilar when the southern teams had to venture north in November, and test football outside of the traditional competitions lost much of its meaning.

With weakened teams being fielded so regularly, the World Cup became the focal point of the rugby calendar. It was recognised as the tournament where excuses couldn't be offered, where the outcome really did matter. Prior to 1987 it had never been important for rugby to have an established and undisputed hierarchy. But by 1999 it very much was. The World Cup was like the Cannes Film Festival – it was the place to be seen to be doing well. Rugby had locked itself into a cycle where the World Cup was dominating the calendar and the more it did, the less value other tests carried. That made it hard for New Zealanders to extract the full emotional value from Bledisloe Cup victories. Tri-Nations victories didn't linger on the palette as long as they should have.

That almost imperceptible emotional downgrading of run-of-the-mill tests also hid the psychological fault line. The World Cup became the single most important feature in rugby and therefore the pressure would always be greatest for the All Blacks at that tournament. The pressure of a close Tri-Nations test might never be enough to expose the mental fragility of some of the All Black players. Only the World Cup could ask the toughest questions of the All Blacks' mental readiness, which again was found to be lacking in the World Cup semi-final of 2003.

In July 2003, when the All Blacks scored 50 points against Australia in Sydney, they slipped once more into their customary role as World Cup favourites. They were a side on the rise, packed with young, gifted players who were maturing at just the right time. They had cruised through the 2003 Tri-Nations undefeated. Talent, though, had never been the issue. The All Blacks of 1995 had been loaded with quality, as had the All Blacks of 1999. It was leadership, decision-making and the ability to deliver on the big occasion that again proved to be the All

Blacks' failing at the 2003 World Cup.

Australia played the 2003 semi-final with intelligence and tactical acumen. The All Blacks played with hesitation, with little variation and a lack of self-belief. Whereas on the same ground four months earlier the All Blacks had run rampant, by the time the World Cup came round they'd lost their voice. No one appeared to be leading the side, cajoling them to greater effort and changing the tactical direction of their game-plan. They were like zombies, roaming the Olympic Stadium as if they were unsure whether they belonged to this world or some supernatural one. Captain Reuben Thorne was every bit as ineffective as Taine Randell had been in the same role four years earlier. The pressure had, once again, got to the All Blacks. The fault line had opened up and – unbelievably – it was 16 years since New Zealand had won a World Cup.

How on earth that went on to become 20 years is a mystery some New Zealanders may battle with to their graves. The All Blacks had been sensational in 2005. They destroyed the British Lions, took out the Tri-Nations with three wins from four games and then enjoyed a Grand Slam tour of the UK where they played magnificent rugby on four consecutive weekends.

In 2006 the benchmark dropped only slightly. An extended Tri-Nations was won before it was barely halfway through and then on an end-of-season tour to France and the UK, the All Blacks played like gods. England were shredded at Twickenham before the All Blacks went on to massacre the French in Lyon, 47-3. Another victory in Paris followed before a thumping of Wales had everyone, even allowing for the All Blacks' uncanny ability to stuff up on the day, wondering whether there was any point in having a World Cup at all in 2007.

The All Blacks had brilliant, experienced, mature players. They had strength in depth. They had an exceptional coaching panel and they had a ferocious desire not to repeat the mistakes of previous World Cup campaigns. They studied the 2003 planning and found much to fault. Where the 2003 side had lacked leadership and quality decision-making under pressure... the 2007 side lacked leadership and quality decision-making under pressure.

Graham Henry's All Blacks of 2007 went splat just as John Mitchell's side had in 2003 and John Hart's in 1999. Just a few months earlier, Henry's All Blacks had hammered the side that put them out of the competition, just as Mitchell's and Hart's teams had done. And in further parallels, Henry picked Mils Muliaina, a regular fullback, at centre just as Mitchell had picked regular fullback Leon MacDonald at centre in 2003, and Hart had picked Christian Cullen in 1999.

It didn't seem to matter whether the All Blacks repeated strategies or formed new ones for the World Cup – the outcome was the same. What the various coaches didn't seem to realise was that the detail of the specific World Cup strategies wasn't the problem. It was the very fact they were forming specific World Cup strategies at all. The World Cup had become an unhealthy obsession.

THE DAY after the All Blacks lost their 2007 World Cup quarter-final in Cardiff, the New Zealand Rugby Union wheeled out its chairman, chief executive and deputy chief executive to answer the inevitable barrage of media questions. The initial onslaught focused on the immediate future – would coach Graham Henry be axed?

When that line of inquiry was eventually exhausted, one reporter inquired of chief executive Chris Moller: 'Does the New Zealand Rugby Union have an unhealthy obsession with the World Cup?' Moller's denial carried little conviction. He accepted that winning the World Cup was a priority, but the actions of the NZRU leading into the tournament pointed more towards obsession.

In August 2006 the NZRU announced that its board had approved a request from Henry to remove 22 All Blacks from the first seven rounds of the 2007 Super 14. The All Black coach, backed by intelligence from the fitness trainers, believed that if the country's best players were not afforded a decent break at the start of 2007 they would be close to exhaustion by September when the World Cup kicked off. The 2006 Super 14 had started in mid-February and the leading players only clocked off that year after hammering Wales in Cardiff at the end of November.

They would have a month off in December before having to join their Super 14 franchises in early January to begin preparing for a competition that had been pulled forward to kick off on 2 February 2007 in order to accommodate the World Cup. Henry said his players would be better skipping the early rounds of Super 14 and instead undergoing specialised, individual training programmes so they could be fresh later in the year, as well as returning to rugby bigger, faster and stronger.

From an athletic perspective the move made sense. From a commercial perspective it was suicide. Sponsors, broadcasters and fans were all being short-changed by the withdrawal. TV audiences in New Zealand dropped nearly 30 per cent. A huge financial risk was being taken to – possibly – enhance the All Blacks' chances of winning the World Cup.

This was an unprecedented gamble. It elevated the World Cup beyond a priority. It said New Zealand no longer really cared about the bread-and-butter competitions that were the financial bedrock of the professional game. It said that the administrators of the game in New Zealand were never going to be content, were never going to believe they had done their jobs properly unless the All Blacks won the World Cup.

It wasn't healthy. The World Cup was an itch the NZRU couldn't scratch. The humming fridge they couldn't stop hearing. The dripping tap that could never be turned off. It wasn't, as they insisted, just a priority. It would have been more than 'nice' to win it, as Moller suggested in Cardiff. It meant everything, which is why the NZRU had not only sanctioned the so-called conditioning break for the 22 players but also, when they extended Henry's contract in 2005 through to 2007, given him greater leeway than any other previous All Black coach to plan and prepare for a World Cup. Henry was allowed to pursue a selection policy that was designed to build depth of talent. He was allowed to plan and prepare year-to-year, rather than campaign-to-campaign like his predecessors.

In 2005 he was required to spend time with Moller, Tew and NZRU World Cup manager Steve Cottrell planning for the 2007 tournament. By January 2006 a plan was in place and in March of that year it was approved by the board. The plan, according to an independent review commissioned by the NZRU after the defeat in Cardiff, proposed a 'paradigm shift' in how the All Blacks prepared for the tournament, based on two central themes: 'A long-term and player-centric focus to All Blacks' selection and preparation; and prioritising the prospects of the All Blacks' success at the World Cup over other All Blacks' and New Zealand team's campaigns.'

The All Blacks had built their legacy on never looking beyond the present. This was indeed a paradigm shift. Henry's All Blacks won 38 of their 43 tests prior to the World Cup. That record allowed the NZRU to argue that they never lost sight of the importance of winning every test.

But perhaps they were just lucky they had a quality coaching team at the helm, who were lucky enough to have a quality group of players available.

The authors of the Independent World Cup Review – lawyer Mike Heron and former New Zealand softball coach Don Tricker – made these observations: 'We consider the emphasis which was placed on the RWC 2007 was too great, principally because of the conditioning programme and its very public nature. We suggest that whilst planning must occur, care should be taken to ensure that the RWC does not overwhelm all else. We note the NZRU did attempt to reduce this emphasis in its communications plan. In our view, winning the RWC was over-emphasised by [the] NZRU, primarily because of the handling of the conditioning programme – future planning should be lower key in terms of player and public awareness.'

The consistent failure at World Cups had acted like an entrenched virus in the NZRU. As the All Black failures piled up, the virus got stronger, making it harder and harder for individuals to think straight, to stay focused on the very thing that had led them to believe the All Blacks were World Cup favourites in the first place. By 2002, the virus was out of control.

Former chief executive of the NZRU, David Rutherford came into the job just weeks before the disaster at Twickenham in 1999. The nation was both shocked and angry at the way the All Blacks had capitulated and having the team come home empty-handed from the fourth World Cup was a little hard to take – especially as Australia won, claiming their second title. Rutherford, like all loyal New Zealanders, was upset by the loss. Yet, despite the pain and humiliation, the key executives at the NZRU did not start frothing at the mouth and wringing their hands like Macbeth.

'Everything we know about the World Cup tells us it is not important commercially,' says Rutherford. 'It's the winning record that's important and we can't sacrifice the winning record to win the World Cup. After 1999 I gathered 12 undeniably great All Blacks and a great former All Black manager in John Sturgeon. I was seeking some guidance on what they thought were the critical values and standards that had maintained that winning record. We talked about our coaching and management structure, the right length of contracts to offer. There had been a tradition to offer two-year contracts and there was a belief that the appointment had become very political. I put in a process to depoliticise [that] and the consensus around contracts was to keep them at two years. JJ Stewart [former All Black coach] was strongly of the view that we didn't leave coaches in there for long enough, but in 1999 we didn't have any intention of appointing for a World Cup cycle.

'We had the view that the only thing that mattered was the winning record and we had adidas [the principal sponsor] telling us the same thing. Straight after we appointed John Mitchell and Robbie Deans, we had a planning meeting and I don't recall sending a weakened team to Europe in 2002 as being part of that plan.'

Unfortunately for New Zealand, Rutherford resigned midway through 2002 and Mitchell sent a weakened team for a three-match tour of England, France and Wales in November. That was in the name of resting frontline players ahead of the 2003 World Cup.

And when the All Blacks crashed out in Sydney later that year, the rot spread further. Moller, who had replaced Rutherford, had not formed a strong relationship with Mitchell. There had been uneasiness about the All Black World Cup campaign. The team's dealings with media and sponsors were publicly criticised by Moller. By December 2003, Mitchell had been axed, replaced by Henry whose mandate also included restoring the image of the All Blacks and improving relationships with key sponsors, broadcasters and media.

The on-field defeat and the off-field conduct of the All Blacks had so incensed the NZRU that a full review of the campaign had been ordered. The key findings of that review included appointing a project manager to oversee future World Cup planning, to avoid a split like that in 2003 between the team and the NZRU, and to present a detailed strategy to the board at least nine months before the tournament.

There was a fierce determination within the NZRU not to make the same mistakes in 2007 that had been made in 2003. That determination was without question too fierce. Perhaps, though, the most damning proof of the union's obsession came after the All Blacks had been knocked out in Cardiff. Moller started one sentence insisting there wasn't an unhealthy obsession with winning the World Cup and finished it saying there would be a major independent review of the failed 2007 campaign. A five-month investigation into why the All Blacks lost a World Cup game – how on earth is that not an obsession?

3
Great expectations

JUST AS OSCAR Wilde could resist everything but temptation, maybe it's true that when it comes to World Cups the All Blacks can live up to everything but expectation. History clings to them like a cheap suit. It sticks to them at times and in places they wish it never would.

The All Black ethos has always been about the application of internal expectation. Whatever pressure is being exerted from outside the camp is never likely to be greater than that being generated within. Those relentlessly demanding, intrinsically generated standards are at the core of the All Blacks' success. Every All Black knows he can't slack off the last five minutes of training, that it won't be okay to drop the ball, or to give 95 per cent instead of 100 per cent. It is by adhering to these standards, through keeping internal expectations so high, that the All Blacks have become the phenomenon they are.

In the normal line of duty the All Blacks are able to cocoon themselves successfully from outside pressures. Or not so much cocoon themselves as keep the external world at arm's length. TV, radio and newspaper consumption can be controlled and while friends and family bring news from the front, it is not intrusive. There is no bombardment of information coming into the camp from outside, more a steady flow that helps the players assess the public mood. It's not that they need to be told that any given test is important or, depending on the opponent and the context, especially important. They always know that, and by setting such high standards from within the All Blacks are able, outside of World Cups, to deal with external expectation.

But World Cups are different. Maybe if the All Blacks had won in 1995 New Zealanders would have been able to brush off the subsequent failures in 1999, 2003 and 2007. Instead, 1987 sits alone in the nation's consciousness and that doesn't feel like anywhere near enough. Failure operates like compound interest – each time the All Blacks come home from World Cups empty-handed the public anxiety at losing becomes more acute and the desire to win becomes greater. That creates a vicious cycle where the more the country wants it, the more pressure they pile on the All Blacks and the more likely it is the team will crack.

All the strategies the All Blacks have in place to absorb and deflect external expectation are rendered pretty much redundant when it comes to the World Cup. There is simply no way anyone living in New Zealand could be unaware of how much the nation wants to win a World Cup. That desire is close to desperation.

Media coverage in the build-up to the World Cup is at saturation point. It's impossible to turn on a TV or radio, or pick up a paper without coming across coverage of the World Cup. The corporate world goes nuts for it too, building marketing strategies around the World Cup so that products from toothpaste to beer have some kind of rugby-themed advertising. People in the street talk about it, school-kids buy souvenir sticker books and the whole country it seems is gripped by World Cup fever.

That's understandable – rugby is the national game and the All Blacks are a much-loved sporting team. Much of that excitement has also been driven by the success the All Blacks have enjoyed in the years between the tournaments. When the All Blacks are continually winning Bledisloe Cups and Tri-Nations and are consistently ranked the number one team in the world, there is every reason to be optimistic about their chances of winning a World Cup.

But the excitement is driven as much by desperation as by optimism and confidence. When people are denied what they believe to be rightfully theirs, they want it even more. The longer they are denied the more they want it. By 2011 it will be 24 years since the All Blacks, the team that have been the undisputed best team in the world for most of that period, have won a World Cup.

If an All Black claimed to be unaware that the nation was desperate for a World Cup victory, either his tongue would have to be deep in his cheek or he'd be in need of institutional care. Measures designed to keep the players safe from external pressure simply can't withstand the weight of emotion invested in the World Cup.

The most powerful and enduring examples of how deeply this passion runs have come in the immediate aftermath of defeat. In 1999 Justin Marshall came to collect his luggage at Christchurch Airport and found that the Auckland baggage handlers had scrawled 'loser' all over his bags. John Hart, the coach of that failed side, became public enemy number one, receiving death threats. Even Hart's horse received death threats and was spat on at a race meet. And in a move mocked worldwide, Massey University suggested making grief counsellors available to the students struggling to cope with the All Blacks' failure.

Disappointment levels were just as high in the wake of the 2003 tournament, although the virulent responses of 1999 were not repeated as the New Zealand Rugby Union moved quickly to implement a massive restructuring of the All Black coaching set-up and national game that took much of the heat and emotion out of the public reaction.

The speed and precision with which the NZRU responded to the 2003 World Cup failure might have appeased the public but it merely emphasised to the players just how high on the priority list the global tournament sat. Which may explain why an already emotional and distressed Mils Muliaina broke down when he was asked the day after the quarter-final defeat in 2007 how he thought the team would be received when they returned to New Zealand.

It might also be why Daniel Carter, arguably the biggest superstar in the world game, started thinking about getting away from New Zealand after the loss in 2007. The 25-year-old Carter was coming off contract at the end of 2008. Usual procedure is for players to start negotiating their new deal a good 10 months in advance of the existing agreement expiring. With the skills to become one of the greatest All Blacks of all time, Carter was expected to negotiate an extension to his contract without delay. But in early January 2008 he met All Black assistant coach Wayne Smith and revealed he was thinking about heading overseas. He was feeling flat about another Super 14 campaign, and the emotional build-up to and then subsequent fallout from the failed 2007 World Cup campaign had drained him.

That led to the NZRU striking a special deal with Carter. He was allowed to take a six-month sabbatical in 2009 with Perpignan in France before returning to New Zealand where he would play until the next World Cup in 2011. So did he just need time to get away from the pressures of being an All Black? 'Definitely. It's tough. There's a lot of expectation playing for the All Blacks,' he said on a glorious sunny Dunedin afternoon before the All Blacks played their second Tri-Nations test of 2008. 'We've got such a tight group that we have really high expectations within the squad, and as long as you're living up to those you don't really read too much of the outside expectations, but at times it's pretty tough.'

What Carter implied but didn't say is that the World Cup is the toughest time to be an All Black, to cope with the expectation and pressure.

IN THEY trooped, all smiles and nervous energy. There was some back-slapping, a bit of laughter and obvious bonhomie.

It was the final farewell for the All Blacks before they set off for France to play in the 2007 World Cup. All 30 of the squad plus the coaches and extended management team were laid out, as neat as place-settings, on the top floor of the Heritage Hotel in Auckland. The team's major sponsor adidas, never a firm to miss an opportunity to get their three stripes in front of the TV cameras, had organised the event. The German-based company had a parting gift for the team and wanted the media to be there when they handed it over.

Their names were called out and up they came to the stage to accept one of the most bizarre gifts they were ever likely to receive.

On the day the All Black squad left for France they had to rip through the goodbyes. There had been a lunch at Eden Park earlier in the day where the players were posted out to the various corporate tables. The lunch was marketed as an opportunity for fans and interested parties to wish the All Blacks well.

Then it was back to the Heritage, where they had to sit politely as adidas went through a laborious video presentation unveiling a new TV advert commissioned especially for the World Cup, and then went into quite extraordinary detail to explain the rationale for the campaign. It finally emerged that adidas had gathered soil from the birthplaces of all 30 players and had combined it in a jumbo bottle. The bottle was presented to captain Richie McCaw and the audience was told the soil would be making the trip with the All Blacks.

A few minutes later it transpired that smaller bottles of the same amalgamated soil were to be presented to each player. Their names were called out and up they came to the stage to accept one of the most bizarre gifts they were ever likely to receive. Most of the players looked bemused, faintly embarrassed that they didn't have a clue what they should do with their bottles. It was at that point that alarm bells should have been ringing. History was repeating itself.

Hubristic marketing had never done the All Blacks any favours in the past. In 1999 Air New Zealand painted the tail of the plane carrying the team to the World Cup with portraits of some of the All Blacks. There was even debate that year about where the victory parade should take place – well before the All Blacks had even left for the UK. Never had the old adage that pride comes before a fall seemed so true, and the optimism that had swept the players into the Heritage in August 2007 quickly turned into a sense of impending doom.

The All Blacks, who had arrived like heroes ready to conquer the world, suddenly seemed more like lambs about to be led to the slaughter, Christians preparing to be tossed to the lions.

They would have preferred to slip off to France quietly, for there to have been no fuss – a quick goodbye to the nation and then on the plane. But their sponsors had different ideas. They wanted to build up the expectation and drama around the World Cup. Not only had adidas come up with the crazy soil idea, but the previous day they had also presented the squad with guitars! Again, that presentation had coincided neatly with the arrival of TV cameras, and the whole of New Zealand knew the All Blacks had taken possession of limited edition musical instruments.

No one knew what if any significance these bizarre gifts might have beyond adidas wanting to make a fuss of the All Blacks. Likewise Air New Zealand, who felt the need to present the players with personalised blankets. There were both commercial and emotional drivers behind all this gifting. Obviously it was an opportunity for the sponsors to gain exposure, but pride also played a part. The All Blacks had amassed an incredible winning record since the last World Cup, and their sponsors wanted to acknowledge their pride in being involved with such a successful team.

Regardless, however, of the motivation for extending and dramatising the All Black farewell, the unintended outcome was to ramp up the pressure on the team. The more they were built up, the more expectation they had to carry and the more they felt the outcome was important to the nation. The standard Air New Zealand blanket would have done, but no, the airline had to go to the trouble of hand-sewing players' initials into the wool.

It might seem like a small thing but it sent a big message. The little things all added up and the players were not oblivious to what was going on around them. How could they be? The 48 hours before their departure to France were a blur, an avalanche of gifts falling into their hands. Thousands slapped their backs and wished them all the best, and there were cameras, cameras everywhere.

And yet, as much as adidas and Air New Zealand and all the many well-wishers and media outlets lifted expectation, they didn't come close to putting the level of pressure on the players that their own employer did. The New Zealand Rugby Union trumped everyone with the reconditioning programme. Modern man takes a bit of stick for not being able to read the signs during personal interaction. No one failed on this score though. Taking 22 hand-picked players out of the first seven rounds of the 2007 Super 14 sent an unmistakeable signal that the NZRU was desperate to win the World Cup. Short of forcing the players to have 'you must win the World Cup' tattooed on their bodies, it's difficult to see how the NZRU could have made its World Cup obsession any clearer.

The reconditioning programme was an extraordinary measure sanctioned with only one goal in mind – to win the World Cup. Extraordinary measures are taken in response to extraordinary circumstances and in this case it was 20 barren years without a World Cup win.

Ken Hodge, a professor at Otago University and one of New Zealand's leading sports psychologists, is in no doubt that the reconditioning programme burdened the players with even more mental baggage to carry. 'My colleagues in fitness and physiology would argue until they are blue in the face that the logic, from a physical viewpoint, stacked up,' offers Hodge. 'But whether they meant to do it or not, the NZRU were sending a very clear message to the players that they were doing all of this to put more pressure on them to win the World Cup.'

And the players hardly needed to have their burden added to. Winning one-off, cyclical events is hard enough as it is. Athletes have to peak for six weeks but maintain their form over a four-year period so they can hold their place in the team. And, as Hodge says: 'Unless you are an extraordinarily good player and exceptionally fortunate with injury, you're going to be lucky to play in one [such event]. So you don't get a lot of practice. Tri-Nations and Super 14 and other tests, they have them every year so you can learn from them as you go and it becomes a challenge that you know. If you haven't been to a World Cup, it doesn't matter what anyone tells you, you won't know what it's going to be like until you get there.'

For the All Blacks of the professional era, there is the inherent pressure of peaking for a one-off event to deal with as well as the increased expectations of a desperate public and obsessive rugby union.

It wasn't like that in 1987 when they won their only World Cup. Back then there was barely any public expectation. In fact, in 1987 there was barely any public awareness that the World Cup was even taking place.

IT WAS all a bit surreal. It was a Thursday, and the All Blacks were playing a test match against Italy at Eden Park. Thursday was not a day for test football and Italy were never normally opponents for the All Blacks. That combination caught the New Zealand rugby public a little unawares, which is why Eden Park was only half full for the opening game of the inaugural World Cup.

The World Cup had come to fruition almost under the radar. The persistence of New Zealand and Australian administrators saw agreement reached that the leading rugby nations would give it a go in May/June 1987. There was no sustained marketing campaign to generate interest. There was no prolonged period, up to a year out from the event, of international coaches messing around with their selections in the name of preparing for the World Cup. The tournament sneaked up on everyone. There was no time to think about what might happen, what might need to be done to prepare and how important it would be to win.

All Black captain, Andy Dalton, who injured his hamstring before the tournament and ended up not playing, recalls that there was intrigue about being involved in something new. 'In terms of how we approached it, my memory is that we had the view that it was no big deal. I wanted to be part of it although it was probably a year too late for me. It was a new concept but we never envisaged it would become as big as it has. We were pretty excited. I still remember sitting in the pre-dinner and seeing the cup and wanting to go and grab it and stick it on our table. It was probably a bit arrogant but I felt it was ours for the taking.'

That was it in terms of expectation – one bloke quietly thinking that the All Blacks, by virtue of the ability in their squad, were the favourites to win the tournament. Probably many more New Zealanders felt the same way but there was no mass expression of such feelings, partly because the All Blacks had endured a torrid year.

Also, people didn't know what to expect. No one could be sure what kind of form the northern hemisphere teams were going to be in as they were coming south out of season with no games behind them. Then there was the uncertainty about the format – knock-out rugby had never been tried. Grant Fox, who played in every All Black game of the tournament, has this memory: 'My understanding of it was that if it wasn't for the southern hemisphere it would never have happened. No one had any idea. We played the first game on a Thursday, I think. There were only 20,000 at Eden Park. It was about halfway through the tournament that people cottoned on that we could be on to something special. We were actually touring in our own country, which was very unusual. Nobody knew what to expect.'

Sadly, for subsequent All Black teams, the genie was very much out of the bottle. As the tournament grew in commercial stature and prestige, so too did New Zealand's desire to win. While Dalton might have thought the All Blacks should really win the 1987 event, every New Zealander, it seems, has verbalised that belief on the eve of every tournament since. No other side has had to contend with so much and the likes of South Africa, England, France and Australia seem better able to keep the World Cup in perspective and not over-analyse the best way to prepare for it. They carry on pretty much as normal, treating it effectively as a series of tests much like any other. The All Blacks, since 1999, have tended to treat the World Cup in a very different light – seeing at as a unique event, which merely inflames the whole cycle of expectation.

In 2003 the All Blacks tried to shut themselves off from the rest of the world in an effort to keep the players immune from the hype. They stayed in Melbourne, which is not a rugby-playing city, for the duration of the competition in the hope of giving the players an unpressured environment. That strategy didn't work – the players complained of being bored and they felt disengaged from the tournament. Many of the other teams were involved in the communities in which they were based, but the All Blacks stayed aloof in that campaign and never felt any of the hype.

In 2007, having learned the lessons of the previous campaign, the All Blacks embraced their hosts at every opportunity. They engaged with the French, moved around the country, showed up at events, smiled, waved, signed autographs – did the full works and suffered their worst World Cup campaign ever.

'Some players are naturally mentally tough. Without being arrogant, they don't give a shit about anything.'

There is only one conclusion that can be reached – the All Blacks can do what they like in terms of preparation but nothing is going to stop the weight of expectation being felt. That is locked into the minds of the players. It can't be shut out and, judging by what happened in France in 2007, it can't be ridden either.

Expectation is not an emotional wave that can carry the players mentally. 'It wouldn't be healthy if the players tried to ignore the outside world,' says Hodge. 'If they did, they'd become very insular. They will also be putting pressure on themselves because they'll know that they haven't won for a while, and they can't help but feel reasonably confident coming into the tournament because they were coming in with a hell of a track record. They'd won most of their games and beaten all of their opponents. Some players are naturally mentally tough. Without being arrogant, they don't give a shit about anything. Sometimes athletes are not particularly pleasant people because of that and some people might perceive that as arrogant, but a lot of athletes have that steely edge where they don't care what anyone says – they are going to do their business. And other people care too much. They might say they never read the paper or watch TV but their friends and family will and they will convey that to the player. The pressure is huge and the expectation is huge.'

Does this mean then that the All Blacks have no hope? That they will always be swamped by the weight of expectation? No, says Hodge. It means that the problem of expectation can't be dealt with by either locking the players in their hotel at the World Cup and pretending it's not there. And neither can embracing it result in a conversion to positive energy. Every All Black will know the importance of the World Cup to New Zealanders. That's the inescapable reality.

The only way to deal with expectation is to replace all thoughts of the significance of the outcome with thoughts about the process required to win. The All Blacks carry expectation every time they play and their winning record suggests they can handle that. They do so by focusing on their preparation, thinking about the process rather than the outcome. They train hard all week and when they play, for the most part, it's a case of doing on the field what they've practised during the week. If the forwards scrum and ruck and the backs pass and run and everyone thinks only about what they should be doing, then winning becomes the product of the performance.

This theory, like many others, makes perfect sense. The problem, though, is remaining focused on the performance and not the outcome. In the heat of the battle, when there are 80,000 screaming fans in the stadium and billions watching worldwide, it's not so easy to stay focused.

That's when the hour-long presentation from adidas can't be forgotten. That's when players start to think about the effort Air New Zealand went to in sewing initials on a blanket. That's when they start to think about what the World Cup means to friends and family, to a nation so entrenched in rugby, so in love with the sport and so desperate to confirm their number-one status by securing the cup. That's when thoughts drift back to the summer months and all those weeks spent pumping iron and pounding the track while their team-mates were playing Super 14.

On 6 October 2007 it didn't look like the players were recalling those summer months as a way of reminding themselves how fit and well prepared they were. It looked like they could only remember that everything they did over the summer was for one reason – to win the World Cup. And it looked like thoughts were drifting towards outcome rather than process because too many players were making decisions they wouldn't normally make.

The All Blacks' outstanding winning record over the previous three-and-a-half years was built on the talent of the players, execution of a well-constructed game-plan and the quality of decision-making. Normally calm, level-headed players like Daniel Carter started to falter. Carter had barely made a mistake in three-and-a-half-years, and yet in the first half of the World Cup quarter-final he kicked the ball across his own 22, which was utterly crazy.

Since 2004 the All Blacks had played a high-tempo, multi-skilled, expansive game where they moved the ball wide and encouraged the natural skills of their players. For the entire second half in Cardiff they played a different game – opting instead to pick and drive relentlessly.

We will never know what was going on inside the players' heads. Based on the result and their performance, we can only assume that many of them were stressed. In other big games leading into the World Cup they had responded favourably to pressure. They had remained focused on performance, continued to make strong decisions and trust in the process to deliver the right outcome. But in Cardiff, and in Sydney in 2003 and in London in 1999, there was panic. Where once players had kept clear heads, in those crucial World Cup games their minds were scrambled. They felt stress rather than pressure and failed to make good decisions as a result. Stress is a killer for élite sportspeople.

During the majority of the games they played in that period outside the World Cup, the players clearly didn't feel stress in the same way. The biggest difference between a Tri-Nations test and a World Cup knock-out game? The latter carries far greater external expectation. Maybe, just maybe, if the nation could scale back its desperation, if the NZRU could hide its obsession and sponsors could farewell the All Blacks with a handshake and a wave, then players' perceived expectations of their performance in World Cups would match those for Tri-Nations and Bledisloe Cup encounters. Grant Fox sees it like this: 'Mostly between World Cups we have been the best side, and I think we are looking at winning the World Cup to ratify that. In my mind it doesn't add up.'

The weight of public expectation around World Cups is torturous for the All Blacks. It's enough to drive individuals mad. In 2007 the All Blacks' preference was to be based at Cardiff's Hilton Hotel in the week of the quarter-final. But the French had first pick of the accommodation and the All Blacks had to stay 15 miles out of town at the golf resort, Vale of Glamorgan. They were a bit disgruntled at missing out on the Hilton, but it was hard to see why. The resort complex used to house a mental hospital, and it felt on the morning of Sunday 7 October like that was exactly where some of the All Blacks needed to be.

4
Root of all evil

THE INTRODUCTION OF money to rugby has done wonders for the All Blacks' winning record. Pre-professionalism, they won about 74 per cent of their tests. Post-professionalism the ratio has steadily climbed to slightly more than 80 per cent. Conversely, the arrival of money has been very bad for the All Blacks' World Cup ambitions.

Their failure to win the 1991 World Cup can be put down to the selection of an ageing team who were well past their best, and being led by a coaching duo barely on talking terms. Defeat in the 1995 World Cup final can be put down to Suzie, the mysterious waitress who supposedly poisoned the All Blacks' tea. Or whatever meal it was she was supposed to have sabotaged. Or it could be attributed to the emotion that lifted South Africa beyond their normal level on the day. There were certainly no similarities between the failed 1991 and 1995 campaigns – the last two played in the amateur era.

But analysis of the three failures of the professional age reveals similarities, consistent themes that show up across all three tournaments. The pattern of exit was strikingly familiar. In all three tournaments the All Blacks encountered teams in the knockout rounds they had beaten, thrashed in fact, only months prior to the start of the World Cup. In all three games they lost, the All Blacks had a regular fullback playing at centre.

These factors, however, are more peripheral than central. The truly frightening aspect was the continually repeated failure to make good decisions under pressure – an entirely un-All Black failing. This was never a problem for All Blacks of old. It was certainly not a failing of the 1987 team who were, to a man, confident and astute while playing on the biggest stage. All Black teams of old had built the foundation of their success on their ability to stay mentally strong. And, even more intriguingly, this trait had generally remained strong even in the professional age – except for World Cups.

In 1996, after losing the World Cup final, the All Blacks bounced back in the first year of professional rugby by winning a series in South Africa for the first time. Of 10 tests that year they won nine, showing immense character and mental strength. When that team came under pressure, they responded favourably. Having won their first five tests of the year, they suddenly found themselves behind against the Wallabies with only a few minutes on the clock. It was panic territory – but no, Andrew Mehrtens felt there was a chance the All Blacks could score a try so he called an intricate move they'd practised in training. It was perfectly executed and broke open the Australians, leading to Frank Bunce diving over to make the victory safe. That try was typical of the way the All Blacks have been able to respond favourably to pressure – except when they get to the World Cup. This selective failure constitutes one of the more peculiar patterns in world sport.

It could be argued that the arrival of money hasn't corrupted the motivation or goals of individual All Blacks. To amass such an impressive winning record, and to continually react positively to pressure in Tri-Nations and other tests, suggests the All Blacks remain a side committed to the cause. The question is, though, are they committed to the same degree as the men of 1987 and the other amateur All Blacks?

We can explain the failures in 1991 and 1995, but we have no real answers to why the All Blacks caved in so spectacularly in 1999, 2003 and 2007. It would be naïve in the extreme not to make a connection with the advent of professionalism. The two are connected. Strongly connected, in fact. Money has dramatically changed New Zealand rugby. It has contaminated the purity of the emotions. It has introduced new targets for individuals, and for many players the black jersey is no longer the end goal. It is, for many, a ticket to somewhere else. It has become the ultimate bartering chip that can add an extra zero to a European deal.

The hardest part of all this is putting the changes into both context and perspective. It would be grossly unfair to portray the All Blacks, en masse, as money-hungry mercenaries. The winning record they have amassed in the professional age guarantees accusations like this won't stick. There is still passion for the jersey; it still means a great deal to the modern player.

For some, like Richie McCaw and Daniel Carter, it means as much as it did to the All Blacks of the amateur era. Both those players chose to stay loyal to New Zealand when they had options to play offshore that were far more lucrative. They turned them down because they couldn't give up the jersey. It meant more than cash.

That's also true of Conrad Smith, the erudite and elegant centre who was happily working towards a career in law when he got his big rugby break. 'I'm a bit different to the others,' he said on the eve of the 2008 Tri-Nations. 'I'm happy here and I'll stay here as long as things are going well. I don't really have any aspirations to chase money around the world. I play where I enjoy it. I love it in Wellington and I love being part of the All Blacks and that's the only thing that I consider. I don't want to think of rugby as a job. It's my passion and when I have that attitude I enjoy it and I play better that way. If I went to a club overseas I'd be playing rugby and that would be it. There might come a point in my life when I want to do that, but I enjoy what I've got.'

So there are still players with the values of their amateur predecessors. Players who believe playing tests carries more value than any offshore contract. Yet Smith himself makes the point that he isn't like the others. Maybe it's easier for Smith – he's a qualified lawyer and will enjoy a well-paid life after rugby – and for Carter and McCaw, who have both already set themselves up for life financially, to put the All Black jersey first. They have financial security. They can make decisions about their careers without ever really having to scrutinise the financial outcomes. That's a luxury few of their team-mates can afford.

For the majority of professionals in New Zealand, the reality is they have to be thinking about the dollar all the time. They give up a normal life to pursue their dreams and few have anything to fall back on when their professional contracts are over. Once they sign their first full-time deal, that's it: they're committed. Committed to making the best living out of rugby they can. At that point, it's no longer a game they play; it's a career. And it's a career with only a brief window for earning.

Best-case scenario, a player will have 10–12 years as a full-time professional. That is best case. Form and injury can reduce that period to one contract. We can't judge the players for wanting to maximise their earnings. They are no different from the vast majority of the population in that regard. Everyone wants to earn the best deal they can. Everyone wants the nice house, the cars, the good schools and the fulfilling retirement. They are no different from us in wanting to provide for their families and to give them the best opportunities. It's just that to achieve those goals they have to regard the All Blacks as only one stage in their career.

For the men of 1987, being in the All Blacks wasn't a phase. Everything was geared towards getting there and once you were there, everything was geared towards staying. That was the ultimate honour. There was no bigger reward than being an All Black. It wasn't financial fulfilment that drove their passion; the amateur All Blacks were paid nothing. It was emotional fulfilment they were after. It was memories they wanted and a sense of achievement. There was a purity to their motivation. All they wanted was the jersey and the chance to say they'd worn it and done it proud. They burned inside with passion for that simple pleasure. That was what drove them in the tightest battles – this desire to feel proud of what they did on the day they wore the All Black jersey. They were driven to preserve and add to the All Black legacy. It wasn't a career – it was a calling. No one made any decisions based on what it would net them financially. They simply played as well as they could and if they were picked for the All Blacks, great, and if they weren't, they needed to work harder.

That is not the scenario facing the professional All Blacks. As the game has become more connected to global markets, the modern player has acquired choices. He can make a good living in New Zealand, or he can make a far better one overseas. Few players here, other than the biggest names like McCaw and Carter, can set themselves up for life by playing only in New Zealand for their whole careers.

A stint in Europe can make a huge difference to the quality of life post-rugby. The money over there is far better, especially if you are a former All Black. If you can quickly win 25–50 test caps – and that only takes three to four years now – you can enjoy a stint at test football before moving to a European club where your value will be sky high.

The professional players still care about the All Blacks. If they don't perhaps care quite as much as their predecessors did, it's not a deliberate choice. It's an inevitable result of the game turning professional. The goals of the modern player extend beyond the All Blacks. Wearing the black jersey means everything, but it only means everything for a finite period now.

THERE WAS an obvious sense of excitement sweeping through Auckland Grammar School on 23 September 2008. The New Zealand Schools team was scheduled to train on the No 1 ground mid-morning. There were TV cameras prowling to capture the next generation of All Black super-stars and NZRU personnel who were there in numbers. For the boys in both the national squad and at Auckland Grammar, it was a little taste of the big time. This was a tiny insight into what life is like for the All Blacks.

No question, all the boys in the national schools side were aspiring to become All Blacks one day. But maybe not for the same reasons previous generations of boys wanted the same thing. Those young men who had to battle the attention of the TV cameras, their peers and a biting wind on 23 September had probably never battled their own thoughts with the same tenacity.

For them, and for so many of their fellow élite schoolboy players, the dream of being an All Black is not simply about being the best. Few young men can evaluate their thoughts or accurately articulate them, but their actions very often speak volumes. The All Black dream is no longer exclusively about playing for your country and winning tests. That's part of it, but only part of it. Now young men want to become All Blacks be-cause it can make them famous. They want to become All Blacks because it will make them rich and provide them with opportunities to move on to other contracts that will make them even richer.

It's a bit like the thousands of young graduates who train to be ac-countants not because of any inherent love of numbers, but because it's a qualification that will open up a myriad of more exciting doors.

New Zealand's young men are not driven by this burning desire to wear the All Black jersey and win tests the way they once were. They might not realise it, will probably even say it's not true, but most of them just want security. If they can last 10 years in the professional game, make some serious cash and have some great experiences along the way, they'll be happy. They will have achieved all they want from their career. Playing for the All Blacks is viewed as a bonus, a great way to enhance a career both for the value of the experience in itself and also for the increased opportunities it delivers. Young men want fame and money and lifestyle as much, if not more, than they want test caps.

The change in motivational drivers during the professional era hasn't ravaged the All Blacks. The fact more and more players are coming into the game with a view to leaving it rich hasn't seen the All Blacks lose their way. There is an alignment of interests here. The players want to enjoy a diverse and financially prosperous career. The All Blacks want to preserve their winning record. If the current generation can make the test arena and keep the All Black legacy intact, it will boost the commercial value of the brand and present them with greater opportunities offshore and at home.

So there is plenty of passion still invested in the jersey. There is still massive commitment given to the cause and there is still this strong desire to win tests. What we have to wonder is whether that desire is as strong as it once was. Has the desire to win been eroded, even by a fraction, since the game went professional? Has the edge the All Blacks carried through the amateur era been blunted?

In 1987 there were 15 blokes whose dedication to the All Black jersey was undiluted. There was no other door to walk through after they'd worn the jersey. For them, it was the here and now – playing in the World Cup was the be-all and end-all. It didn't get any bigger. There could have been no greater honour. 'For us,' says 1987 World Cup hero Grant Fox, 'rugby was our passion. It is for these guys too, but it's also their profession. Our vocation was elsewhere and the demands of our time were not so great. To get paid to indulge your passion is a dream. But how difficult would it be? I haven't been through it so I'm not that qualified to comment, but I think it would be challenging. Can you retain that excitement that you need to consistently perform? It isn't easy.

'I don't know the answer, and it's difficult for guys like me to make a direct comparison. Professionalism is an attitude. I think rugby players here still dream of being an All Black but I think that dream is broadened out to "I want to be a professional rugby player". Maybe that's the first thing that comes to mind now – that I want to be a professional, rather than I want to be an All Black. They now grow up knowing if they're good enough that's an option, and the option is no longer just in our backyard.

'I know of one All Black who could earn several hundred thousand dollars more playing overseas. But he wants to be remembered as a good All Black and I think he will be, too, because that's the rest of your life. If you are regarded as a great like Pinetree [Colin Meads], that stays with you forever. And in our society that's got currency. They have to ask themselves "do I get currency for the rest of my life?" and currency isn't about money, it's about kudos and standing, "or do I take hard currency?" How do you qualify that? People say they [the modern All Blacks] are chasing money but no one knows what they'd do if that sort of money was waved under their nose.'

It is apparent the All Blacks of 1987 had the most incredibly fierce passion for the national team. Measuring the importance or the impact of that desire in any scientific form is impossible. But there is enough reason to believe the intensity of that commitment, the ferocity of that desire and the purity of their emotions had a bearing on results. Rugby at test level is about inches and the All Blacks of the amateur era always seemed to be able to stretch things that little bit further than their opponents.

The All Blacks of the professional era have seemingly managed to preserve much of that same ability. Except they've only managed it up to a point. World Cup tests are won and lost around margins that are even tighter. The team that wins is very often the team that, from deep within, finds that little bit of energy to stretch an extra metre to make a critical tackle; or to push the lungs that little bit harder to get in support; or to jump that little bit higher in the lineout.

At World Cups it becomes more critical that players are so firmly dedicated to the jersey they will find the extra inches. This is where the new attitudes in New Zealand rugby are being exposed. The men of 1987 were able to find those inches. The All Blacks of the professional era have not.

Dr Jane Magnusson, a psychologist at the Auckland University of Technology who works with sports stars and sports teams, believes it's possible for players to reach the highest levels before the flaws in their internal drivers show through. 'In rugby, if you aren't intrinsically motivated it's going to be a lot tougher to ride those bumps as you're not going to be riding them for yourself. You're riding them for the little biscuit of money or sponsorship. The danger is that if you are solely motivated by the outcome then you are not going to be as successful. What you'll see is a lot of going through the motions if they're only doing it for the money. Really talented players can go through the motions for a long time. Talented players can go quite a distance.

'As the levels get higher the margins get tighter. Once you're at the top the fractures will start to show – you won't be as competent in those core areas. Passion and determination and commitment… that's when the cracks will start to show because you didn't drive up there on intrinsically motivated factors.

'What's interesting now is this offshore opportunity. Instead of thinking, gosh the ultimate is becoming an All Black, now it's just one option. If you don't have good intrinsic motivation, what we can do is make you very focused on the task. Make you very task-focused so you know what you're doing every moment on the field. From there you might get more success, and that might nurture some intrinsic motivation. The idea being that if a player says, "I don't want to play this game", my job is to make them click on. I say to these guys all the time that they don't know who's in the stadium. You have to make the best of that time. I can stimulate the intrinsic drive a bit. I can give them the tasks to help them focus.

'Ideally, you want them to be intrinsically motivated but you can work around it. If you have a scenario where you have one player with more talent but less intrinsic motivation, against a guy who has less talent but more intrinsic motivation, the guy who has the heart could probably squeeze out some more effort. In the long run those guys pull ahead because they want it, because they'll put in the harder yards than the guy with just talent.'

It's easy to make simplistic, generalised comparisons and suggest the 1987 team had the intrinsic motivation and the professional sides have been relying more on talent. Quite easy, because to a large extent, it's true.

THERE IS an irony, not missed by those who played for the All Blacks in the 1987 World Cup, that they as amateurs were more professional than the men who followed them into the jersey and were paid for the privilege. For the All Blacks of 1987, professionalism didn't mean accepting payment. Professionalism was a culture, an attitude, a way of life – a way of making sure every possible care was taken in the preparation phase to deliver victory.

Some of that culture was lost when money entered the game. We could blame the players, but it wasn't really their fault. It wasn't really anyone's fault; it was more a consequence of the circumstances in which the game crossed the divide between amateur and professional.

Jim Blair, the enigmatic Scotsman who trained the 1987 All Blacks, has been involved with professional sports teams for more than 50 years. His view is this: 'I think half the trouble was that we jumped into professionalism. We did it out of fear and we shoved a whole lot of money in front of players without a great deal of thought. I am just wondering what sort of attitude a 23-year-old will have if he is on $300,000 a year and he knows he's got a contract. Sometimes the best guys are a little bit hungry. Some guys, they lose it and you have plenty of people in soccer who are like that. Plenty of people are brilliant players but they can't handle the pressures that come with it.

'I am just wondering what sort of attitude a 23-year-old will have if he is on $300,000 a year and he knows he's got a contract.'

'If you look at the best teams you'll see a name in there that you don't really recognise but you'll see it in there every Saturday. He quietly gets on with the game and he's never looked upon as a star. He's the professional. He doesn't moan, he just gets on with the job – now that's the true professional. That 1987 All Black team, they became professional before they were paid. Now we're paying people and expecting them to become professional. In a professional team, you learn about teamwork and team spirit and you don't worry about whether you're being patted on the back or not because you know you've done your job. You know you've got value and you don't need to read your name in the papers or see yourself on TV.'

Professional rugby caught everyone on the hop. It was ushered in as a consequence of the threat being posed by a rival professional competition. That meant there was no controlled review process as to the best way to make the transition. It had to happen on the hoof and that was always going to be dangerous.

David Moffett, the chief executive of the New Zealand Rugby Union in 1995, remembers seeing an immediate change in attitude among the players. 'The conversations in the dressing room, and not just the All Blacks but in Australia as well, changed quite a bit,' recalls Moffett. 'Players started to talk about properties they'd bought or were looking to buy, or cars they'd seen and what kind of stereo systems they had and all that kind of stuff. There was a shift. I'm not sure the players today realise what it means to be a former All Black. I think the likes of Richie McCaw and Dan Carter do, but not enough of them realise how many doors it can open being a former All Black. Too many don't realise the value of their brand beyond the immediate contract. A guy like Sean Fitzpatrick understood the value of his own brand. Now players see the All Blacks as a means to an end, rather than an end. For so many, being an All Black means they've just boosted their value overseas.

'I was involved in putting together the Tri-Nations and Super 12 deals in 1995. We had to buy four or five players out of their Nike contracts when we were putting together the adidas deal, and I think that was evidence it was becoming more about the money. The biggest evidence though that it was all about the money came at that World Cup when the players all signed with Ross Turnbull's World Rugby Corporation. They had all the signatures and no money, while we had all the money and no signatures. The players all came with us in the end because that's where the money was. We'd been trying to get money into the players' hands as best we could during the end of the amateur era by bending the rules as much as we could. The players were of a mood that they wanted professional rugby.'

And once they got it, the foundation values of the All Blacks became increasingly hard to preserve. In the immediate aftermath of professionalism, there was no dramatic change as the players carried over the heavily ingrained ethics and culture of the amateur era. The likes of Fitzpatrick, Michael Jones, Zinzan Brooke and Ian Jones knew no other way. For them it was business as usual, except they were finally being paid. But as those players who'd straddled the two eras retired from the game, a new breed of athlete replaced them – one who had known nothing but life as a professional rugby player.

These were the sorts of player who formed the bulk of the 1999 World Cup squad. These were men who hadn't been grounded in the old school of what it meant to be an All Black. These players were, in fact, given almost no support to help them understand the world in which they worked. They trained and they played and that's about all they knew. Given how insular and under-prepared these players were, is it any surprise they lost five tests in a row in 1998 and bombed at the 1999 World Cup?

It wasn't until the formation of the New Zealand Rugby Players' Association in late 2000 that the support networks were put in place for the country's top players. And even then it took the NZRPA some time to build its development programmes, to build structures to educate the players and get them to understand fully the concept of being a professional athlete. There was enough talent in New Zealand rugby to continue winning tests – while the players were ignored off the field they were exposed to the best sports science practices and the best coaches in the world.

But there wasn't enough of a professional culture in place to win World Cups. Too much of what the 1987 team had was lost in transition. 'We've been doing this for nine years,' said NZRPA boss Rob Nichol in August 2008. 'The guys who played before 1996 had a good grounding. Then we had the situation of young kids coming straight out of school and becoming professionals at the age of 18, 19 and doing nothing else. Between 1996 and 2001 there wasn't a lot out there to balance those guys – in fact there was nothing. The NZRPA started in 2000 and it was late 2001 before we got our first programmes running and got stuck into this issue.

'We could call them the lost generation, but I don't think that's it – it's more like, you look at what we do now and if you talk to any of those guys you get the response that they wish this was around when they were playing. It's lost opportunity. If he's given good tools and guidance about who to deal with, then you are just going to be able to do so much more with that player. If you've got a young player, and the foundation is good and he's well organised off the field and understands about all the core competencies he needs for a professional career. If he's not fazed by the media and is a little bit confident in that area and understands that as his profile grows what are the various things that can influence the risks around young females, alcohol, all that sort of stuff.

'We had a generation that missed out on that and it's pretty sad. If the right foundations are put in early then those players are going to be so much better down the track. You can go so much further with them. We have to get those foundations as solid as possible.'

The solidity of those foundations has been suspect for much of the professional age and no World Cup triumph is ever going to be built on sand. New Zealand rugby needs concrete. It needs the players to be less focused on money. But that is going to be hard until they are set the right example by their employer – because the NZRU has placed the dollar even higher up the agenda than the players have.

5
Too much of a good thing

THE HOME UNIONS had always feared that money would flow through the game as destructively as Coca-Cola through a toddler's mouth. In New Zealand the fears were entirely different – the big worry was not what money would do to the players, but whether they would have enough of it. Since the game went professional in 1995, the New Zealand Rugby Union has been as active as a market 'geezer', ducking and diving and looking into every conceivable and inconceivable scheme to generate revenue.

The desperate need to raise money was understandable – still is. New Zealand produces superstars in much the same way as fast-food joints produce burgers. Top All Blacks have been in demand globally from day one of professionalism and unfortunately for the NZRU, the European and Japanese buyers have deeper pockets.

The ability of major European and Japanese clubs to lure New Zealand's top players has made the All Black legacy that much harder to preserve. The constant departure of players puts pressure on the development systems. It means there've been times when young, inexperienced players have been forced into playing test football possibly before they were quite ready.

For most of the professional era, the All Blacks have managed to deal with the talent drain. They have maintained their winning record and have somehow, miraculously almost, managed to unearth world-class player after world-class player.

Since 2006 the battle has intensified. Rugby in Europe has enjoyed a financial boom, allowing top clubs to increase massively the wages they can offer high-profile All Blacks. The numbers of players leaving New Zealand has crept up to near damaging levels and in 2008, as a result of so many players leaving at the end of 2007, the All Blacks ended up fielding five forwards, with only 19 caps between them, against South Africa. It's the fear of losing players that fuels the NZRU's desperation for money.

The NZRU has been under threat from offshore predators since 1995 and the governing body hasn't had much in the way of effective defences. It has been hampered by the most frustrating paradox. Here is New Zealand, with a disproportionate share of the world's best players. That has enabled the All Blacks to build and maintain the most phenomenal winning record in international sport and, as a result, the All Blacks have become one of the most recognisable sporting brands in the world. Few Americans know much about rugby at all. But show them the iconic black shirt and they get it – it's the 'Noo Zealand' All Blacks. In France at the 2007 World Cup, there were more All Black replica shirts being worn on the streets than there were French jerseys.

As a brand – and in the modern world, sports sides of this magnitude have long since ceased being simply teams – the All Blacks have been shown to be up there with the likes of Manchester United and Ferrari in terms of recognition and potential commercial appeal. So really, given the ability of the team and the strength of the All Black brand, the NZRU should be up to its neck in cash. NZRU staff based at HQ should find themselves tripping over suitcases of the stuff.

The problem is that with only four million people in the country, the NZRU can't leverage the full value of the All Black brand in New Zealand. The All Blacks are just too big for what, when you strip out primary produce, is a lightweight economy.

In 2007 the NZRU's income was slightly more than $101 million. In the same year it cost almost $25 million to fund the All Blacks and other representative teams. It had to plough $42 million into the running of the Super 14 and provincial championship, with another $15 million going into community rugby. By the time it had paid another $8 million to its administrative staff, given all the unions an additional $8 million in grants and lost a nominal $5 million on the value of its foreign assets, it made a total loss of almost $2 million. That loss followed on from 2006 when it had dropped almost $5 million into the red.

The reality for the NZRU is that it has a cost base that has no room to be cut. The success of the All Blacks starts with the quality of the players from which it can select. Many are world class, or close to it, and they have to be paid a remuneration package that reflects their global standing. The global market says the top players are worth as much as £400,000 pounds a season in England, possibly more if they go to France. Depending on the exchange rate, that can be as much as $1.2 million. The top players here earn between $500,000 and $700,000 a season and only then if they continue to be selected for the All Blacks. (They earn All Black fees of $7500 for every week they are assembled with the squad. If they are not selected they don't get paid. They sign a retainer that is guaranteed but the All Black fees are worth close to $200,000 a season.) So big money has to be found just to offer the top players a salary that is in fact not really comparable to what they could earn in Europe.

The top players in New Zealand have to be developed, and that costs too. The All Blacks are only the tip of the iceberg. Vast sums of money have to be pumped into the age-grade ranks, the provinces and Super 14 teams to ensure the best coaching, facilities and sports science are available. The travel costs alone of playing in the Super 14 are enormous and then there is the accommodation; even the food bills – these guys like to eat – are phenomenal. If the NZRU started to cut costs around any of these core structures, the quality of the All Blacks would start to erode. The need for money is ferocious.

There are standard ways for all national rugby unions to make money. In New Zealand, selling broadcast rights is the biggest earner. Rupert Murdoch's News Corporation accounts for around 40 per cent of the NZRU's annual income. The value of the contract is relatively high because the rights can be sold into global markets. New Zealand might only have around 750,000 Sky subscribers but, fortunately for the NZRU, there are millions of other TV viewers who will pay to watch All Black tests.

The TV deal does come with one major drawback, though. Sure, the money is just dandy – the Sanzar alliance sold the five-year rights to Super 14 and Tri-Nations in 2006 for US$323 million, of which New Zealand takes almost one-third. But News Corporation want plenty of content for its investment. When the first Sanzar broadcast deal was signed in 1995, the All Blacks found themselves locked, for 10 years, into a Tri-Nations format that would see them play both South Africa and Australia twice a year. They were obliged by both the IRB and their domestic broadcast partner, Sky TV, to play three home tests in June and three northern hemisphere tests in November. In 2006 the broadcast deal was renegotiated and a new Tri-Nations format agreed where the three teams would play each other three times. From then on, the minimum number of tests per year would be 12.

Most international coaches believe 10 tests is manageable; concerns are raised about playing 12, but the All Black coaches of the professional era have all been told the same thing by their employer – there is no other way to raise the necessary cash to keep the game afloat.

The other traditional way of raising money is to sell sponsorship packages. In the case of the All Blacks, given the strength of their brand, that should be no problem. And it isn't, but there's a catch: the value of the contracts is not particularly high given the size of the New Zealand market. The basic rule of thumb is that the bigger the population in a sponsor's key market, the more money they will have to pay to clinch the deal.

The NZRU has an extended family of domestic sponsors including the likes of Mastercard, Ford, Coca-Cola, Air New Zealand and Lion Nathan. These companies have tie-ups with the All Blacks but they are only allowed to market that association in New Zealand. Ford, for example, can't have an advertising campaign in Japan with Dan Carter behind the wheel of one of its cars. It can't advertise its sponsorship internationally because it's not willing to pay for that type of contract. These big multinational firms use different methods to reach different markets and while the All Blacks are a big brand, there are other ways to sell bottles of fizzy drink and motorcars in Europe, Asia and North America. So the money paid for these domestic packages is tiny in comparison with what a sponsor would have to pay to gain a relationship with, say, Manchester United.

Ideally, the NZRU would like to have four or possibly five international sponsorship partners, all paying top dollar for the link. It has two in place – one is adidas and the other Italian truck manufacturer Iveco. But even these international deals have a sting in the tail. The New Zealand dollar has enjoyed a prolonged run at unprecedented levels. That's a major problem for exporters, which is what the NZRU basically is. The News Corporation deal is paid in US dollars as was the adidas contract until 2009 when it switched to Euros.

If the exchange rate between the US and New Zealand dollars was averaged out over the last 20 years, it would come in at around 60 US cents. The NZRU has, since 2005, worked its budget on the basis of the New Zealand dollar being worth about 66 US cents. For much of the period between 2005 and 2008, the Kiwi was trading well in excess of 70 cents and on occasion touched 80 cents. That is why the NZRU posted a $4.5 million loss in 2006 and a $1.8 million loss in 2007.

And while the union, through a clever hedging currency deal and also a $23 million boost from hosting the British Lions in 2005, had built up cash reserves in excess of $70 million, its position has still been precarious since the birth of professionalism. Much of its reserves are in foreign currency and it has, since 2005, been forecasting a loss of around $30 million through hosting the 2011 World Cup.

The NZRU has every reason to worry about money. The game in Europe remains a sleeping giant. It might feel to the NZRU as if the European clubs have long been packing a major financial punch, but the game over there is nowhere near its commercial peak. The wealth gap between the hemispheres continues to grow and the NZRU, for most of the professional era, has been frantically looking for ways to close it.

It has been a scramble just to keep things on an even keel – to keep most, but by no means all, of the best players here and committed to a decent stint in the All Black jersey. Since 2004, the NZRU has been in full-on give-us-your-money mode. It was uneasy about being so reliant on the broadcast contract and, with sponsorship just about saturated, it began looking at innovative ways to raise revenue.

The NZRU touted the All Blacks on simple terms: you want them, you pay for them.

The NZRU was sure it was following the right financial model. It made sense, it thought, to promote the All Blacks, to see them as the cash cow for the national game and exploit their popularity and global standing. Given the power of the brand – this fantastic team that was theoretically worth millions – it felt there had to be other ways of making money.

But it was proving too hard to leverage off the brand. So it was decided to make it easy for global markets and potential corporate backers – give them the All Blacks in the flesh, in their full glory. This was a much more direct ploy – it was pay for play. The NZRU touted the All Blacks on simple terms: you want them, you pay for them.

And because the likes of England, Wales and France knew they'd sell out their massive home stadiums in a flash if the All Blacks were in town, they agreed. It was great business for everyone. The All Blacks asked for a fee – usually about one million pounds to play at Twickenham – and the host kept the rest of the gate takings, probably worth about double that. Even this avenue had restrictions, though. The NZRU could only ask for a fee when the All Blacks were playing outside the designated IRB test window, which usually runs for three weekends in November. They played for cash against the Barbarians in 2004, against Wales in 2005 and England in 2006.

It was such easy money that the NZRU started to think beyond traditional venues and arranged a game in Hong Kong against the Wallabies in 2008. Fledgling plans were also formed to play the Wallabies on neutral soil again in 2009, and the Irish in Boston or New York in 2010. It seemed like a great way to get some extra money pumping in. And it would have been, but for the fact it came with a hidden cost.

WITH THE world experiencing a sustained commodities boom from the turn of this millennium, the price of cheese and butter rocketed for New Zealanders. But the dramatic rise in the price of dairy products was nothing compared with the rampant inflation in the All Blacks' playing schedule. Back in those halcyon days when the country came to a standstill to watch the All Blacks, it was rare for there to be more than six tests in a calendar year. Most years there would be a maximum of four, sometimes even just two.

It was partly the rarity of tests that added to their value and prestige. It's a simple numbers game. Christmas only comes around once a year so we cherish it. Mondays come around 52 times a year so we hate them. That's pretty much how it was with the All Blacks. If they were only playing two tests in a year, there was a sense of occasion.

From the players' perspective it was much the same; there were only going to be two chances to make the team. And if you made the team, there were only two chances to win. Or, seen from the flip side, there was no leeway to lose. It was a simple numbers game again. The fewer tests scheduled per season, the greater the chance the All Blacks could go through unbeaten. The fewer tests the greater the expectation, both external and internal.

By 1996 the numbers were stacking up very differently. The All Blacks played 10 tests that season and that meant there was more likelihood of a game being lost. And 10 tests per season became the norm. By 2004, that number had started to rise again as the NZRU pursued its pay-for-play strategy. In that year they played 11 tests and a non-cap game against the Barbarians. In 2005 the All Blacks played 12 tests. In 2006 it was 13 and in 2007 it was 12, although of course everyone had been planning to play 14. In 2008 that number jumped again to 15 and for the foreseeable future, between 13 and 15 each calendar year is the probable number of tests the All Blacks will be lumbered with.

That inflation has changed the mind-set of both players and fans. Certainly for the fans, the thinking has softened. When the All Blacks were playing only two or three tests a year there was genuine expectation they would win the lot. If they were only playing two tests and they lost one, the winning ratio would be a paltry 50 per cent. Play three and only win two and it was 66 per cent – nowhere near good enough to preserve the legacy. With so few tests, each loss was felt that much more acutely.

Now, with 15 in a season, there's recognition that the All Blacks can't win them all. The last few All Black coaches have lamented this fact while at the same time calling for realistic expectations.

Professionalism has allowed a number of other countries to improve greatly. If the All Blacks have to play 15 tests a year, mostly against the best teams in the world, it has to be accepted that on at least one or two occasions they will be a few percentage points off their peak against an opponent running at maximum power, and some tests will inevitably be conceded. That is the nature of international sport. With 15 tests, the All Blacks can drop two a season and still hold a near 85 per cent win ratio. That ratio is in excess of anything consistently achieved by other international sides.

Statistics demonstrate the law of probability has been obeyed. Since professionalism kicked in and the number of tests per season jumped dramatically, the All Blacks have only gone through one year, 1997, without dropping a test.

No All Black ever has or ever will run out onto the field ambivalent about whether they win. There is passion for the jersey. There is a desire to win. The issue is degrees. When the 1987 team played there was no leeway. There was no sense that winning 85 per cent of the time would be acceptable. If they'd lost in the final of the 1987 World Cup, they wouldn't have been consoled by coming second. For them, there was no plump calendar to hide behind.

A loss in any test was taken very badly. Captain of the 1987 team Andy Dalton said there was never any solace to be found on those days the All Blacks lost. 'You were absolutely determined not to have an L written next to your name. I played 35 tests and only lost six or seven, I think. I remember them well. The memories from those games we lost have stayed with me more vividly than the memories from the games that we won.'

Losing a test no longer carries the burning humiliation it did in 1987. Now the players know that, at some point in the year, they are going to lose. They don't enjoy it, but they do have to accept it more readily than their predecessors. They can console themselves in defeat the way the men of 1987 and earlier generations of All Blacks couldn't. They can point not only to the laws of probability, but also to the physical and mental demands of the extended season being greater. If the All Blacks have to front on more weekends, to play a game that is seriously more physical in terms of the size and athleticism of the players and the impact of the collisions, then it increases the chances that on one or two, maybe even three, occasions in the season they will be a little off peak performance.

That's not to say the modern All Black thinks it's okay to lose – rather that some of the mental edge has been blunted by repetition. That defeat, while it still hurts, doesn't leave him distraught the way it did Dalton and his 1987 team.

Jim Blair, the trainer of the 1987 team, puts it this way: 'They [the 1987 All Blacks] had a sense of the jersey and knew at the end of the game they had to be able to look in the mirror and not feel any shame. There was a sense with the All Blacks back then that they were very special. You only ever saw them together every so often and there wasn't the same amount of TV coverage. It's pretty exciting to see a star you only see occasionally but if you see too much of [him], it can lose that something special. It can become ordinary. I'm certain the players today still idolise the silver fern, but it remains true that the more you do something the more normal it becomes.'

The prospect of defeat is now built into the All Black psyche. It's like a currency market predicting interest rate rises – they show in the price before the decision is confirmed. The modern All Black can deal with defeat more readily than his amateur counterpart.

And despite the hype, the pressure, the expectation, the modern All Black might not view the World Cup as anything other than another test to be fulfilled in the bloated programme. If it's accepted that some tests will be dropped, then why not the World Cup? After all, the chances of losing a game at the World Cup are higher than they are in the regular season. Every team has tried to peak for the World Cup. Every team has conditioned and prepared to give its best at the World Cup.

Defeat at the World Cup carries the same statistical weighting as defeat in any other test. The All Blacks lost in 1999 and still managed a near 80 per cent win ratio that year. They lost in 2003 but still won 84 per cent of their games, and in 2007 the loss to France in the quarter-final left them with an 83 per cent ratio. There was some heavy-duty disappointment to cope with in the fallout from those defeats. But once that had been endured, once the players had put things in perspective, they could still hold their heads high, look at their overall record and feel proud.

For the modern All Black, success is not evaluated explicitly in terms of wins and losses. Maybe the best way to put it is that the modern All Black is determined not to lose, while the All Blacks of the amateur era were desperate not to lose. It's about degrees.

For the All Blacks of 1987 there was despair waiting in the changing room if they lost. In those closing minutes, if they were behind, there was a frantic welling of fear. To lose was to be plunged into a dark place. For the All Blacks of today the dark place has light fittings. The changing room is an unhappy place in the wake of defeat but not quite the morgue of old. Defeat is something that can be overcome. That's the mind-set and it's no different at World Cups.

Failing to win a World Cup does not forever damage an individual's career. Look at the 2007 team. Luke McAlister, Carl Hayman, Aaron Mauger, Doug Howlett, Chris Jack, Anton Oliver and Byron Kelleher had all signed massive overseas contracts before they left for France. Their individual reputations didn't suffer in the wake of Cardiff. The deals weren't called off and neither was the value of their contracts reduced.

And for those who were staying in New Zealand there was no sense of their star having faded. Richie McCaw was still massively respected, as were Ali Williams, Tony Woodcock and Mils Muliaina. Winning a World Cup would be great. But a career doesn't stall if the silverware is not secured. The modern All Black has different goals, a different view of what constitutes a great career. In 1987 all that mattered, the only way the players could etch their names in folklore, was to win the World Cup. Now there are so many routes to fulfilment that we have to suspect that the hunger, while still there, is not quite what it was.

IN 1987 an All Black defined his career by the number of tests he played and the number he won. There was no other measuring stick. Since professionalism, the parameters have shifted. The biggest change has come in the opportunities that exist overseas. Like every other young New Zealander, your typical All Black wants, at some stage, to spend some time working overseas. Unlike your average traveller though, an All Black working in Europe can earn serious money – almost $1 million a season if he's got a good agent and a decent pedigree.

It's not just the lure of Europe that has changed the means of evaluation. It took Colin Meads, the greatest player New Zealand has ever produced, 15 years to win 55 caps. Now a player can win that many in four or five seasons. A whole career can be crammed into four years, and that leaves many of the players mentally and physically exhausted at a much earlier age. When Hayman left for the UK in 2007 he was just 28, a relative baby in propping terms. Mauger was 25 and was nowhere near a spent force, while McAlister was only 24 and very much on the rise.

All these players talked of how special the jersey was to them. They all said they loved being All Blacks and there is no question they gave it everything throughout their test careers. Yet, despite their assurances that it meant the world to them, they were prepared to give it up when they had the opportunity to win so many more caps. Buck Shelford, a critical figure in the 1987 team, probably would have died for his jersey. Hayman and his departing team-mates could give it up because it had served its purpose; it had scored them the major European contract. It had made them rich and famous.

David Kirk, the on-field captain of the 1987 team, says, 'It's a life-cycle issue. We had three motivations. Get into the team; stay in the team; and be a great All Black. The early part of the cycle is the same. You want to get there, to represent your country and be the best you can be. No one wants to be dropped. In some ways it's worse than never playing. Once you get over those hurdles and get up to 20–25 tests, for the first time now, people have other options. You have a limited time period to make money. What happens if you're injured, or you are dropped? The last part of the career is about getting the most money you can, wherever that might be. And that's what has changed. That transition is occurring earlier.'

For Hayman and Mauger the period between 2004 and 2007 had been so intense, they had invested so much in building up for so many tests, they felt they needed a break. They had to get away, refresh their minds and try something new. That desire to leave was understandable. Maybe if Shelford and his 1987 chums had been asked to play as many tests as the current All Blacks, they too would have felt the same way after four or five years of relentless slog. Maybe if there was a life-changing deal waiting in Europe, Shelford and his chums would have signed up for it the way modern players do.

It's not fair to be critical of the choices made by the current All Blacks, or to judge them for viewing their career in different terms. They've made a choice to become professional rugby players. They give up everything in pursuit of that job and, with a limited earning window, they have to bank it while they can.

But this isn't an exercise in blame; it's an attempt to determine the consequences of the changing landscape. And one of the most obvious consequences has been the development of an entirely different evaluation of success, which in turn has created an entirely different team culture. Now the players can look at their test caps and feel proud. They can also look at their endorsement deals, the value of their overseas contract and their media profile, and feel proud. Now they see the All Black jersey as one part of their career. It's a link to the next stage – which is usually a well-paid stint in Europe.

For the players of 1987 it was all so different. 'The fear of losing in those days was tremendous,' said John Drake, prop in the 1987 team. 'You just couldn't lose. That seems to have changed now. I listen to these current All Blacks and they say that isn't in their psyche at all – it was definitely in our psyche. The next saying was there was no point being an All Black [if you could accept losing]; you [had] to be a good All Black otherwise you shouldn't [have] even be[en] there.'

We're talking chalk and cheese in terms of attitude, and it would be foolish to believe this isn't in some way linked to the failure to win the World Cup. The All Blacks of the professional age have developed a culture that allows them to maintain their winning record. They remain mentally tough and physically good enough to win most of their tests. They have, perhaps astutely, factored in defeat as an inevitable part of the process. They have downplayed internal expectation and tried to reduce external expectation about just how many tests the All Blacks can win.

On that basis, can we really believe the players of today are as desperate as those of 1987? We can believe they're fiercely determined. We can believe they hurt when they lose. But it's back to degrees. Can we believe they hurt as much as the All Blacks of old when their bank accounts are bulging and the offers to play in Europe come flooding in regardless of whether they've bombed at the World Cup or not? Can we believe they have that same desperation when they play 15 tests a season? Can they feel as passionately about test football when their own employer sees it, primarily, as a means to raise revenue? Could it be that even major World Cup games are just another test – just another game to be updated on the CV? We can't rule all this out as a possibility given the continued failures.

The introduction of professionalism has seen the All Blacks lose that chronic fear of defeat. The 1987 team played with stark consequences attached to failure. Losing would have prevented them from achieving their key goal of becoming good All Blacks. It also meant they would have to look at themselves in the mirror the next morning and hate what they saw in the reflection.

6
Fear and loathing in New Zealand

IT'S THE STRANGEST thing. Given how many tests the All Blacks won during the amateur era, it's natural to assume the players were motivated to perform by the elation they felt in victory. That they revelled in the culture of success, and found fulfilment in the knowledge they were the best.

That assumption is not correct. What drove the All Blacks of the amateur era, and particularly the World Cup-winning All Blacks of 1987, was their ferocious fear of losing. It might seem there's little difference – whether you want to win, or don't want to lose, the desired end is the same. But appearances can be deceptive. There is a major difference between the two mind-sets, and between the resulting team cultures and outcomes.

No one from the 1987 team is pretending otherwise – they all accept the fear of losing was potentially a negative driver. They all accept it could have promoted an environment where some players became too nervous to perform. And if everyone was focused on not losing they would make conservative decisions; they would play to avoid mistakes rather than to express their skills. They all accept that was the risk.

But while there were risks, the men of 1987 saw no evidence that their team culture prohibited individual expression. They never clammed up. When they were under pressure they reacted positively. No one felt inhibited. No one felt they were prevented from playing the way they wanted.

Far from being a negative force, the fear of losing was the burning fire in their bellies. It was this omnipresent shadow that spurred them on to bigger and better things. The intensity of that emotion was off the scale. It made them desperate and when people are desperate they are capable of extraordinary feats. That All Black team of 1987 had a depth to their belief that they couldn't lose. For them, that was the one thing that could never be allowed to happen. They could play badly, and it would be okay as long as they didn't lose. They could play well, and it really would matter if they lost.

There was no grey area in defeat, no straw left to clutch at. Defeat was seen in absolute terms – it was hideous. Defeat meant you had let yourself down; you had let your mates down; you had let your family down. It meant you had let down the great men who had gone before you. It meant you had let the nation down. There was only shame to be found in defeat. The only emotions losing brought on were pain and humiliation.

There was no smile to be found for loved ones waiting for the fallen heroes at the airport the next day. There would be no striding into work on the Monday morning after a defeat.

As Alan Whetton, the great All Black flanker of the 1987 team, puts it: 'You can talk about winning, but I always talk about the fear of losing. It's not a nice feeling. It's not about winning. It's about not losing. The losses were very unfortunate. The loss far outweighs any form of winning. You suffer a loss and boy, I tell you we're at a funeral. The beer tastes flat. The jokes are hollow. We can go out and get pissed and lose it in alcohol, but it only lasts a night. It's a reality the next day that stays with you – all week, when you're on tour. If it's a huge game it stays with you for the rest of your life. If that isn't motivation enough, I don't know what is. Once you've suffered a major loss, it's someplace you don't want to go.'

This is a strange concept to get your head around. Here was a phenomenally successful team that had been driven by its desire to avoid a certain outcome rather than achieve its opposite. For the 1987 All Blacks, as daft as this sounds, winning was the consequence of not losing. They didn't set out to win. They set out not to lose.

The emotional pathway to avoiding defeat varied in direction from the one they would have followed if their motivation had been to achieve victory. It probably varied in intensity as well. The passion for not losing was greater than the elation felt at winning. The All Blacks of 1987 didn't revel in the euphoria of victory. They merely felt relief when they won. That sounds bleak. It sounds like being an All Black in that era was more of a chore than anything else, that there was no upside. Win, and all you'd done was live up to expectations. There was no partying, just relief that you'd been part of a team that had avoided the humiliation that came with defeat.

But there are two things worth noting about the culture of the 1987 team. First, it worked for them. They won a World Cup motivated by the fear of not losing. No other All Black side has won a World Cup since. And, by and large with the same team that won the World Cup, the All Blacks went on one of the longest unbeaten runs in history. Between 1987 and 1990 they didn't lose a test.

Since the game went professional, there's been a gentle erosion of the culture so firmly endorsed by the 1987 team.

Second, and almost paradoxically, by continually avoiding defeat the All Blacks built an internal confidence that they would win. 'You never went into a game thinking you were going to lose,' said John Drake. 'In the Auckland team, and I'm sure it was the same in the Canterbury team, we just never thought we were going to lose a game. We had that total confidence. I never thought I was going to lose a rugby game in my life.

'You just have it and also I guess it's in the psyche of the teams you're playing in. I was in a cycle of teams right through my schoolboy rugby, like Auckland Grammar where Graham Henry was the coach, and I didn't lose a game at school. I played 90-odd games for Auckland and I only lost about four or five. But that's the way you think. And to have the fear of losing I think is fantastic, and I'm amazed when I listen to guys like Anton Oliver [say] they don't believe in that, and that they always worry about the positives. I don't know – I think the fear of losing is a great motivator; it certainly doesn't stifle the way you play. I don't think we ever thought we wouldn't do something because we were scared to have a go. Probably the opposite. We knew we had to have a go to win.'

The players, coaches and sports scientists of the modern era haven't shared Drake and his team-mates' conviction about the fear of not losing. Since the game went professional, there's been a gentle erosion of the culture so firmly endorsed by the 1987 team. Dismissing the fear of not losing as negative has been just one of the many ways the professional game has distanced itself from the amateur game.

Perhaps unconsciously, or perhaps deliberately – it's hard to tell – those involved in the professional game have adopted an almost sneering attitude towards the amateur era. They give the impression there was little to be salvaged from the period before 1996. Training methods, nutrition, recovery, game-plans, psychology – everything that has any kind of input into the make-up of the athlete – is regarded as infinitely superior now.

The modern men try to be kind; they soften the blow by saying the differences between professional and amateur athletes are so vast it was inevitable everything would evolve. They try to suggest that the thinking, the preparation and planning of the amateur era were good for that period. It's just that everyone has moved on since then. The thinking has become more sophisticated as a consequence of having more clever people specialising in this, that and the other. The modern game adopts this patronising tolerance of the amateur era.

That supercilious attitude is hard to understand. The men of 1987 won a World Cup, an achievement no All Black side of the professional era has come remotely close to emulating. So much of what went before has been treated like a scab, something unsightly and in need of removal. The All Blacks of the professional age will refute that. They will bristle at the very suggestion. But there is a truth they have to acknowledge. The modern All Blacks have picked away at the culture, tradition and institutionalised bonding rituals that made the All Blacks of the amateur era what they were. The first step was to move away from the fear of losing. The new breed of professionals wanted positive reinforcement. They were driven by the lure of the carrot, not by the fear of the stick. Why not chase the victory they said, rather than run scared from defeat.

Grant Fox understands that the culture is now firmly about winning tests. 'The fear of losing has always been part of the All Black psyche. I think that was never going to survive when the game went professional. They play more tests than we did and they have a level of rugby only just below test rugby. For us to get up [there], we only had to do it so infrequently, [whereas] for these guys the hardest thing about playing élite sport is the mental approach. The more they play the harder it is going to be. There is no doubt.

'So they start to take the process away from that emotional fear of losing. You can't keep playing on that. It happens so often that it is too hard to play it. It is about process. Winning is a by-product of the process. So if we get the process right, and back ourselves... but if they happen to be better on the day, we'll move on. I think that times are different, and they were different for Colin Meads who played before us. You need to factor in some modern-day landscaping.

'I think there are a number of assumptions people make based on history without taking into account how different things are now. There's an assumption that they don't care as much, that they don't care as much when they lose, they don't have the same pride. I know a lot of these guys quite well and that is absolutely not true. They care deeply. And they understand the history and legacy. But they're playing more often, both tests and Super 14, and there's a bit more quality across the board. So it's harder with the amount of contact the top nations have with each other, it's going to be harder and harder to win.

'Given all the contact we have, the All Blacks still have a remarkable record, apart from the World Cup. Because we haven't won it for so long we're becoming obsessed with it, and I think the obsession is damaging. I can't speak for how our guys think, but I do know the internal workings of an All Black set-up. Guys place much more pressure on themselves than the public do. Much more.'

Fox makes an entirely valid case to justify why the culture had to evolve. Maybe the fear of losing was a culture that had to be buried in the amateur era. Maybe with so many tests now it would leave the players emotionally burned out if they had to live in fear of defeat. The problem, though, is the cultural revolution of the professional era didn't end with the shift to positive reinforcement. The danger when you pick a scab is that it becomes itchy. Then the temptation to pick it intensifies and you keep on picking. The more you pick it, the itchier it becomes and you end up with an awful mess.

WHAT BINDS most of the world's greatest and longest running institutions is an assumed culture. That is to say, there is no written code of conduct as such. The All Blacks weren't presented with a manual when they were first selected, detailing how they should behave, what and whom they were representing, and what was expected of them.

All that was assumed. It was assumed that by being good enough to win selection, they would be good enough to work out what they were doing there and how they were supposed to behave. In an assumed culture, it's the senior players who hold the power. They set the tone. The new men learn by keeping quiet at first, by keeping their heads down and seeing what the senior players do.

That assumed culture can be intimidating for new entrants. There is uncertainty, a sense of fear that they might break a code they know nothing about. They might say or do the wrong thing. For new All Blacks of the amateur era, the first few months in the All Black camp could be a difficult and lonely time.

Even a hard man like 1987 prop Richard Loe could find it tough. He was playing for a club in France when he was first called into the All Black side as cover on an end-of-season European tour. 'I played one game against the French Barbarians,' recalls Loe. 'We got to the hotel and Cowboy [Mark] Shaw said, "You're with me." We went up to the room and I put my bags down and he said, "Milk, no sugar," and lay on his bed. And then he said bugger-all until we were on our way to the game, when he said, "Hey, pal, don't be a oncer." That game, I was carried through on adrenaline. When a legend like Cowboy Shaw says don't be a oncer, it means everything. I played the rest of the season absolutely on fire.'

There was no mechanism to break the new boys in gently. There was no desire either. The All Black culture was built on the notion of survival of the fittest. The team had built an astonishing winning record over a very long period. Much of the success was due to the ability of the players to sort things out for themselves when they were on the field. There was enormous pride in the culture of self-reliance. There was a clear sense that becoming an All Black was a rite of passage. The journey began with being selected. It most certainly didn't end with winning a cap.

Once a new player was called into the camp, he had to serve his time. He had to learn how to fit in. He had to learn the internal workings of the team. He had to prove he was a good bloke, that he could fully absorb what was expected of him and then deliver. It was a bit like boarding school. There was an apprenticeship to be served.

No one, no matter how good they were on the field, could swan into the All Black camp as if they owned the place. That was not what being an All Black was all about. It didn't matter what you'd achieved in the provincial game. It didn't matter that you might have lifted the Ranfurly

Shield 10 times or more. Respect only came with test caps and good performances. Even then it only came when you had honoured and respected the values of being an All Black. There was no one there to help. There was no guidebook to consult. It wasn't the kind of place where a friendly face would appear from behind a hotel room door with a cup of tea and a bucket of sympathy.

'When you first came into the team you watched, learned and listened,' says Whetton. 'It was tough coming in when you were green and being spoken to by senior players when you were still learning the game. You had to earn your stripes, be the duty boy. You relate to the guys who are in the same age group. You know some of them but you don't really know them. It was tough at times and some guys fell between the cracks.

'But once you'd been there and had a taste for it, when you put your mind to it you tried to be successful, but it was tough early days. There weren't any of the support groups around. It was, you are an All Black – go and do it. I had to room with John Ashworth once. You look back and laugh now but you had to earn your stripes. I roomed with him for three days and I saw him for about half an hour. That geriatric front-row had earned their right – they had done their time. When he did come in it was "watching TV. That's my bed". I had nothing in common with him. He was 31 and had played test matches, what did we have in common? We were All Blacks and we played together, but we were separated by the hierarchy. It was tough certainly, not for the faint-hearted.

'Those older guys were characters and they loved a bit of fun, especially teasing the new boys. It was a tradition they inherited and that they were going to pass on. Now whether they were right or wrong it didn't make any difference – this was tradition. I can remember being at the front of the bus and getting the call – "Whetton. Alan. AJ. Back seat." Oh shit, that's when you start sweating. Cowboy Shaw, because he's a loosie, says, "So you think you're any good? You're just a snivelling toffee-nosed nothing." It was intimidating.

'Axle [Gary] Knight was there on the back seat with Trapper [Dave] Loveridge, and this is what they'd been through so this is what I had to go through. I said, "I want to make sure I don't let anyone down." Then they would say stuff like, "You going to buy us a beer? You going to buy us some fags? What else?"' Then I'd reply, "I just want to make sure I fit in and do whatever I can for the team." "That's right. Whatever you can for the team. Don't you forget it. Now bugger off." '

Whetton survived those early days. He went on to become a great All Black. He had the character, the mental fortitude and the ambition to plot his way through those tough times. Looking back now, he has mixed emotions. As he progressed up the hierarchy he became more conscious of the need to soften some areas of the culture.

Every All Black had to be a problem solver. Every All Black had to be self-reliant. He had to be able to work things out for himself. That bred a culture of defiance.

There was a need, in his view, to tone down the intimidation, to make the new players feel more at ease earlier in their careers. 'You were always thinking about what you didn't do, and what I did wrong,' says Whetton of his days as an All Black. 'I could talk to my brother or some of the other guys in the team, but they were in the same boat as well. I had a close mate, Lee Walsh, who I could confide in and he was a good sounding-board. I could talk to him about things I couldn't talk about with people in the team. I was very fortunate. There were no structures, there was no management and it was not something we spoke about unless you had a poor result and then it was cards on the table – what do you think went wrong? And that was usually led by the senior players.

'When you've spent time in that environment, you think, how can I make it easier for the likes of Michael Jones and Zinzan Brooke? You went out of your way to make sure they didn't have what I had and that there were ways of doing it better. Possibly a strength of the Auckland team was that we made it easier for guys to come into the side. It wasn't about who we are and what we've done. It was about, how can we help? We know you're good to be selected for this team. We want to make you look good, because that way you make me look good. We took some of the things that happened in my day and made them easier for new people coming in. But how far do you take it?'

And that is precisely the question that needs to be asked. Whetton and his ilk wanted to soften things. They didn't want to eradicate the very framework that had built such a phenomenal winning legacy and landed a World Cup. The mixed feelings kick in for Whetton because, as tough as those early times were, they were what made him. They were what made his team-mates. They were what made the All Blacks. It was those lonely days that built character. It was through having no one to turn to that individuals developed strength of character.

Every All Black had to be a problem solver. Every All Black had to be self-reliant. He had to be able to work things out for himself. That bred a culture of defiance. It bred a culture where no one was looking around for someone to come in to sort out problems. When every day in the All Black camp was a challenge it made dealing with pressure on the field that little bit easier. The All Blacks of 1987 were not in need of external help. They knew how to make strong decisions. They knew how to survive. They were tough physically and mentally, and they were streetwise. They also had faith that every player around them deserved to be there because he too had completed his rite of passage.

What that meant for performance was significant. It meant that players were less likely to be fazed by the biggest occasion. It meant they were conditioned and expert at making decisions under pressure. It meant that every player held himself accountable. It meant that every player had been close to breaking point just to make it on the field. Collectively that made the All Blacks of 1987 a powerful unit. It meant they had no soft underbelly that would be exposed at a World Cup. This was a team full of independent leaders who had learned the hard way. This was a team that could respond when they went behind. This was a team that didn't panic. This was a team that was scared witless about losing. This was a team that knew they couldn't look to anyone else for help when they were losing.

Every man in that 1987 side knew that the responsibility to deliver the correct outcome lay with the players, and exclusively with the players. They all knew that because, at some stage in their career, they'd been hauled in front of their peer group and made to feel six inches tall. They had all, at some stage, roomed with a monosyllabic senior player whose only communication was ordering tea and biscuits. They had all, at some stage, felt the humiliation of being the equivalent of a boarding school fag. They had all, at some stage, felt lonely, insecure and unworthy. But to a man, they'd overcome those feelings. They'd graduated to the next level of the hierarchy and they'd all succeeded without a support group. They owed their survival to their instincts, dedication, perseverance and sheer bloody-mindedness.

'When I first made the team I was called down to the back of the bus, it might have been while we were going to the airport,' says Andy Dalton. 'I was made to stand in front of the back seat and Bryan Williams said, "What are you going to do on this tour to help us?" So I explained, and then he asked, "What does it mean to you to be an All Black?"

'That had a huge impact on me. It showed me just how big my responsibility was. I told them I wanted to be in the team that won the series and if I could be part of the team that played the game then great, and if I wasn't then I would do my best to help the team be successful. As far as being an All Black was concerned, that was being the best; the best I could for the best team in the world. It seemed to satisfy them, because I went back to my seat and kept my head down for six months. That had a really powerful impact on me.

'As I got older I never consciously thought, I am now a senior member of this team. But I was very conscious of my responsibility in the team and to the team. Being captain you don't sit at the back of the bus anyway. John Ashworth and Gary Knight and I always used to sit up the front. We could have easily taken the back seat and beaten the crap out of everyone but they chose not to. The modern-day structure of having your senior leadership taking on responsibility for off-field stuff, then a mid-tier group, and the new boys – we never consciously wrote this up on the board and said this is what we are doing and this is who is going to be in the senior leadership team.

'We had that, but it was never stated properly. That dropped away and from what I saw when I was involved with the NZRU as president, I believe that was lost in the 1990s. The senior leadership of that team in 1991 – and I was just on the fringe, so I would have to be careful in terms of judgement, but my perception was that they had lost some of that leadership from that senior crew.'

What was evolution in the early 1990s became more like revolution in the professional era. Bit by bit, the culture of the 1987 team was destroyed. It started with the desire to make the environment less hostile to newcomers and then snowballed to the point where the sink-or-swim style of apprenticeship had become anathema to the failed 1999, 2003 and 2007 World Cup campaigners.

STRONG ARGUMENTS can be made to support the many cultural changes the All Blacks have made in the last 20 years. In 2008 there were six new caps selected in the first squad of the year. It's a sign of how much things have changed that those six players were handed a manual when they checked into the camp detailing the various protocols and expectations being an All Black involved, and then they were greeted with a haka performed by the rest of the players.

The days of exclusion are long gone. The days of having to fend for yourself are long gone. In 2008 Jimmy Cowan was perilously close to having his NZRU contract terminated. The 26-year-old All Black was arrested for a second time in June for committing offences while under the influence. The NZRU decided to give him a final warning and allowed him to stay employed on the condition he attend alcohol counselling and abstain from drinking. Rather than cast him adrift and leave him to sort his own problems, the NZRU gave Cowan access to all the support he could ever need.

The week Cowan had to front for his disciplinary hearing, the All Blacks were in Wellington preparing to play South Africa. Cowan was given Brad Thorn, a former wild boy who had experienced his own drink problems earlier in life, as a roommate. Thorn is a reformed character, a born-again Christian, and the All Black management team thought he could offer Cowan guidance.

The modern systems are definitely worthy of commendation. The experience of being an All Black is far less lonely now than it was in the amateur era. The environment is more relaxed. Younger players are encouraged to have their say. Younger players are given some responsibility in team affairs. When new caps come into the squad they can more readily access senior players. They have a raft of specialist coaches from whom they can seek both technical and emotional guidance.

The fear of losing is no longer there. Instead the modern All Black sides have focused on performance with a view to it delivering victory. Now there is joy and elation in victory. Now the players take the time to enjoy the experience of winning and celebrate accordingly. Now the players can take something away from defeat. They can more objectively evaluate their performance in a loss and find things on which they can build.

There is no assumed culture any more. The modern teams have tended to be more communicative, more willing to define and discuss the make-up of leadership groups so everyone knows their position and responsibility. The back seat of the bus is no longer the reserve of the senior men who literally fought their way back there. That culture has died. The greatest sin a new player could commit is keeping a problem to himself. The team is set up so no one has to feel he is alone. If they are unsure, they just have to ask. If they have a problem there will be someone who can fix it.

At the 2007 World Cup there was a head coach, a forwards coach, a backs coach, a scrum coach, a kicking coach and the team manager. There were two conditioning coaches, a doctor, a physiotherapist, a muscle therapist, a bag man, a mental skills coach, a nutritionist, a video analyst, a media adviser, a lawyer, and Sir Brian Lochore as a fourth selector. Every angle was covered and then covered again. There was a specialist for everything. There was no possible way any player could ever feel he was alone, that there wasn't someone there for him to turn to.

In fact, the All Blacks' win record in the professional era has increased slightly.

When Graham Henry took over as coach in 2003 the All Blacks even began to have role-playing sessions where the players divulged their greatest fears. They talked about what it meant to be an All Black, all in the hope that the men who would be serving together in the trenches would better understand each other – would have bonded that little bit tighter. Those players whose careers straddled the amateur and professional eras all say they were much happier in the modern environment. What they saw was progression – the rejection of a system that had made the All Black experience unnecessarily fraught, and almost joyless. To back up those views, the modern men can show results that stand comparison. In fact, the All Blacks' win record in the professional era has increased slightly.

But – and it's a but that can't easily be dismissed – the All Blacks of the modern era have failed spectacularly at World Cups. It can also be argued that while they have a better win ratio, in 12 years of professional rugby they have actually lost more tests than they did in the last 30 years of amateurism. Although the modern culture has many admirable elements – the inclusive, progressive thinking has made the All Black squad a happier one and improved the experience of playing for the national team – it also carries one major flaw that has been continually exposed at World Cup competition level.

By having such strong support structures in place, the professional All Blacks have killed the rite of passage and undermined the self-reliance and independence that was the bedrock of the All Blacks' success. In 1999, 2003 and 2007 the All Blacks were lacking on-field leadership. Individuals failed to make good decisions under pressure. They failed to take responsibility for their performances and it looked to those on the outside as if too many of the players were waiting for someone else to come up with a solution to their problems.

And why should we have expected anything different? When the modern All Black has a problem off the field, he seeks help. One of the many specialists sweeps in and solves things. The modern All Black doesn't need to be self-reliant – his problems disappear without any input from him.

The definitive test of a team's culture, the robustness of its systems and their ability to cope, comes at the World Cup. For most of the professional era the June tests have been a joke for the All Blacks. They play half-baked sides from the north that they could beat with 12 players. It's much the same in the November tests, and neither South Africa nor Australia has sustained high enough standards since 1996 to constantly put the All Blacks under pressure during the Tri-Nations.

Too many Tri-Nations in the last 10 years have been won too easily by the All Blacks because neither the Boks nor the Wallabies have been able to offer much in the way of resistance. Neither is the Tri-Nations a knockout competition. The All Blacks can lose a game and still win the tournament, and it hasn't often boiled down to New Zealand having to win a specific game to take the title.

It's different at the World Cup – a loss in the knockout rounds and you're gone. And that's where the failure of the modern All Black culture to deliver the same robust players that emerged from the tougher culture of 1987 is continually exposed.

'The thing is, life is tough – get on with it,' says Whetton. 'You learn through mistakes. Are we taking the challenge out of playing for your country? You can't play for the players. You can't think for the players, or take the emotion away from the players. The only way you find out is standing on your own two feet, and you know what? Life sucks at times. When you're playing international rugby it can be lonely at times. It shaped me as a person and as a player and I think you have to hit those brick walls. What do you do? Do you get over them or under them? If you have people telling you what you should or shouldn't do, or should or shouldn't feel, it takes away all that individuality. You have to work things out for yourself.

'If I don't like something [in the All Blacks], do I go straight away and tell someone? No, I should plot this out, otherwise it becomes too easy, too repetitive to go looking for someone to help you out, and they may not help you in the right way or give you a fallback like a security blanket. Or they might tell you the reasons why it is not your fault – things like the coffee wasn't hot enough. Or the guy beside you didn't pass or make the tackle. Give me a break. Stand up and be counted – that's why you wear the All Black jersey, because you're the best.'

The modern system is typical of the convenience society. It's typical of the way so many procedures have been softened to the point where all risk has been removed. Children used to turn five and go off to school. Now they have trial visits. They have to be gently integrated, have their parents by their side during those first few traumatic visits.

Without risk, without pushing people out of their comfort zones, New Zealand is creating individuals who expect others to make decisions for them. A generation of leaders has been lost, and that is arguably the single biggest reason why the All Blacks have failed to win a World Cup since 1987.

7
Lead thyself

LIKE SOME SORT of modern-day Artful Dodger, leadership has slipped into the rugby lexicon without anyone realising it. These days a coach can barely complete a sentence without mentioning leaders or leadership in some capacity. Players, too, prattle on about their desire to be leaders and the need to be a leader within the team. It would all be very engaging and worthy were it not for the fact that no one in the game uses the term with the faintest idea of how they would actually define it. And because the term is used so loosely, the professional rugby system in New Zealand is able to convince itself that leaders are cropping up everywhere.

Someone throws all the used jerseys into the kit bag after the game and they're a leader – they are, after all, showing initiative. Someone else asks a question in a team meeting and they're a leader – seeking clarity is showing concern for detail. This goes on until everyone in the team is considered to be a leader, or at least suspected of showing leadership ability. It's nonsense and lulls New Zealand's professional rugby sides into believing they are stacked with strong, self-reliant characters who can make good decisions under pressure. The truth is not so palatable – a whole generation of leaders was lost at the beginning of the professional age as a consequence of this inability to understand precisely what constituted leadership.

In the transition from amateur to professional, a host of value systems were lost. The amateur All Blacks had a clear understanding of leadership. For them, it was all based on the knowledge that for the team to work, for it to achieve its potential, there had to be a culture of responsibility.

Individuals had to take ownership of their performance. Each one of them had to drive his own preparation. It was up to them as individuals to seek advice and guidance on the best ways to get fit, and it was up to them to find the time to implement the programmes, to fully understand their role in the team and to know how best they could contribute. If things went wrong, if mistakes were made, there was no one to blame but themselves. Everyone was individually accountable.

They were also collectively accountable, as the failure of one was effectively the failure of all. Everything, the whole structure of accountability and responsibility, started with the individual. And that's where the modern game lost its way in the early professional period. The culture of individual responsibility disappeared. The strength of the 1987 All Blacks was their understanding of where leadership started.

Each player had a responsibility, a duty, to lead himself. Leadership began with setting the alarm early enough to get a weights session in before work. Leadership was about following through and actually getting up when the alarm went off. It was about packing your own kit bag and getting along to training on time. It carried over into making sure that if a tackle had to be made, no one held back and thought it wasn't their job, or assumed someone else would do it for them. It was often said of the 1987 All Blacks they were a team of 15 leaders. That was true, in the sense that there were 15 players who led themselves. There were 15 players who were self-reliant, self-motivated and sold on the concept of accountability.

Too many modern rugby players have lost the art of self-leading, and that's a major contributing factor to the All Blacks' World Cup failures. The great All Black captains and leaders of the past – Sir Brian Lochore, Sir Wilson Whineray, Ian Kirkpatrick, Graham Mourie, Buck Shelford and Sean Fitzpatrick – were all men who were gifted at leading others. They were players who had mastered not only the art of leading themselves but also of leading the unit. They could see beyond their own frontier and how the collective needed to operate to achieve the goals.

Iconic leaders have not been so easy to find in the professional era. Tana Umaga carried himself with poise and authority and was maturing into an excellent leader when he decided to retire in 2005. His successor, Richie McCaw, may well become a great captain in the same mould as Fitzpatrick as he continues to develop his skills in the role of leading others. What is overlooked, or simply not understood, is that the great captains of the amateur era were all supported in their role by the strength of the self-leaders around them.

When Lochore captained the All Blacks, he usually had seven other provincial captains in the pack alongside him. These were men who had experience at leading others but, more pertinently, they were men who had all taken responsibility for leading themselves. The same is true of the sides Fitzpatrick, in the latter part of his career at least, and Shelford captained. Their respective jobs were made that bit easier by the self-reliance and self-motivation of the players around them. It was easier to guide the team when the component parts were all operating as they should.

'We just got on with it,' says Alan Whetton. 'We had a captain and, in my day, he was someone who had respect and leadership qualities. He did the toss and the after-match speeches, but the culture of the teams I played for – Auckland in the John Hart era and Bryan Williams and Maurice Trapp eras – was about being a leader or the best in your position because that was why you were selected. You were the best in your position and you took a lot of pride in that. When you were playing some of the finest rugby players in the world – the likes of my brother Gary, Grant Fox, John Kirwan, Michael Jones, Fitzy, Buck Shelford and John Drake – those guys were the best in their positions and we became, from my point of view, leaders in our positions, and that was my speciality.

'I was supposed to be the best and take ownership of my position. With experience and the confidence I gained in long-term selection, I became a leader. Was it thrust upon you? I don't think it was so much like that; we just grew as a team, and then within a team of three loose forwards we became leaders. We took ownership and were leaders in our own roles, and if something wasn't working we were confident enough to say so and admit it. We had the guts to admit we'd made a mistake. If you fucked up you needed to fix it. Sometimes it would just take a look or a glare and you knew. If you couldn't fix it, you would have asked for help.'

Somewhere along the line, this idea of everyone taking responsibility for their position disappeared. That became obvious in the 1999 World Cup semi-final. It was apparent no one within the All Black side was taking responsibility for fixing the problems they were encountering. There was a sense of 15 players standing back and looking for someone else to offer a solution. The culture of responsibility just wasn't there. Clearly, there weren't 15 players on the ground who were self-leaders.

But how much help did he have from his team-mates? How many of them were taking an active role in fixing the problems specific to their own positions?

When a team fails, as the All Blacks did in the 1999 event, there is a tendency to focus on the captain and the coach – to blame them for not leading the team to victory; to blame them for not finding the inspiration to lead others. That criticism is valid, but only up to a point. Captain Taine Randell probably could have done more to change the tactical approach of his side. He probably could have brought his team close and told them it was time to try a different approach.

Coming into the game, the All Blacks had been concerned about their discipline and had talked about not losing it should the French start provoking them with off-the-ball shenanigans. When the French did indeed start getting on top and niggling the All Blacks, maybe Randell should have ordered a free-for-all to deter them. Certainly, in the years since that loss, Randell has been held increasingly culpable for the failure to deviate from Plan A and react to the situation. But how much help did he have from his team-mates? How many of them were taking an active role in fixing the problems specific to their own positions? How many of them were clearly demonstrating leadership of their own performances?

The same questions could be asked about the 2003 World Cup failure. Again, Reuben Thorne as captain has been accused of being too quiet and not doing enough to alter the All Blacks' game-plan to counter the Australians. Again, this is valid. Again though, how much help did he have from his team? Who of that 2003 team could have walked off the field in Sydney and, hand-on-heart, said they had taken ownership of their performance? How many of them could hand-on-heart say they were a strong self-leader? The answer would make depressing reading.

Everyone involved in the professional game is culpable for this demise of the self-leader. Professional rugby teams in New Zealand have been guilty of defining leadership in vague terms. Not enough was done in those early years of professional rugby to hammer home the need for individuals to retain the majority stake in their own development. A rugby jargon was born where terms like 'leader', 'environment' and 'group' all became commonplace without anyone having sat down and explained what they really meant.

Auckland University psychologist Dr Jane Magnusson has worked with the Auckland Rugby Union, and she spends much of her time explaining to aspiring players exactly what is meant by leadership. 'Leadership is an interesting concept because not everyone can lead, and not everyone should lead. As we are telling people more and more now that everyone should be a leader – and we do have a society more and more now where everyone is the same – we're losing a little bit of that hierarchy that does need to happen. Leadership starts with individuals – can you lead yourself? Can you get yourself up at 5.30 am three days a week to get to the gym and train? Can you lead yourself to have clean gear and good boots? Can you self-lead? And that's where it starts. I don't know that it's been made all that clear what a leader is, and what we're looking for. There are entire courses on leadership and we're tossing the word around because it's kind of flavour of the month.

' "We need a leader" is a catch phase. But I don't know that we know who we're targeting. There's leadership by dominance, by ordering around and being the bossiest person; there's leadership by inspiring, by setting a good example for people to follow. I don't know that we've defined it well enough to start churning out good leaders. It has to start with self-leaders.'

IT OFTEN happens, when standards have slowly and imperceptibly been slipping, that there comes a point when it's obvious the nadir has been reached. In the case of the All Blacks, it wasn't the failures at the 1999 and 2003 World Cups that shook the system into facing up to its shortcomings. The ability of the All Blacks to recover after World Cup losses and continue on their winning way lulled everyone into believing there was no systemic failing. The World Cup failures could be attributed to a host of factors, all of which were deemed to be specific to the tournament.

It was easy to be convinced by such an argument. Outside of World Cups the All Blacks remained the world's premier team. They lost to France in the 1999 semi-final but, come 2000, they showed mental fortitude, leadership and strength of character to defeat Australia in a test many believe could have been the greatest ever played. Likewise, the All Blacks kicked off the 2004 season by annihilating England, the team that had won the 2003 World Cup.

The ability to keep winning outside the World Cup encouraged the provincial, Super 14 and national coaches to believe in what they were doing. They couldn't see that there was much wrong with the set-up when the system continued to produce a winning All Black team. The World Cup failures could be down to the quality of opposition and the tighter margins.

The All Blacks were also in the unfortunate position of being the team everyone saw as the benchmark; therefore they were more likely to face opponents who were going to play above themselves. Throw in an unfortunate bounce of the ball here and there, the odd poor refereeing call, a couple of mistakes by the All Blacks, and it could all be written off as a bad day. That's why, in the wake of the 1999 failure and, initially in the wake of the 2003 failure, nothing dramatic was done to make a difference to the way the players prepared.

The catalyst for change came in August 2004 when the All Blacks suffered back-to-back Tri-Nations defeats in Sydney, then Johannesburg. Those two games were the first time the All Blacks had played away from home under coach Graham Henry, who had been appointed in December 2003. In both games the All Blacks demonstrated a lack of accountability. They played, as they had in their previous World Cup failures, with no sense of individual or collective responsibility. The self-leadership was missing. The senior players in the team also failed to lead others.

Henry and his assistant coaches, Steve Hansen and Wayne Smith, as well as selector Sir Brian Lochore, were quite disturbed by what they'd witnessed. It wasn't just the nature of the defeats that got to them. They were concerned at the way some individuals had prepared and, in particular, they felt there was not enough dynamism in the camp off the field. The experience of touring, albeit for one week for one test, should be a highlight in a player's career. It's an opportunity to be embraced, to enrich the experience of being away from home; a negative attitude opens the way for travel to become a chore, for players to become bored and disengaged.

When the All Blacks played at home, there were various distractions for the players during the week. There were friends and family to catch up with, favourite restaurants to be visited – whatever constituted the security blanket that helped the players feel comfortable in their environment.

It was when the team left the crutch of home comforts behind that Henry and the other coaches saw something which disturbed them. The players were nowhere near as self-reliant as they'd hoped. There was a culture of train, rest, train, rest, and then play. There was too much time spent around the team's hotel – time that sapped energy and immersed players too deeply in the rugby mode. The players didn't show a lot of initiative when it came to entertaining themselves. There was not enough self-driving of the preparation routine. Too many players waited for someone else to tell them what to do.

This, as far as Henry was concerned, had to change. The talent within the All Blacks was such that they were always going to be able to win a fair proportion of their games. There were just enough self-leaders and senior players to guide the team through some tight games. But there was no doubt that a strong enough base to guide the team to victory in the really tight games – like World Cups – was missing.

Lochore says those two weeks in August 2004 left an indelible impression on him and the coaching team. 'I was in Sydney in 2004 and watched them lose quite badly. Then they went to South Africa and were given what was a tanning really. We [the management team] sat in Wellington for a couple of days after that and asked why it was that a team could play so well on a good day and so badly on a bad day. We felt there was a lack of responsibility and not enough people putting their hands up in the professional era. It's something that happened over a period of time and something that happened when they were playing badly. It was the nature of the professional game that everyone wanted to look after their own contract and think about No 1. But if you get 15 people who go into their shells, then you can get into a disastrous situation.

'That led to the implementation of the leadership programme. The youth of today are not into leadership. It's not cool to be a leader. They'd never sampled everyday situations where they had to make decisions. They hadn't held down what we could call a proper job for any length of time. They were told what to do and when to do it all the time. They would go to training and be told what to do. They would be told what to eat. How to train – yet when you get to the game of rugby, it's all about being able to make decisions for yourself. I was quite staggered by the lack of self-reliance.

'Gilbert Enoka [the mental skills coach] and I invited them to come and talk one-on-one with a view to building their self-belief and self-esteem. At first they were reluctant to come, but after the initial break-through some of the players started asking if they could come for a chat. They would come in and talk about this house they'd bought, or something they were getting into, and it was so much better than having them lying on the couch watching DVDs. I was staggered until I realised they were just victims of society. I don't think they were into a DVD/PlayStation culture in the All Blacks, for the simple reason they just didn't have time. But I think it probably did happen in the Super 14 franchises, and a number of them even admitted that they didn't really know how to fill in their time.

'Those who had an outside interest produced 20 per cent more effort.'

'We were supposedly looking after them, but we were mollycoddling them. I read an article where a guy had done some research in the US and he made a comparison between people who had an outside interest and those who just trained and played. Those who had an outside interest produced 20 per cent more effort. Even if it was just half of that, it would be enormous. We wanted the guys to be busy and to keep themselves occupied, and we wanted them to be self-reliant, to make decisions and look after one another. We had to get them to change the way they were going and [start]viewing the team differently.'

Lochore has always been recognised as a fair man of considered judgements, which is why he didn't blame the players for their own failings. The source of the problem was far deeper. The lack of self-reliance was, as Lochore saw it, indicative of both society at large and the professional rugby system.

The All Blacks, in Lochore's view, really were a product of their environment. They struggled to lead, to show initiative and take responsibility because they had come through a professional rugby system that didn't require them to be in any way independent. The system catered for their every need in terms of access to training aids and advice. The pathway was cleared so all the players ever had to do was train and play – the peripheral stuff was taken care of.

It's easy to understand why the system was set up that way, to provide the athlete with the maximum possible time to prepare without distractions. The intentions were good but the outcome was one that few had the foresight to predict – the players ceased to think or fend for themselves.

The societal factor can't be underplayed either. The personality of the players was shaped well before they reached the All Blacks, and Lochore quickly became aware of the fragile ego of the modern player. Again, that should have been no surprise given how protected the typical modern child was from hard knocks.

Modern parenting is more about risk avoidance than risk management. Auckland's clogged roads are a testament to these changed attitudes; children were expected to walk to school once, but now most get driven. Sports are cancelled when it rains, and the safety net of continual assessment takes the pressure off the old-fashioned exam-only system.

Anxiety and paranoia have taken hold and we can only speculate what this frantic parenting does to the spirit of adventure and the attitude of children to risk. We warn them off exploring their surroundings, against using their initiative to discover things for themselves. It's a stifling environment and one that is far less effective than letting nature take its course. Personal experience is everything for children. If they fall off a climbing frame because they've taken on too much risk, that experience stays with them. It allows them to evaluate future risks better.

Anyone with children will know that if they fail at something, their natural response is to try again. They fight hard to succeed and to complete what they started. Encouraging children to persevere, not to stand back when they're in mild danger of a scraped knee, is the parental attitude that nurtured Sir Edmund Hillary. Colin Meads came through that school, as did Sean Fitzpatrick and Buck Shelford.

Over-protective parenting means most children lack exposure to direct criticism. We have, en masse, dropped standards to promote equality. Rather than reward those who achieve excellence and encourage others to aspire to it, we have a philosophy now that says everyone has to succeed. Back when schools set exam papers there were clearly defined parameters marking success and failure. Now the stigma of failing has been removed and everyone gets a pat on the back even if they've only managed to write their own name.

Not everyone has the necessary skills, drive and ambition to succeed, but we create a false environment in which they're rewarded nonetheless. Take for example the way Pass the Parcel is played now. For Generation X and those who went before, there was only one prize at the centre of multiple layers of wrapping. Now there's a prize under every layer. Everyone wins.

And what about the practice at many schools of discouraging score-keeping in junior sports? This is done to prevent children from feeling stigmatised; participation is promoted above everything. But competition is healthy. Competition prepares children for life – when they get out into the real world, it's fierce. When they go for a job interview there'll be other candidates and there won't be a prize for everyone.

But positive reinforcement is seen as the only way forward, which is why most of the All Blacks Lochore encountered had to be handled delicately. They had emerged into adulthood without ever having faced constructive criticism. 'We had to start at square one,' says Lochore of re-building the self-esteem and self-reliance of the All Blacks. 'You couldn't be critical. We weren't starting halfway up the ladder. That was what surprised me. We had guys who had a bit of experience but in terms of responsibility they were miles behind. I think if a guy has potential to be an All Black you have to bale into them.

'I'm being very general here, but there are some guys who haven't been disciplined. There are some whose preparation has been very poor. They should know what to do, but their experiences have been less than what ours were [when we played]. They are probably not as mentally tough as we were. They have never been growled at. I had to be careful not to upset anyone. I liked giving them a bit of hell. I wouldn't be straight critical. I would use a bit of humour. If you're going to be critical you have to be fair and you have to give them the opportunity to come back. I don't think the modern player is criticised as much.

'It's the same in life. It's the same in marriage, too. It seems they have one argument and they get divorced. People are much more sensitive to criticism, but I think that's where you make your gains – when someone points out where you've gone wrong and you learn from it. How can you even know if you are going wrong if no one ever tells you? The modern parent doesn't put a line in the sand and I think they need to.

'I don't think we can point the finger here. This is something that has just evolved. It crept up on us. I was with the team in 1995 just before the game went professional. Most of them had part-time jobs. Their preparation was a bit stronger at that point, because now they have their agents and their managers, all the people telling them what to do every minute of the day so they don't have to think for themselves. It comes back to the fact we had jobs, families and responsibilities and yet we had to find the time to get fit. It was self-motivation – which is the best kind.

'The thing that we did [in 2004] was give them more responsibility. [We] made them feel that they were running the team. The coaches were very good at taking the senior players into their confidence and talking to them about tactics and in a lot of cases the guys came up with some very good ideas. The most frustrating thing from my point of view is that we took the time to try to change the culture from [one of] selfish, self-interested people into total team people, and in the end it all came to nothing.'

When Lochore says it all came to nothing he means it didn't deliver the World Cup. It didn't necessarily all come to nothing though. Lochore had been at the helm of a cultural revolution. He had been invited into the All Black fold and encountered a culture that had been allowed to drift; a culture that too closely reflected the societal drift that had eroded traditional values such as self-reliance, independent thought and re-sourcefulness. He discovered players who were too sensitive to accept direct criticism and absorb home truths and instigate change.

When he'd been coach of the All Blacks in 1987, it was not so different. His players back then were also a product of their environment. It was just that the environment in the late 1980s had fostered a grittier individual – players who were used to struggle, hard knocks and hurtful truths. The players of 1987 never had any choice but to lead themselves – no one was there to do it for them. Almost to a man, the team of 1987 had better self-leaders, or at least it had an ingrained culture of self-leadership making it less likely that individuals would hide on the big occasion.

They had more than that though. They also had men who could lead others – men who were adept at getting the best out of themselves and those around them. Self-leadership has been lacking in the professional era, but just as damaging has been the dearth of inspirational leaders, cool-headed players who can look their team-mates in the eye and elicit more effort. Strong decision-makers, those who can read the game, instigate tactical change and take responsibility for it, have been conspicuous by their absence at World Cups.

8
Follow the leader

RUGBY USED TO pride itself on being a simple game. You had big blokes who beat each other up in the forwards and smaller blokes who tried to dance past each other in the backs. There was a coach, usually a former player, who vaguely organised things at training, picked the team and maybe gave a rough idea of what strategy to employ. And that was largely it.

The best rugby sides kept things uncluttered. Most important of all, the best rugby sides had a captain who was unmistakeably in charge. When there was a decision to be made, the captain would make it. When an inspirational speech was required, the captain would give it. If someone needed to be brought back into line, it would be the captain who would do the pulling. No one was ever confused under that system. The captain was in charge and everyone knew it.

Just to make sure there was no doubt whatsoever, even in test matches, coaches were not allowed on the field at half-time. Teams would have a few minutes break out on the field and hear from their captain where they were going right and where they were going wrong.

That was the way right through until the introduction of professionalism and it was a system that served New Zealand rather well. The All Blacks, over the years, never had any problems producing strong captains, iconic figures who bore the responsibilities of office as effortlessly as French women accessorise. The names reel off – Sir Wilson Whineray, Sir Brian Lochore, Graham Mourie, Buck Shelford, Sean Fitzpatrick. These men were great captains. These men could lead themselves and they could also lead others.

It would be a major study in itself to determine just what made these men such influential and successful leaders. There are, however, two key factors that can be singled out, neither of which is inherent in the individuals themselves. The first, as has been discussed, is that for most of the time these men were at the helm they were lucky enough to be surrounded by a number of strong self-leaders. When a captain has strong characters around him he can concentrate more on his job as a player and less on worrying about everyone else.

The second factor is that all these great captains of the amateur era operated in a system where they had responsibility thrust upon them because it came with the job. Even in the late amateur era, the captain was the undisputed central figure in the team. He, and not the coach, was the first port of call for most of the players. He, and not the coach, had to make snap decisions on the field, assess what was working and what was not and adjust accordingly. It was a different job back then. There was no ambiguity and that helped. The lines of jurisdiction were clearly defined; there was never any confusion about who was responsible for what. If things were not going right on the field, it was pretty much down to the captain to read the situation and react. The coach was responsible for selection, for providing a game-plan and coming up with a few moves. But if the game-plan wasn't working, then it was up to the captain to change tack.

The All Blacks relished the simplicity of that environment; the captain having to adapt and work things out on the run suited the Kiwi mentality perfectly. New Zealand, after all, was a pioneering society. This was a country that prided itself on ingenuity, innovation and initiative. Many great All Blacks held jobs that required them to continually assess and react to their environment. The challenge of planning on the hoof, of responding smartly and creatively to a problem no one saw coming was seen as a Kiwi trait – one of the many qualities behind the nation's growth and success. The skills of assessing, planning and executing were in operation throughout the New Zealand economy for much of the amateur era. So there was existing aptitude in leadership generally.

Throw in too the fact that so many New Zealanders knew rugby inside out, that they were great readers of the game, clever thinkers and tacticians, and it's no wonder the All Blacks produced so many great captains.

That quality of leadership – in both the large number of self-leaders, and the men who could lead others – was a key All Black strength throughout the amateur era. Under pressure, the All Blacks had men who made good decisions. They had leaders who could steady the ship, use their wisdom and experience to make bold tactical calls.

Test football is a brutal environment. There's no time to think. Everything happens that much faster in the test arena than it does at provincial or club level. The sense of occasion is magnified, the intensity is greater, the expectation is greater and during the amateur era, the capacity for opponents to surprise was greater. There was no detailed analysis of video footage back then. There was no satellite TV to bring the nuances of play of various overseas test stars into the living rooms of the men they would face in tests. There was much less training. Game-plans were not as detailed or as complex and games tended to swing more on instinctive brilliance. A captain could make a significant difference in those less structured amateur days. There was a much greater capacity to make relevant and defining tactical decisions. The All Blacks, as well as having great players, had great leaders.

The spontaneity of the game was lost under a deluge of intelligence.

It all changed when the game turned professional. The entire rugby hierarchy became confused. Lines of responsibility became harder to read. The key role was no longer that of captain; the job was effectively reduced to front-of-house work, post-match analysis for the media and coin tossing. Bloated management teams made all the key decisions.

What was once a simple game became unduly complex. Everyone had time to analyse opponents, time to come up with clever strategies to beat opponents. The detail of the analysis was phenomenal. Clever computer programmes were written to track the every move of various players. An All Black would enter a test knowing – or at least he should have known – whether his opposite man preferred stepping off his left or right foot. He should be able to pick up cues, obtained from video evidence, about where opponents were going to attack. The spontaneity of the game was lost under a deluge of intelligence. The capacity to surprise was all but gone and the power of independent thought was almost totally stripped from the players.

If the process of selecting a team and preparing it seemed frighteningly scientific, the process of actually playing had become formulaic, regimented even, with players, by and large, working to predetermined plans. Decision-making wasn't supposed to be instinctive any more – it was about choosing which one of the prescribed options to execute.

That was the way rugby evolved in New Zealand in the earliest days of professionalism. Maybe the heavy media intrusion that came with professionalism, and the subsequent awareness within the All Blacks that they were a brand rather than a team, led to a different emphasis being placed on the skills required to be captain. The iconic captain was no longer in vogue. The preference was to have an articulate, corporate-style executive who could deliver the key messages to a wider audience and set the right tone off the field. With the coaching panel of most professional teams having such a major input to the tactical approach and the game being so structured on the field, there wasn't the same need to have an instinctive thinker as captain.

The art of captaincy in New Zealand changed quickly from the outset of professionalism. That probably wasn't deliberate or even conscious – it was just the way things evolved. Professionalism came in such a rush that there was an awful lot being made up on the hoof. It wasn't easy for anyone to stand back and see the big picture, to assess what affect micro decisions would have on the macro climate. The evolution of the role of the captain was an area where there were no obvious signs of bigger problems looming. But they were there.

Although the captain became increasingly impotent in the greater scheme of things, a strong leader on the field was still important. There still had to be a clear head in the midst of battle capable of instructing others and making sure the game-plan was implemented. There was less room for a captain to manoeuvre but he still had a job to do – he still had to execute the coach's instructions, he still had to keep a handle on the mental and physical state of his team-mates to determine which of the available options was going to work best, and he still had to have an influence on the referee.

The All Blacks had many strong leaders with skills honed in the amateur era who crossed over into the professional code. That was both a blessing and a curse. It allowed the All Blacks to produce some of the finest rugby ever seen in 1996 and 1997, but it also blinded coaches and administrators to the fact that their brave new world was not producing a new generation of leaders.

New Zealand suffered a triple whammy in 1998 when captain Sean Fitzpatrick, pack leader Zinzan Brooke and senior player Frank Bunce all retired at the same time. The All Blacks, after years and years of brilliant leadership, were suddenly scrambling for a captain. They lost five games in a row in 1998, but it wasn't until the failed World Cup campaign of 1999 that New Zealand really learned how important on-field leadership remained in the modern game, and the consequences of failing to produce strong leaders.

THOSE WHO saw the semi-final between France and New Zealand at the 1999 World Cup will never forget it. It was, and may indeed remain, the most extraordinary game of rugby ever played. A thousand and one images from that game may stick in the memory but there's one that will last forever, one that many followers of the game thought they'd never see – an All Black side totally lacking in leadership. The image of 15 All Blacks unable to sort things out on the field, unable to determine the best course of action and then implement it, was the most shocking part of the afternoon. The All Blacks failed to make strong decisions in the second half. They failed to respond to the intensity of the French. They failed to stand up and think their way out of the problem.

It's easy to eulogise the old-timers and say that such a meek surrender would never have happened on BJ Lochore's watch. That Graham Mourie would have died trying to change the outcome, or that Sean Fitzpatrick would have found a way to slow things down, to unsettle the French, regroup his troops and see his side safely through to the final. Sometimes we conveniently forget the faults of the old-timers and insist they would have delivered success where others failed. But we can predict with a reasonable degree of certainty that virtually every All Black side of the last 100 years would have shown stronger leadership if placed in the same position as the 1999 team.

Some blame has to fall on the shoulders of captain Taine Randell. He had a chance to be a hero, to make a name for himself. It was sink or swim and he sank – without a trace. There was no problem-solving on the field. There was no assessment of the threat being posed and no plan formulated to counter that threat.

With the benefit of hindsight, Randell was not the right choice as captain. He wasn't ready or maybe he just didn't have the skills required to operate under pressure. He was the perfect choice for the brave new world, however. He was young, articulate, intelligent and Maori. He was the perfect front man for the modern All Blacks and their desire to be seen as a brand, as a corporate, multicultural, inclusive entity. But Randell wasn't an iconic on-field leader. He wasn't instinctive, and he didn't have the strength of personality to enforce his will among those around him.

However, to focus too hard on the failure of the players to make critical decisions is to miss the real problem. As Lochore realised when he came on board as an All Black selector in 2004, the players were merely a product of their environment.

Those players who came into the professional game could leave their brains at the door; they could expect to sit back and be told what to do by the coach. The notion of on-field leadership wasn't quite alien, but it had certainly become less of a priority. Professional teams in New Zealand concentrated on building top-quality athletes to implement the clever game-plans dreamt up by their coaches. There was no need to worry too much about building strong leaders as so much influence was being wielded by the coach. If the players trained well and then followed the plan, the All Blacks would be just fine.

That faith was misplaced. As the 1999 semi-final demonstrated, the best teams still had smart generals on the field. The All Blacks didn't. The secondary danger of the All Black system was that it created ambiguity about who was responsible for fixing problems during the game. Was it the captain's and senior players' responsibility to implement tactical change during the game? They came on to the field with a plan, and presumably variations on the plan should things not work out. But what if they went through the available options and still had no success? Should Randell have thought, to hell with the coach; let's do things our way? Or should coach John Hart have got a message to the players to try something radically different?

Nothing is clear-cut now, not as it was in the old days when it came down to the captain and the senior players to fix things. And they knew it was down to them. That sense of responsibility was missing at the 1999 World Cup.

When the All Blacks were cruising through their June tests and the Tri-Nations, the cracks went undetected. It took severe pressure to expose the truth – that none of the players on the field in that second half actually knew how to climb out of the hole they were in. More disturbingly, most if not all of the players didn't believe it was their responsibility to find a way.

Peter Thorburn, the former North Harbour and US Eagles coach who took over as an All Black selector shortly after the doomed 1999 campaign, makes this assessment of that day at Twickenham. 'In 1999 they were under the Hart regime where they were totally under the thumb. In fact if you get a tape of the game against France and look at it just after half-time when there is an injury or a stoppage, Randell and those guys are looking up into the stands. Dave Abercrombie [the team physiotherapist] came out and they were looking to Hart to find out what they should do. The French were getting into the ascendancy and they [All Blacks] didn't know what to do. Hart was a control freak. I'm not saying he was a bad guy but he was a total control freak and he had the players under his thumb and they weren't allowed to breathe.'

This was a long way from the simple game rugby had once been. There was confusion about who should be doing what – and that's hardly surprising. The players were being pushed through a system in which they weren't really encouraged to think too much for themselves. They were asked to follow instructions most of their waking hours, when they could be controlled or influenced by a wider management group. But once they were on the field, the influence the coach and the wider management group could exert was vastly diminished. The most the coach could do was get messages on to the field to tinker with the tactics, to hammer a certain theme that had been learned on the training ground.

The strangest thing, though, was that after telling the players what to do during the week, when to do it and for how long, coaches generally had the attitude that the team were on their own come match-day. Once they were on the field it was pretty much up to them, and particularly the captain, to work out how to implement what had been practised during the build-up. If things weren't going to plan, the coach had 10 minutes at half-time – in the changing room – to get his point across again. The actual 80 minutes of rugby, however, was down to the players.

When you stop to think about this it doesn't make sense. The players were not empowered on the training field. They were not empowered to take responsibility for the team culture off the field. Even the captain was reduced to delivering the coach's message, albeit in his own style. As they prepared, the team were in no doubt as to the authority of the coach and the control he exerted – yet, come the game, the players were being asked to take responsibility.

The picture became even more confused when the coach was able to get messages on to the field through water carriers, physios, medical staff and the like. No wonder the players at Twickenham in 1999 stood looking hopefully toward the stands.

Everyone wanted answers in the wake of the 1999 disaster, but strangely enough very little was done over the next four years to address the obvious failings in the system. Come Sydney, 2003, the failure of leadership fiasco was repeated. Reuben Thorne was just as poor a choice for captain as Randell before him. A lovely bloke, and a great inspiration at provincial and Super 12 level, Thorne was not a strong leader in terms of being able to own the game-plan and work the right areas of it. And, just like Randell, he was not supported by a crew of strong self-leaders. There were some great players in his side, but they were mostly young and inexperienced, hoping to be told, or shown, what to do by somebody else.

Just like 1999, there was no sense of the players taking responsibility for the outcome in 2003. They followed through the game-plan as rigidly as their predecessors and were just as unsure as to whether it was their responsibility or that of coach John Mitchell to try something different. The danger with blurred responsibility is that players can hide. They can fail to make decisions and later suggest it wasn't their fault, and no one can really argue the point.

The similarities between 1999 and 2003 were quite alarming. The wrong captain was chosen for the wrong reasons and in neither team were players given anywhere near enough input into team affairs. Under pressure, both the 1999 and 2003 All Blacks cracked and that really is no surprise. These teams failed because they had very little experience in leading themselves and their on-field general didn't have the required strength of personality. Nor did they fully understand their own responsibilities as against those of the coach.

It was a different story in 2007. Coach Graham Henry had spent most of his tenure addressing the key weaknesses that led to ineffective decision-making. He gave the players responsibility for team affairs and asked them to lead in various aspects of their professional and non-professional lives. He built a leadership group to ensure a body of strong thinkers, men who would be able to input solid intelligence, around the captain.

There was also greater clarity around jurisdiction between the players and the coaches. The very essence of Henry's thinking was that he was never going to be on the field, so he had to do all that he could to build strong generals who would always know it was their responsibility to lead on the field. The greatest crime a player could commit in the first four years of the Henry era was failing to make a decision. He could make mistakes, but to opt out, to simply hope someone else would do it for him, wasn't on.

Henry's other great success was in his selection of captain. He always had a vision of the type of leader he wanted and the relevant skills he would need. He started his tenure with Tana Umaga and then handed the armband to Richie McCaw.

Both were excellent choices and when McCaw took over in 2006, there was every reason to believe many of the issues that surfaced when the team was under pressure had been eradicated. In Brisbane that year, the All Blacks were under intense pressure against the Wallabies but they continued to make effective decisions through the 80 minutes. No one did more in that regard than McCaw.

A year later, they were well down after 60 minutes against a strong South African side in Durban. There was potential to panic, to try some high-risk football. Instead, the All Blacks continued to believe in their skills, in the game-plan, and McCaw led them to a dramatic late win that was secured with some stunning rugby.

It felt, in July 2007, as if the one great flaw in the All Black make-up, their inability to respond well under pressure, had been fixed. It was a major surprise then, to see the All Blacks capitulate as they did.

There were extenuating circumstances. The All Blacks were battling a referee who wasn't biased, just staggeringly incompetent, and who awarded the French 10 penalties and New Zealand only two. The All Blacks also suffered an unusually high injury count on the night with Dan Carter, Jerry Collins, Nick Evans and Chris Masoe all being forced from the field – the latter two only minutes after they had come on as replacements. With Anton Oliver substituted and Thorne, Aaron Mauger and Doug Howlett not selected, there were precious few members of the leadership group on the field in those critical final 15 minutes.

All that led to the independent report into the World Cup, which concluded that: 'The combination of these factors put enormous pressure on the All Blacks leadership and decision-making. We consider that on-field leadership and decision-making was a factor in the loss in the quarter-final. Arguably, the team and its leadership group had only occasionally been tested to the same degree over the last four years. The trend, as witnessed in Melbourne earlier in 2007, was for the leaders to revert to type and let McCaw make the calls.

'In the dying minutes of that critical game, the leadership model failed to deliver what was its most important objective – decisions which give the best chance of winning the game. With the benefit of hindsight, the team failed to ensure that the right decisions were taken. As with the philosophy underpinning the leadership model, the players, coaches and management must take responsibility for that.'

Given the work done by Henry to strengthen the leadership of the side and to better equip the All Blacks, it is baffling that the 2007 campaign failed in such a similar fashion to previous meltdowns. Many astute judges were convinced they were going to see McCaw lift the trophy aloft on 20 October as the All Blacks were not only the best team, but they were also finally a team with backbone and a strong captain. That of course did not turn out to be the case or, at least if it was the case, the All Blacks still failed to display leadership qualities and make strong decisions under pressure in a World Cup.

Could it be that the All Blacks are simply destined to bomb at World Cups? Is that the cruel fate afforded them by the rugby gods – a malign karma earned by their dominance at all other times?

A more likely explanation has been put forward by David Kirk, the 1987 World Cup-winning captain. He is of the view that to create the right strength of character within both the team and the man chosen to lead it, you have to do more than set up a leadership group within the All Blacks. He believes the concept of leadership and of taking responsibility for decision-making begins far earlier. 'It's important that you have a group of leaders who are responsible for winning on the field. It's important that you have a group of players where leadership is inherent, not just the captain. You have to remember that team [1987] went on to be very successful for a long time. There were players in that team who were among the top in the world. Look at the facts and the sort of careers those people went on to enjoy.

'To win an important test match under pressure you have to go back to education. The physical stuff just about evens itself out. We have been the most successful side before World Cups. England [in 2007] were a joke. They had a powerful set-piece but they were well off the pace and reached the final, so we know it's not the physical capabilities. That's not distinctive. It's the mental capacity that's tied into the tactical approach. Great players adapt – how do you find a way to win during the 80-minute period? What causes mental strength – life experiences and education provide the bedrock and what follows from that is the decision-making, the analytical problem-solving. You've got to do that for yourself, both in real time and emotionally.

'You need raw intelligence. Can you think through a problem and solve it? Identify the problem and analyse it? The emotional side is, are you able to keep making decisions under pressure? Analysis can be clouded by anxiety – you worry so much about losing that you can't focus on what you are doing, then the one place you lose control is in your head. Can you come up with the goods and control your emotions? Can you assess the potential options? – work out that this is what we can do, then have the courage to do it. It's easy to just keep doing what you've been doing. What can you do to change the flow of the match, or are you going to do what you have always done? I don't know enough about how they communicate during the match. How we used to do it was the coaches were not even allowed on the field at half-time. It was the captain who spoke, you had to take responsibility and you had to have courage. If there's a division of that emotional strength, it's damaging.'

THE ANALYSIS of the 2007 failure could go on forever. It is possibly the most intriguing of the failures in light of the stronger leadership base that the team was given. Why that model broke down at the critical time may never be fully understood. There were so many variables on the night, so many factors that all led to the failure.

But Sean Fitzpatrick, arguably the greatest All Black captain of all time and a key member of the 1987 team, offers a simple take on things and one that is worthy of deep consideration. Fitzpatrick doesn't see leadership as something that should be over-analysed. He's not one to get overly complex. His view is that the number one rule to being a good leader is to focus first and foremost on being a good player. That is the foundation stone on which great captains are built. If the captain does his job as a player, if he deserves his place in the team, then everything will flow from there.

'I'm a believer that leaders can be made – sure, some are born – but I'm a believer that if you give people an opportunity and throw them in at the deep end and give them the right tools then they can become a very good leader. In 1992 I didn't want to be a leader, I didn't want to be the captain of the All Blacks. It was our centenary year and for me it was a case of growing into the job. It wasn't until 1994 or even 1995 that I actually felt comfortable being in that position. It was a position that I fell into and in the end it was a position that I enjoyed.

'I didn't feel like I had the right skills. I knew I could play rugby and that's what I'd done for my previous six years in the All Blacks. And to do that, I had to do my own job. The biggest thing about leadership is to make sure you are the person that's going to get selected anyway, and secondly winning makes a huge difference. When you start winning, you start developing confidence, you start trying things, but when you're on the back foot you're going to really struggle.

'I'd captained age-grade teams, the New Zealand Under 21s, the First XV at school, but I came into the All Blacks at a very young age and I was educated and taken along for the ride. I played for very, very good teams. I played for Auckland and I played for the All Blacks. So from a young age I was exposed to different forms of leadership – some good, some not so good, some not good at all. It gave me an overview. When I came into the position I was trying to piece together a Buck Shelford and Andy Dalton and a David Kirk instead of concentrating on being me.

'I was fortunate, I didn't have a bad leader in a broader sense. There were some [aspects] of particular leaders that I didn't really like. There were good attributes among them all. I sat down with Andy Dalton after I was made captain. I rang Kirky [Ian Kirkpatrick], spoke to different players and then one day I sat down with John Sturgeon, one of the great All Black managers. He said: "Sean, you don't need to do anything else other than play well. All you have to do is lead by example." The other guys like John Kirwan and Grant Fox, they were there and they said, "Look, we'll tell you if you're saying enough or not saying enough, or if you're talking rubbish."

'So to have that was unbelievable. I had this belief that I was going to be the next David Kirk or the next Andy Dalton straight away. I came in at a young age and I was leading a team that was pretty average and the expectation was that we were going to have a better year. Maybe I wasn't given the right tools early on, I don't know.

'There's a lot made of leadership. We had Laurie Mains. He was a total dictator and he didn't give us any leadership. He sat us down said, "Get out there, this is what you're going to do." I didn't like that at all, it wasn't the way I was brought up. I was brought up in terms of group leadership. But we were in a situation where we weren't capable of doing it, so we were stripped back to the bones and told this is what you've got, boys. If you don't like it, get out of here. A lot of my team from 1991 couldn't foot it because they didn't like the team being stripped back to the bare bones.'

At first the Fitzpatrick theory doesn't seem to stack up in regard to the 2007 captain, Richie McCaw. The openside flanker was, by some distance, the best No 7 in the world. In 2008, All Black assistant coach Steve Hansen even went so far as to suggest McCaw might in fact be the best openside New Zealand has ever produced. It wasn't a claim that was laughed out of town. McCaw was absolutely worthy of his jersey – no question of that.

But the effects of the reconditioning window earlier in the season shouldn't be underestimated. McCaw missed a lot of rugby as a consequence and his game was all about timing and instinct. He needed more game time to be at his best and while he was hardly shabby in 2007, it wasn't his best year. His standards, albeit remarkably high standards, were not fully achieved in 2007. His lack of sharpness was perceptible to those who'd followed his career closely. His confidence might have been slightly down, and if the Fitzpatrick theory is correct, that may well have had an effect on McCaw's decision-making ability. While he wasn't playing badly, he wasn't at his peak – a point McCaw would have felt within himself. Many of his leadership group were in the same boat and if every key decision-maker was feeling just that little bit lower in confidence, that might explain why the All Blacks failed again in 2007.

Certainly the Fitzpatrick theory stacks up in 2003 and 1999. Thorne was by no means a unanimous choice on the blindside of the scrum. There was a vocal lobby who wanted him out of the team, not just removed from the captaincy. There were genuine contenders for his position and genuine arguments to be made that Thorne was not the right player for the number six jersey. While he always tried to give the impression of being immune to the constant criticism, the deluge of protestors campaigning against him must have had an effect on Thorne's confidence. Could he really be an effective captain if he was constantly under pressure to prove he was even worthy of selection in the first place?

The same is true for Randell, who was dogged by stories that he never had the support of his senior team-mates throughout his tenure. He had shown some ability when he had come into the team in 1997. He was fortunate then to be playing as part of an established and brilliant team. When he was thrust into the captaincy the following year and the All Blacks lost five games in a row, Randell never looked the same player. It would be next to impossible to become a great leader if you harboured doubts your team-mates respected you as either a captain or as a player.

Fitzpatrick on the other hand was a great captain on the back of being a great player. He was also fortunate that he came into the All Blacks at a young age and was exposed to various forms of leadership so he could determine what worked and what didn't. There was more to his success than just that, though. As Kirk said, the process of building great players and great leaders begins well before they reach the All Blacks. Fitzpatrick, like the rest of his 1987 colleagues, was one of the last to be afforded a genuine rugby apprenticeship.

9
Death of the apprenticeship

WHEN THE PLAYERS of 1987 were out pounding the roads during their pre-season work, it wasn't the thought of one day being an All Black that drove them through the pain barrier. In the amateur era, there were no shortcuts to the national team. There was a defined apprenticeship to be served. Players dreamed first of winning a regular place in their club side. If they were good enough at that level to stand out, they might gain selection for their provincial side. It was only at that point, when they had earned the provincial blazer, that they started to dream of maybe, just maybe, becoming All Blacks.

The modern players will say that things are no different today. That the apprenticeship still has to be served, that there are still various points that have to be reached along the way toward national honours. But that is only partly true. The professional structure has made it possible for players to skip parts of the process. Players can jump from an age-grade side to the All Blacks without being halted by much in between.

Examples of fast-tracked All Blacks are numerous these days. By the end of 2003, Joe Rokocoko had played more for the All Blacks than he had for his Super 12 franchise. He was an integral member of the World Cup side that year and yet he had never even played for Auckland. He didn't actually wear his provincial jersey until September 2004, by which time he had won almost 30 test caps and was sitting high up the list of all-time New Zealand try-scorers. His journey was one of the more extreme examples of a player reaching the top end of the game in a big hurry.

Isaia Toeava was another. He had started just one game for Auckland when he was selected for the All Blacks' end-of-season tour in 2005. He'd won the coaching panel over earlier in the year with his performances at the Under-19 World Cup. He hadn't even played Super 12 when he was asked to wear the black jersey at Murrayfield.

The roads travelled by Rokocoko and Toeava were not quite typical, but they were certainly indicative of changing career paths in the professional game. Yes, there are still players who make the national side after years of honest toil with their provincial and Super Rugby sides. Jono Gibbes, Steven Bates and Craig Newby were all granted All Black caps in 2004 on the back of their loyal and dedicated service to their provincial and Super Rugby teams. They had stuck it out in the trenches year after year and they were called into the All Black camp on the basis they were good guys, hard workers who wouldn't let anyone down. But the path to the All Blacks is becoming increasingly shorter. Players are selected younger. They are selected with far less experience, and professional rugby stands accused of killing the apprenticeship.

There are two key ways in which the professional game has altered the path to international honours. Since 1996 the process of monitoring players has become not only more sophisticated, but more extensive. It used to be that a player would only really come onto the radar if he managed an extended run of decent games for his club. At that point, the relevant provincial coach would be notified there was someone worth taking a look at.

If the player in question took the coach's fancy some inquiries would be made about the individual's temperament and background, and slowly, if that player continued to progress, a limited data bank would be built up. By the time a player reached the All Blacks, a reasonable amount of knowledge about his strengths and weaknesses would most likely be in circulation. That's very different to how things are now.

Players are now coming on to the radar at the age of 15. Schools have sophisticated assessment systems that have been built in conjunction with provincial unions. Most unions design a selection template for each position and players are then marked accordingly on the various criteria. As players progress through age-grade sides more and more data is collected to monitor their development. In addition to the selection template criteria, age-grade coaches are encouraged to learn more about

Captain quiet: The 2003 semi-final was slipping away from the All Blacks, and captain Reuben Thorne had no answers. *(NZ Herald)*

Captain courageous: In contrast to Reuben Thorne, England's Martin Johnson is in his element, punching the air after his side's 22-7 semi-final defeat of France. *(NZ Herald)*

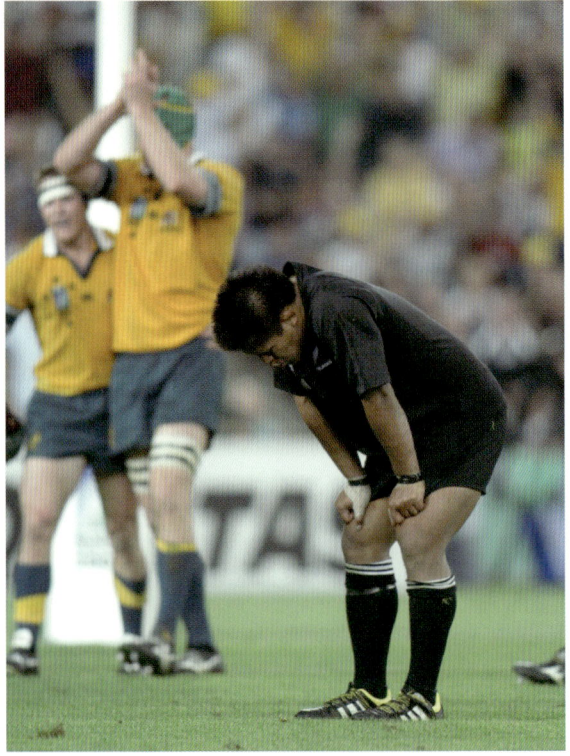

Lightning strikes twice: All Black hooker Keven Mealamu drops his head as the horror of another World Cup defeat, this time the semi-final loss in 2003, starts to sink in. *(NZ Herald)*

Lost leader: The decision not to start or even put Aaron Mauger on the bench in the 2007 quarter-final loss was one that came back to haunt the All Blacks. *(NZ Herald)*

Don't cry for me: All Black centre Mils Muliaina holds back the tears the day after the 2007 World Cup loss. They would flow later when he started to think about how the nation would react after the team's return home. *(NZ Herald)*

Third time unlucky: All Black Rodney So'oialo (centre) stares in disbelief after referee Wayne Barnes blows the final whistle at Millennium Stadium, Cardiff, on 6 October 2007. *(NZ Herald)*

Magic dust: All Black captain Richie McCaw scatters some of the 'magic' adidas dust that was presented to the team before the 2007 World Cup. *(Photosport)*

Another catastrophe: All Black supporter Dan Heijer had the misfortune to be at Fox's Tavern at Auckland's Viaduct Harbour in the final minutes of the 2007 quarter-final. *(NZ Herald)*

Golden boot: 1987 hero Grant Fox showed he was one of the most professional amateurs with his dedication to his goal-kicking. *(NZ Herald)*

Blood and guts: Former All Black captain Wayne 'Buck' Shelford was happy to take some punishment in the 1988 test against the Wallabies in Sydney. He knew that there would be plenty of opportunities in the future to exact his revenge. *(NZ Herald)*

Not on my watch: Auckland Grammar headmaster John Morris will not tolerate boys coming to his school just to play rugby. *(NZ Herald)*

Staying grounded: It's hard work keeping young men focused when rugby carries such prominence. Here it seems that the whole school has come to support the Auckland Grammar First XV. *(Auckland Grammar School)*

Giant impact: Jonah Lomu remains the best example of how young men from a Polynesian background can be physically destructive at a tender age. Lomu had just turned 18 when this picture was taken at his school, Wesley College. *(NZ Herald)*

Golden boy: Richard Kahui is the model new professional whose career will be as much about endorsement deals and media profile as it will be test caps. *(NZ Herald)*

Get to the beat: Former All Black captain Tana Umaga liked to listen to his iPod while warming up ahead of All Black tests. *(Photosport)*

Director's cut: The modern All Black is never without his gadgets. Here Rico Gear (rear), Isaia Toeava (left) and Ma'a Nonu film their team-mates while on tour with the All Blacks in 2006. *(Photosport)*

the personalities of the players, to build relationships with their parents and take an interest in their holistic development as individuals.

By the time a promising player reaches his final year of school, his file will be bulging. There will be data showing how his tackling has developed over the last three years. There will be marks to show he improved his kicking but regressed in his decision-making. For the young player of today, there's no hiding. If he has a flaw in his game it will be picked up and every resource provided to eradicate it. And the system has to be that sophisticated, because major decisions are made about these kids when they reach their late teens.

When they left school, players used to join their local club, but now they become part of an academy programme. Every union in New Zealand has developed an academy programme that effectively tries to incubate individuals for professional rugby. The typical academy programme provides between 10 and 35 of the region's most promising players with the resources they need to win a full-time contract. These players are given specific training programmes. They are given advice about nutrition, lectured on the right mental approach and briefed on the wider responsibilities they will carry should they become professional players.

The academy is there so the sophisticated monitoring process can continue and gather pace. The academy manager will be in close contact with the provincial coach; the provincial coach will be in close contact with the relevant Super 14 coach; and the Super 14 coach will be in close contact with the All Black coaches. The depth of the intelligence means that players can be selected for professional teams on the strength of their potential rather than what they might have actually delivered on the field. The athletic ability and attitude of a young player are deemed as important as his actual performance on the field, if not more so.

So what tends to happen is that players are selected at a younger age for their provincial side because their progress has been closely followed since they were 15. The provincial coach will have been through the dossier on the player, assessed his athletic potential and mental strength, kept in close dialogue with the academy manager and convinced himself that the 19-year-old in question has the ability and skill set to deliver.

If the system is doing its job, and everyone has to trust that it is, then those who make it to the academy will deserve to be there – the system has flagged them as the most likely of their peers to make it to the professional ranks.

The system has merit. The world is often left agog at how effortlessly New Zealand unearths players of incredible talent. Now that New Zealand operates in a global market where the financial strength of European rugby grows ever greater, the exodus of labour has increased. The turnover of players is phenomenal and every year a host of Super 14 rookies are billeted to the franchises. Most of those youngsters manage to hold their own; some do much more than that, while a few never quite make the grade. The system is identifying talent, carefully and accurately monitoring it and nurturing it through to the professional game. But there is one thing the system is not giving the talent – it isn't giving players the same weight and diversity of experience that their predecessors enjoyed.

THE REST of the world is fiercely jealous of New Zealand having a development system that identifies, promotes and nurtures talent; that production line keeps the All Blacks in business. The English, the French and South Africans in particular tend to churn out bigger individuals who are bulked-up but without the inherent skill of their New Zealand counterparts. For the last five years or so New Zealand teams have either been in the final or have won the under-19, under-20 and under-21 World Cups. The junior Boks and Poms are bigger and more physical, but they can't cope with the pace, power, skill and rugby genius of their New Zealand counterparts.

What tends to happen is that those players who star for New Zealand age-grade sides are either already in Super 14 squads or are called in shortly after impressing on the world stage. Guys like Jerry Collins, Luke McAlister, Dan Carter, Richie McCaw, Christian Cullen, Aaron Mauger, Chris Jack and Carl Hayman were All Blacks only a couple of years after they were playing for national age-grade sides. Those who possess talent in New Zealand will advance quickly and they owe their accelerated progress to their ability to score highly in the various assessments made along the way.

Even when they get to the All Blacks, their ability to stay there depends largely on their ability to score highly in the unfortunately named Key Performance Indicators, or KPIs as they're called.

In this technological age the volume of statistical detail is frightening.

Thanks to state-of-the-art software, the All Black coaches receive detailed feedback about each player's performance during his Super Rugby games. If they want to know how many tackles a player made off his left shoulder, they can find out. If they want to know whether a player was tackling opponents round the chest or legs, they can find out. Kicks made off the left foot, kicks made off the right foot and metres gained are all on record. Coaches no longer go with gut feel. They select based on the overwhelming knowledge available about each player, and that player's ability to achieve his KPIs.

Meanwhile, junior players from France, England, South Africa and most of the other major rugby nations tend to return to anonymity; they will go back to their clubs or provinces and play a limited role. It will be back to the coalface where they'll do the hard yards on muddy fields. Those youngsters still serve an apprenticeship in the way New Zealanders of the amateur era did. And the strength and value of that apprenticeship becomes apparent in times of adversity, in times of extreme pressure – such as World Cups.

In the amateur era, aspiring youngsters in New Zealand had it tough. They left school and joined a club where no one had mercy on their soul. There was nothing a gnarled old prop or a heavy-duty provincial lock or an international loose forward loved more when he donned his club colours than seeing a baby-faced newbie as his opposite number. Those were the fun games. Those were the games where the old-timers could take on the role of educator, where they could get away with some of their tried and tested tricks without fear of retribution.

For the unfortunate youngster the game would be tough, but the lessons learned would be stored away. It was up to the new boys to plot their way through the season. It was up to them to take care of themselves when they encountered All Blacks and provincial stalwarts. There was no malice in those encounters – far from it. The old timers were doing the nation a favour. They were giving the next generation a rugby education that couldn't be bought. They were passing on trade secrets, the little nuggets that had kept the All Blacks at the top of the world game.

That was life for New Zealand's young players. They had to survive the brutal world of club rugby. They had to prove they could handle the physical and mental intensity. It was intimidating. It was often violent, probably scary, but if a young player could hold his own, if he could stand up for himself, he was going to come out the other side all the better for the experience. If he could graft his way through club rugby, deal with all that was thrown at him there, then he was going to have some great mental tools in his kit to cope with provincial rugby.

And that was the way it went. No one, bar the odd freakish exceptions like Bryan Williams and John Kirwan, got anywhere in a hurry. It was all about serving time in tough places. It was about fronting up on wind-swept, sodden training grounds on Tuesday and Thursday nights, and then to be left black and blue on a Saturday afternoon by a bunch of nasty blokes who would quite definitely say boo to a goose.

'In that 1987 All Black team and that great Auckland team the average age was about 26 or 27,' recalls Jim Blair. 'They'd been through the clubs where there were 22 guys trying to change in a tiny space, the jerseys were torn, it was pissing rain but they went out there and they gave it everything. They became professional before they were paid.

'Now we're paying people and expecting them to become professional. It's very difficult for guys in their early 20s to suddenly get all the adulation and all the money and they haven't played the number of games at a lower level that their predecessors had. The players that eventually came through to Auckland learned a lot from playing against the likes of the Whettons, Andy Haden and Grant Fox in club rugby. But somewhere along the line we have more of an academic apprenticeship. I could read a book about how to ride a motorbike, but I only start learning when I get on it.'

The benefits of the old-style apprenticeship were many. There was the self-confidence that came with survival. There was the self-reliance that was necessary to work out how to survive. There was the courage that came with standing up to the intimidation. There was the increased motivation that came through enduring so much hardship – when a player finally stood in black vowing to God he was going to defend New Zealand, he remembered all those cold showers after brutal club games, the crappy changing sheds, the abuse hurled from the touchlines. All those experiences created individuals who were equipped to make strong decisions. It created players who were capable of leading, of being bold, of taking control and ownership of their responsibilities.

The modern player can't match the 1987 team for depth and variety of experience. The modern players have tended to leave school, join an academy programme where they quickly win a provincial contract, and soon after make Super 14. Most Super 14 players have barely played for a senior club team. They will have had some experience with their Under-21 club side and with an age-grade provincial and/or national side, but no one these days has to slug it out in the club scene.

Playing rugby and achieving KPIs was pretty much all new entrants into the professional game knew how to do.

The typical pathway for the very best players will see them break into their provincial side in their second year out of school, win a Super Rugby contract on the strength of that campaign and then possibly be called into the All Blacks in the same year they make their mark in Super Rugby. That was the path for Carter, Woodcock, Ali Williams, Hayman and Jerome Kaino to name but a few. Others such as McAlister, McCaw and Toeava made it to the All Blacks without even playing Super Rugby.

Is it fair then that we expect the modern player to be able to lead just because he's an All Black? The answer is no. There were plenty of players in the 1999, 2003 and 2007 World Cup squads who were barely two or three years into their professional careers. They hadn't served the same sort of apprenticeship as, say, John Drake, Andy Dalton, Sean Fitzpatrick, Buck Shelford and David Kirk.

For too many players in those doomed World Cup campaigns there was no variety of experience in their backstory. After leaving school they'd been channelled into an academy where they lived a limbo existence, preparing to become professionals without actually earning a living from the game. When they made the breakthrough and earned a professional contract they continued to live much the same life except their bank balances were a lot healthier.

For some it only took a couple of years from leaving school to becoming an All Black. The system had prepared them to be marvellous rugby players. But it hadn't provided them with any other focus or distraction. Playing rugby and achieving KPIs was pretty much all new entrants into the professional game knew how to do. They hadn't learned the same skills as their predecessors. They hadn't faced the same battles and therefore hadn't developed the same self-reliance or ability to lead.

As Blair says of the 1987 All Blacks: 'They all had good jobs and they all had a good education, so a certain work ethic had been embedded in them. Guys didn't turn up late for training and they knew if they didn't play well they wouldn't be picked. Then, you weren't regarded as a real All Black until you'd played a certain number of games. So there was a hard apprenticeship.'

Blair's first point is worth focusing on: 'They all had good jobs'. Removing the need for players to hold down other paid employment is the second key way in which professionalism has changed the apprenticeship. Rugby is now a career option. Most players who've made the All Blacks in the professional age have never held down a nine-to-five job. They haven't been able to do so because of the demands of their training in the academy programmes. This is significant.

Many of the leadership skills that came so naturally to the 1987 All Blacks had been learned in the workplace. There were so many synergies between success in business and success on the rugby field. The All Blacks of 1987 had to learn self-discipline off the field – they had to take responsibility in their day jobs. They had to learn the importance of everyday hard work, professionalism and commitment because that's the glue that sticks companies together. For some high fliers, corporate life provided an advanced leadership course. All this added to the quality of the apprenticeship. The need to hold down paid employment added more diversity to the athlete's experience – picking up valuable life skills was a great way to enhance the apprenticeship. The trials and tribulations of the office could help prepare a young player for the trials and tribulations he was going to experience, first at club rugby, and then when he graduated to his provincial side.

The modern player of course doesn't have either the same on-field or off-field apprenticeship. His only exposure to the real world prior to becoming a professional is being part of his region's academy programme. And as hard as all the staff in these programmes work, as much as they keep implementing the very latest thinking from the sports science world and as much as they care for the welfare and development of their players, the academy system is very definitely a long way from the real world.

ON THE surface, the academy programmes across New Zealand are doing a grand job. Every year good players emerge into the professional game as a result of the training and support they have received in the programme. Yet, come the World Cup, All Black teams keep bombing. It has to be asked whether these programmes are the right development vehicles. It has to be asked whether the academy system is failing to provide players with the quality apprenticeship they need.

To be a good player is not enough when it comes to World Cups. As New Zealanders know only too well, the biggest games of rugby are not necessarily won by the teams with the best players. The ability to perform under pressure is critical. Teams need good leaders and good decision-makers when they go to a World Cup. Does the academy system develop good leaders in the same way as the old-style apprenticeship of the amateur era did?

There's no question that the programmes are doing their best to provide the robust apprenticeship of the amateur days. They are trying to give their players the tools to succeed on the rugby field, to immerse them in a daily routine that isn't about fast cars, golf and too much leisure time.

Mike Wallace, the high-performance manager at the Auckland Rugby Union, says of his academy programme: 'We're trying to do two things. We're trying to produce players capable of playing professional rugby. We're trying to build players who are capable of going on the field with the necessary physical attributes and skill sets that will allow them to express themselves at the professional level.

'But further to that, what I'm trying to do is develop players with the ability to think for themselves, and not only make decisions for themselves but be confident that their decisions are right. And even if they aren't right they follow through, and to transfer that into life. I'm not building footballers, I'm building people who just happen to be élite footballers. That's my biggest goal. There's a lot of stuff chucked about suggesting sportsmen don't have to be role models, but in my opinion that's part and parcel of what you do if you're an élite sportsperson.

'By right or wrong you're a role model; people will look up to you, therefore you have to understand that you have service within the community and that the decisions you make do affect people in the wider community. We're trying to produce winning professional footballers. If we can produce footballers with character, then we'll have more success than if we just went after bigger, faster and stronger.'

This all sounds great. It all makes sense. The physical demands of the professional game are so great that the only way a young player can make it is to spend the bulk of his time training to ready himself for the enormous challenges that lie ahead. 'We run a pre-season programme from November until February/March,' says Wallace. 'We train at 6.30 am and our guys will be doing a combination of weight training, skill development, aerobic development and speed development. That's the physical programme.

'Sitting alongside that technical, tactical, physical programme, we have professional development and that entails them doing work on nutrition. That might be one-on-one with the nutritionist, it could be cooking classes, supermarket tours, learning about the right things to eat and the way to prepare food that's going to be appropriate. It's essentially good food education and we have sessions on understanding recovery, and a sports psychology programme. We put a huge emphasis on mental skills. Mental toughness, anger management, controlling arousal levels, time management, goal-setting and then the holistic programme that is life skills – getting the players to ask, "What are the things that impact my life outside rugby and how do I make sure I give all of those things enough time and priority so the balance of my life is good?"

'We run an earn-or-learn policy. Unless you're working or studying full-time you can't be in the programme. We don't have professional PlayStation players. They come in at 6.30 am and they're gone by 8.30 am. They're in, do their workouts and then they'll come back in the afternoon.'

Because he's spending the bulk of his time training, there's no way the academy athlete could hold down a full-time job the way his predecessors did. The players are asked to enrol for study or to work part-time. Those who are working tend not to be involved in positions that could lead to a more engaging career. The sorts of jobs they are able to hold down are gap-fillers. They keep the players busy, give them somewhere to be, provide a bit of pocket money and allow them to fulfil the programme requirement of having some form of paid employment. Those who study often have to delay their exams so they don't clash with age-grade team commitments, or even if they do stay on schedule many players neglect their study once they become full-time professionals.

The academy programme is trying to fill the gap, to instil the skills the

1987 team learned in their jobs. The problem is the synthetic environment; real life is a far better teacher. Sitting in a lecture learning about leadership is not the same thing as living it in the field. A bollocking from an angry boss is a sharp way to discover the need to be accurate. Having someone explain the consequences of inaccuracy is not the same thing.

But what can the programme directors do? Should they just ignore the shortcomings in the life skills of their protégés? Should they say their job is to teach rugby, to make better rugby players and be done with it? Should they abandon academy programmes altogether and just throw players back into club rugby and see what happens?

After all, that worked in the amateur era. That kind of apprenticeship helped New Zealand win a World Cup. Grant Fox is not only a World Cup-winning All Black but he also has detailed knowledge of the Auckland academy programme, having been assistant coach for the province in the late 1990s through to 2003. 'I think it's quite complex,' says Fox. 'I know times are different and I'm not one of those who look back to the past through rose-tinted glasses. But we were brought up in the school of hard knocks in senior club rugby. You had gnarly old buggers looking to kick the shit out of you every week. Guys like Barry Ashworth played well into his 30s and you didn't get on the bottom of a ruck when he was around. You learned a lot from that environment, so I think you were pretty well equipped to deal with the next levels of rugby.

'I think that the school of hard knocks in senior club rugby would better equip guys to deal with the next level of the game.'

'I just wonder whether what we do here is identify talent too young, and they know they've been identified. They are on the treadmill and I wonder if they – subconsciously, because I don't think this is a deliberate thing – think the opportunity is going to come. It's almost like they know they don't have to play to earn it, like they know it's going to come.

'Maybe that's being uncharitable and perhaps they're doing much more in the academies than I give them credit for. But I think that the school of hard knocks in senior club rugby would better equip guys to deal with the next level of the game, which then has knock-on effects for the higher levels again. When we got picked, unless you were a superstar like JK [John Kirwan] – but he'd been working in the butchery, getting up at God knows what time anyway – there was a bit of sacrifice involved. These guys don't have that experience. Having said that, there are not that many gnarly old buggers playing club rugby. That's a societal issue, with things being open seven days a week and Mum and Dad [both] having to work to pay the mortgage, so guys are giving the game up pretty early because they have to get ahead in life. So maybe I'm arguing against myself.

'But maybe [the academy programmes] need to say to guys, we'll help you develop but not as an identified academy system. It's more like we'll somehow facilitate you guys helping yourselves to become better. We'll have access to three or four gyms around the place, you guys pay your membership. We'll help you with the programme but you're on your own. We'll come to check you every now and again, but it's not a regular thing. It's more like you're on your own performance-wise. We'll give you a leg up but we're not going to do as much as we currently do.'

The new school will point out that if they disbanded the academy programmes the players would be snapped up by overseas clubs or by rugby league scouts. If that happened, New Zealand would never win a World Cup. But they haven't won a World Cup as it is, and it feels like some tough love wouldn't go amiss.

As Fox says, the academy environment by its very nature breeds an élitist culture that sends the players a strong message they've already made it. It cossets the players, no matter how much the programme directors believe otherwise. The players certainly serve a tough training apprenticeship. They have no time to lie in of a morning. The Auckland cadets have to report for duty at 6.30 am and that is standard for many regions. It takes self-discipline and mental strength to get to a public park that early on a freezing winter's morning to complete a sprint endurance session in the dark. That part is tough.

But the rest of the programme isn't building the type of character that emerged under the old system. It's just too soft. Most players in the Auckland programme will play club rugby. But they don't start off in the senior team the way the likes of Fitzpatrick and Michael Jones had to when they'd just emerged from school. 'Our first years out of school play Under-21,' says Wallace. 'I want guys to adjust to club football and I want guys to gain confidence and to learn to play with their mates, to learn to be a leader. If they are 18 and go straight into senior grade, they will be physically assaulted. At Under-21 they'll have a chance to develop other attributes while coming under pressure physically. As we get further into the season, if the guys show they're ready to play senior football we'll talk to the coach about that. Physically ready doesn't equal being emotionally or psychologically ready.'

No one was thinking this way the year the All Blacks won the World Cup. Back then young bucks were thrown to the lions. If they made it through it was because they were tough enough to survive. There was a culture that said perseverance was to be encouraged. That life was tough and trying to cushion young people from the blows would only deny them the experiences they needed to develop.

Now we have a society that is outraged when youngsters have to do it tough. Everything is done to protect them from the vagaries of fate, the nasty little curveballs that arrive from nowhere. Now we have teenagers who have cruised through life without wanting for anything. They have mobile phones, computers, iPods, DVD players, financial wherewithal and attitude. That's why, over the years, the academy programmes have found they really need to hammer home the holistic development. 'It's about making them accountable for their decisions,' says Wallace. 'We look at a decision-consequence model so that they understand that every decision they make has a consequence in the community. They learn that if they make a decision they own the consequence. Once they accept that they're responsible for their own decisions, they become better people.'

It is incredible that 19-year-olds need to be taught that there's a consequence to every decision they make. It's incredible that they need to be told they are responsible for their decisions, and that they need to own the consequences. It's not just the apprenticeship of old that has died. It seems that the modern education system is also failing élite rugby players.

10
Just like America

THE SPORTING HERO falling behind in his studies has become a favourite Hollywood storyline. Countless films have been made probing the American college scholarship system where athletes with limited academic prowess are granted places at renowned tertiary institutions on the basis of what they can bring to the sporting programme. The scholarship athlete is supposedly there to learn, not just to play. There are expectations to be met when it comes to study in terms of achieving grades. There are requirements to be in class, to produce assignments on time and failure to do so results in serious consequences – the loss of the scholarship.

Filmmakers know the reality is often very different. Some institutions run a tighter ship than others. Some schools clearly don't care too much about their scholarship athletes' academic achievements, or lack of. For some schools the sporting programme is too important to worry about whether critical players know their Shakespeare or their calculus. As long as they are performing on the field, whether it's basketball, gridiron, athletics or whatever, that's all that matters. And it's all that matters because in America college sport is huge.

In the States, college football games are broadcast live. They can have crowds in excess of 60,000. Some colleges have stadiums that we in New Zealand would kill for and spectator interest is such that many people prefer to follow their old school rather than the professional NFL. With so much interest in college sport, there are commercial opportunities everywhere. Corporate sponsorship is significant and so is direct investment from former students. All this makes prime fodder for scriptwriters. Universities are supposed to be the highest seats of learning. They are supposed to be where a society's brightest and most gifted can be nurtured into top-performing contributors to the culture and the economy.

And yet it seems some universities feel it's more important to encourage young people to excel at sport. The very idea of a sporting scholarship is hard to fathom. Why should a university care if it has a renowned golf programme? Why should it care if its football team is the best in the country? Education should be holistic and valuable lessons can be learned from playing sport. But playing sport alone doesn't constitute an education. To offer a scholarship on the grounds that someone is highly gifted at a specific sport and only moderately gifted academically is placing the emphasis in the wrong place. The message to the individual is clear – they are there to excel in their chosen sport and to get by academically.

That message is powerfully endorsed by the financial backing sporting programmes receive. When, as is the case sometimes, former pupils are pumping millions of dollars into the college in return for sporting success, what does that say to the students? It tells them that sport is vital and that success in sport is vital. It tells them that the success of their education can be measured by the success of their sporting achievement.

But what kind of person does that produce? If an individual has been allowed to operate above the law because of his sporting prowess, will he have the foundation values of independent thought, self-discipline and self-reliance? If he has faced no consequences for failing to fulfil the academic obligations of his scholarship, will he have the drive to work at things that don't come easily? And just how big will his ego have become? When there are 60,000 people watching the team on a Saturday, and when your peers are slapping you on the back and calling your name every corridor you walk down, it can't be easy to stay grounded.

The system divides opinion. There are those who feel it provides an opportunity for talented performers to advance their sporting careers while building an academic foundation to serve as back-up in case their dreams don't come true and they have to make it in the 'real world'.

There are others, though, who doubt if placing such prominence on sport and providing financial assistance leads to scholarship athletes graduating as well-balanced, deep-thinking, grounded people. *The New*

York Times carried a piece on scholarships in 2008 that said: 'The best-laid plans of coaches do not always bring harmony on teams, however, and scholarships can be at the heart of the unrest. Who is getting how much tends to get around like the salaries in a workplace. The result — scholarship envy — can divide teams.

'The chase for a scholarship has another side that is rarely discussed. Although those athletes who receive athletic aid are viewed as the ultimate winners, they typically find the demands on their time, minds and bodies in college even more taxing than the long journey to get there. There are 6 am weightlifting sessions, exhausting practices, team meetings, study halls and long trips to games. Their varsity commitments often limit the courses they can take. Athletes also share a frustrating feeling of estrangement from the rest of the student body, which views them as the privileged ones. In this setting, it is not uncommon for first- and second-year athletes to relinquish their scholarships.'

By the end of their college days scholarship athletes may well have greatly improved their sporting ability, but very few walk away having advanced their life skills. But that in itself doesn't kill their dreams. The big three American sports – basketball, football and baseball – aren't games that require instinctive decision-making from the players. They're heavily structured games where the coaches do nearly all the tactical thinking. The players merely follow instructions, which is why in some cases a flawed college education is not detrimental to their chances of making it to the professional ranks. In some ways it's even beneficial, given the culture of self-promotion and the lack of humility in America's professional sports.

That whole scholarship system is ugly. At its core is a rotten principle, and it churns out athletes lacking basic life skills and modesty when in fact they have plenty to be modest about. We're fascinated when Hollywood dips its toes into that pool and heave sighs of relief that it isn't happening in New Zealand. But our complacency is misplaced. The same thing *is* happening in New Zealand, and it's even worse because rugby players are being enrolled to do well at sport and absolutely nothing else, and this culture has invaded schools and is warping the minds of boys barely into their teens.

IT MIGHT sound over the top to suggest New Zealand's schools have become like America's colleges. Rugby has always been a prominent part of the larger schools. The First XV is a big deal. Make it and you are instantly idolised. Every other boy in the school will know your name. You can do no wrong.

Ask an All Black to recall the detail of some of the biggest tests he has played and the chances are he'll be vague. He'll struggle to dredge much from the memory banks. But ask him about the biggest games he played at school and the detail pours out. All First XV players will be able to recount which other schools they beat. For some, it remains the greatest source of regret that they never managed to beat their fiercest rival.

The First XV culture has always been huge, and it provides lifelong memories for those involved. But in those pre-professional days, while it was big, rugby only formed part of the package. There was never any suggestion that anyone was coming to school just to play rugby. Back then, rugby was just a game – a great way for young men to express themselves physically while learning all the positive benefits of a team sport. For the 1987 All Blacks, it was education first, rugby second.

Since professionalism, the emphasis has shifted. Those in education say it hasn't, and there are certainly some schools where that remains true, where rugby is a potential career option for some pupils but not one that is necessarily actively encouraged.

'It's increasingly difficult,' says Auckland Grammar principal John Morris, speaking of the challenge of controlling the influence of rugby in pupils' lives. 'The importance of having a strong First XV here is vital. Any decent boys' school has a strong sporting programme – you have to. You have 2,500 boys and testosterone galore, and you've got to offer them things outside the classroom. We've grown our sporting programme to accommodate 39 different codes. But having said that, rugby is still number one so we have to have a strong First XV. It's interesting when we win on a Saturday and have an assembly on the Monday that spirits are noticeably higher than when we lose.

'But at this school the number-one priority is always academic. It's really important for us to make it clear to the boys that they're not just here for the rugby. They might think that's the case, but it's not – it's to get a good qualification and get out in the world and do well. Sport is an add-on, a very important one, but the academic focus is paramount.

'If you're in the First XV there are no priorities or privileges. You're in class like everybody else. In my time here we actually had a First XV member who decided he wanted to take liberties and he didn't want to come to school, he just wanted to play rugby, so we dropped him – he didn't play. That has happened a few times. We aren't going to let them just turn up and play rugby; if you do that it's a slippery slope down.'

The problem for New Zealand though, and the problem that's hurting them at World Cups, is that not enough schools are doing as much as they should to promote education ahead of sport. They might say they are, but the evidence to the contrary is damning – indeed, overwhelming.

Standards have slipped on so many fronts it's hard to know where to begin. The poaching of pupils is probably as good a place as any. Everyone denies it happens, yet every year an inordinate number of pupils in their final year choose to switch schools. Changing school is a major, and few teachers or educational theorists would say the child in question is going to benefit academically or socially by switching in their final year. It's disruptive and unsettling and there really needs to be strong justification for pupils to switch schools in that late stage.

The schools where the pupils end up deny enticement; it's entirely coincidental, they say, that their new pupils happen to be rather good at a particular sport. Those who say it doesn't happen must realise how far they're stretching credibility. Of course it happens – it's just next to impossible to prove it. If a teacher has a quiet word with a pupil from another school after a game and makes it clear he'd be a great addition if he switched institutions – is that poaching? Or is the teacher just expressing an opinion? It's very murky, and only the truly naïve would think schools aren't making promises to talented rugby players all the time.

In 2008 College Sport, the independent body that organises and manages secondary school sports competitions, had to arbitrate in 15 cases where pupils had switched schools. College Sport had a ruling that prevented transferred pupils from playing premier-grade sport for their new school unless they had written permission from their old school to do so.

The suspension was for 12 months, but when 15 cases in Auckland went to mediation as a result of schools refusing to grant playing permission, an independent review of the body's by-laws was commissioned with a view to delivering a fairer system that wouldn't punish the students so severely. The review was conducted by lawyers Andrew Brown, QC, and Paul Pa'u, and would have carried significant expense. That's a long way to go if there was no problem with schools poaching sports players.

Poaching is even more rife in the private sector. The state schools are limited in how many stars they can go after because of their zoning. But at the bigger boarding schools there are no barriers. A private school can recruit from wherever it likes as long as the fees are paid. There is a fair chance that in any given year most boarding schools will have some vacancies in their hostels. The school might have a few areas of weakness in the First XV and decide they need to shore those up. So into play comes the scholarship. The school can poach the players they need to bolster their First XV, offer to drop all the tuition fees and use the cash reserves to pay for the living expenses.

And that passes as a scholarship. The school is not terribly bothered whether the students on these scholarships contribute much academically. If they contribute to the First XV then it was money well spent, because a successful rugby team will act as the best recruitment advert going.

Mount Albert Grammar School headmaster Dale Burden says boarding school scholarships are handed out all the time. 'I know for a fact there is a school here in Auckland whose team came fifth in the 1A rugby championship and the old boys whipped around and came up with a six-figure package to put kids in boarding houses.' The kids who were recruited hadn't shown any aptitude in anything other than rugby.

And just how rife these 'scholarships' are became apparent when the Northland Union submitted a document to the New Zealand Rugby Union in September 2008 pleading to be retained in the professional Air New Zealand Cup. Northland had been told they were going to be relegated at the end of the year, and one of the points they made was that their work in developing young, talented players was not being fully recognised because so many of them were whisked off to the bigger Auckland schools.

'Northland produces great rugby talent,' said the submission. 'For example, this year alone our sub-union Hokianga has lost more than 15 outstanding age-group players to Auckland schools, while other age-group players have been identified by talent scouts and taken to other regions. These players include Sonny Henare, a Northland age-group player who represented New Zealand in the Under-17 competition and is now at King's College, Auckland; Mar'u Grace, Isaiah Mulitalo and Louis Rogers, all Under-14 players now attending Auckland schools, and Under-15 player Ted Lolo Campbell, who is now playing for Counties. The NRU also wishes to bring the NZRU's attention to the fact that there are more than 15 former Northland secondary schools players playing in the Auckland First XV competition for 2008 alone (excluding the age-group players from Hokianga).'

Kids go to school and they can say they are part of the rugby academy programme. At 13 years old they can be part of an élite set-up.

These issues are not unique to Auckland. There are more examples to draw on, but poaching is just as big a problem in Christchurch, Wellington, Dunedin and Hamilton. In fact, the problem exists everywhere. And it exists because it seems too many schools have lost the plot and decided that gaining kudos through sporting achievement is more important than gaining it through the quality of the overall education package.

Clearly the private boarding schools think so; the evidence is there in the way they fling around their so-called scholarships. But many state schools are just as determined to excel at sport and now run academy programmes. Yes, that's right – kids go to school and they can say they are part of the rugby academy programme. At 13 years old they can be part of an élite set-up, giving them licence to brag to their peers and feel just that little bit above their station.

For old-timers such initiatives are new-age nonsense – further evidence that the youth of today are given too much too soon. But the headmaster at Mount Albert Grammar in Auckland, which runs one of the best programmes in the country, sees it like this. 'In many ways we are no different to any other secondary school. We provide opportunities for kids. If you are good at music there should be a good music programme. If you are good at sport there is generally a good sporting programme. I'm a big believer that in New Zealand you should be able to walk to your local school and what they get there should be as good as what they get anywhere. But the reality isn't quite like that.

'We have a situation in New Zealand now where we probably have some schools that are doing some things better than others. That's for a whole variety of reasons. Here, and this is probably due to economies of scale, we're providing all-round programmes. I think our cultural activities are as strong as our sporting programme. So if you are really good at music you can excel, or if you just want to learn an instrument there'll be something there for you. It's the same with the academics. In our sports programmes we have some outstanding talent and we've also got kids who just play sport. If you have a big school you can have these special programmes.

'Sports academies are what we run here. So in year nine you are eligible to apply for a range of sports academies. You enrol in the school, and then you get selected into those areas by virtue of how good you are. So if you're a good cricketer you go down to the nets and try to show the coach you have a good eye for the bat. And that's run as a subject. That's not a lot different from having a whole lot of maths tests. To me, that's in keeping with working with kids who have talent in a particular area.

'The academy programme looks at a range of things, such as the technical aspect of being a hooker. How do you throw the ball in properly? Each programme also has a generic focus on things like diet and health and leadership. They work on this about two or three hours per week until they hit Year 11.'

Mount Albert Grammar has become one of the strongest sporting schools in the country in the last decade. It has an expanding roll, with people from all over the city desperate to get lucky in the annual ballot that allows 30 per cent of students in from out of zone. Given its success on the sports field, its growing reputation as a must-attend school and the media profile it gains as a result those sporting achievements, there is an overwhelming sense amongst teachers, parents and pupils that the school is doing everything right. As Burden says, there's expanded choice now across every frontier, catering for every level.

There is an alternative, much less positive view to be taken. Far from advancing the educational experience, the inception of sporting academies has fostered a culture of aggrandisement on false foundations. It is building children so insular, so focused on sport, so lacking in basic skills, that they can't even tell the time on a numeric clock.

Dave Syms, a former teacher at Auckland Grammar before becoming the long-serving principal of Palmerston North Boys' High School, is now operations manager at the Auckland Rugby Union. Having been an educator at two of the country's top schools for almost 25 years and now in day-to-day contact with the young men in the Auckland academy programme, Syms is well qualified to pass judgement on the road many schools have chosen to go down.

'With the development of sporting academies in schools there is a lack of balance,' he says. 'I remember having this debate at Palmerston North Boys' – saying, "Yes, we do want a sporting academy but it can be academic with sporting tagged on to the end." Not a sporting academy. It was driven by people saying the boys could now make a living out of rugby so therefore we should be assisting them. My argument to that was that half a per cent of a half per cent were going to make it through, so to throw all your eggs into that one particular basket was bloody stupid.

'This was being pushed by staff members, mainly young staff and good on them for wanting to develop things, but it was about sitting back and saying, "Righto, yes, let's give them this opportunity and provide niches for them, but sitting on top of that is the whole education programme."

'Mount Albert Grammar has been very successful at soccer and rugby and they have this great sporting academy. I haven't looked closely enough at the academic qualifications of these kids to see how they come out of it. Clearly they are doing a great job from a sporting perspective, but I don't know if they've helped the kids who've missed out [on making the professional ranks], because there'll be a lot of them asking, "What do I do now? I had a great time playing rugby but now where do I go? I have no qualifications and I can't go to tertiary, so what do I do?"

'I take my own situation in Palmerston – and the desire to set up academies and do well at sport is all driven by kudos. It's old boys. The best attract the best. People will want to go there if you're doing well at this and well at that. You'll attract more kids and that should be part of it. It's how much you want it to be. There is no question that there are plenty of environments where kids are just coming to play rugby. You can get obsessive people in schools who think it's the be-all and end-all that they have to win the First XV championship. I was like that myself for a while when I was a young teacher.'

For professional athletes like the All Blacks, obsession is a quality. The most successful people are always dedicated to the point of obsession. But in education it's certainly not a quality. It's a dangerous emotion that can stunt the mental growth of young people and leave them horribly under-equipped to cope with life in the adult world.

WE EXPECT the All Blacks to be able to make snap decisions on the field; to have the confidence to lead and to work things out for themselves. We then expect them to be fantastic role models. We expect them to be articulate, intelligent, worldly and engaging; to uphold the strongest moral values; and to behave in an exemplary manner at all times.

We expect all this and when we don't see it, when an All Black stands in front of a TV camera barely able to string a sentence together, or is photographed coming out of court for some late-night alcohol offence, we express outrage. Or when they fail to win the World Cup, we just can't believe it. But why on earth should we be surprised when even the education system, the last bastion of good values, appears to have given up on building the type of people who created the All Black legacy?

Schools, with the odd exception, are no longer pushing academic success to the top of the agenda. There is no longer a conviction across the board that they should produce young people who can excel in the classroom first and show their rugby prowess second. There doesn't even seem to be an acknowledgement in many schools of a link between rounded people and All Black success. Educators are taking short cuts. They see rugby as a legitimate career option for many of their pupils and they allow, even encourage, many young men to prepare for life by immersing themselves in rugby and nothing else. That has never been the New Zealand way and it certainly wasn't how the country produced a World Cup-winning side.

Intriguingly, both Morris and Burden expressly made a point of saying you wouldn't find kids loafing around in their schools' corridors during lessons – just throwing a rugby ball around and waiting to train. They said this not so much to highlight the holistic culture at their own schools, but more to point the finger at others – to make it clear that an increasing number of schools are simply providing pupils with a rugby team each Saturday, which they can use to chase their professional dream.

It's no wonder, then, that the likes of Mike Wallace at Auckland Rugby and his fellow academy directors have to instil the most basic principles into their recruits. Too many schools simply haven't bothered. Too many schools have fallen into the trap of believing they are doing their pupils a massive service by allowing them to focus so heavily on rugby.

Worse still, too many schools have allowed a culture similar to that of the American colleges to develop. Promoting the importance of sport, and in particular rugby, sets the wrong tone. The scholarship recruits at boarding schools and the poaching of star players from state schools exacerbate that. Those factors alone can easily inflate the ego of a young man who makes the First XV.

It's a culture that breeds arrogance and an environment that erodes self-reliance.

Even in more rigid, traditional schools such as Auckland Grammar, Palmerston North Boys' High and Christchurch Boys' High that try to downplay the significance of rugby and the First XV, it's a tough battle keeping pupils grounded. It's hard work trying to keep talented players up to speed on their studies – if rugby can make them a living, a very good living, why should they bother with maths and chemistry? Why should they even bother attending class at all?

So many other factors contribute to that sense of rugby being all that matters. There are corporate sponsors knocking the door down to get exposure. Provincial rugby in New Zealand struggles to make ends meet, yet there are many big, traditional schools awash with cash secured from persistent backers. What kind of message does that send to the pupils? It's not a natural culture and is every bit as distorted as that in the US. It's a culture that breeds arrogance and an environment that erodes self-reliance. For those with talent, rugby is all they know by the time they leave school.

The plus side is that New Zealand schools are producing large numbers of young men who are hugely talented at rugby. They have all the skills. They know the game inside out and they can do clever things on the pitch. That talent gets them into the provincial union academies and then, at frightening speed, into Super 14 and, in some cases, the All Blacks.

And for a long time their weaknesses can go undetected. Their ability to play the game carries them through right up until the point they find themselves in a World Cup knock-out match. Then the system fails them. Then their lack of an all-round education reduces their impact. Under pressure they have nothing to fall back on.

The men of 1987 had strong values drummed into them from the day they turned up at secondary school. They had no sense of entitlement the way their successors do. The men of 1987 knew how to solve problems because that's what they'd been encouraged to do at school. They knew how to think for themselves because they'd been encouraged to do so at school. And they knew that while rugby was a big deal – that everyone at the school loved it and wanted the First XV to be successful – it wasn't the only reason they walked through the school gates each morning.

Compare that with now. 'Very often some of the sports, rugby in particular – and this is a generalisation and doesn't apply to all of those kids – is the only thing that they tend to do particularly well,' says Burden of the academy students at Mount Albert Grammar.

'They have a track record of not being tuned into school. They have a track record of issues at home – things around diet and decision-making and that kind of stuff. So when they get to that élite level there's a lot of effort put into things like homework. There are some kids who do so much sport that their schoolwork gets left behind. So we've set up a system where their manager and their teacher monitor them to make sure they are making progress. They make sure these kids have a 100 per cent attendance record.

'What we try to do is to create the balance. And that's quite hard, to be perfectly honest. Many of the top kids are under immense pressure from rep coaches. Many of the kids watch TV and read the paper and see that rugby is a professional sport. They can see that there are even average rugby players making lots of money overseas. They see that as their ticket out of where they are at, in the same way football players in America and soccer players in the UK do – it's a smaller version of that.

'I think the danger is when they get into the First XV. It's very difficult in a traditional school where every time an old boy phones he wants to know how the First XV are doing. Every time you go into the community there's this First XV thing. Rugby is the national sport in New Zealand. You can't pick up a newspaper without rugby being in it. Rugby players are treated like celebrities so it's quite difficult for us to play down all that. We've got a high-profile coach whose son is a recent All Black. It's hard to play it down, but we go out of our way not to play it up.'

Syms is greatly concerned about the long-term impact of having rugby too heavily emphasised in schools. He sees the problems at first hand. 'Here at Auckland Rugby Union we have an education programme called Prosport. We've had guys like John Afoa, Jerome Kaino, Isaia Toeava and Joe Rokocoko who've come through that system. They were iconic First XV players and they did nothing more than play rugby when they were at school. So when they came out of school they had nothing else.

'To qualify for this programme you've got to have nothing or next to nothing academically. Our programme is really a bottom-of-the-cliff thing that says, here are these kids, great rugby players, but they could just go poof into the ether. But we hang on to them here and put them through these courses and they get their feet back on the ground. A lot of them, because the transition is so quick nowadays, go straight into careers as professional rugby players.

'Isaia is a classic example of a guy who came out with no life skills, who had only ever played rugby in his life, and it's no wonder they struggle. The effect of having so many players in the professional ranks who only went to school to play rugby – that's something that we don't know. We're guessing what it does. We're only just finding out. Not only are we having these kids coming into our environment who are very good sports players but not very well educated, but we've also got the age coming down to meet them. From them coming out of school to becoming professional, the time is getting less and less. The outstanding ones are almost walking straight in.'

This scenario is not unique to rugby. Over-confident, under-educated young people everywhere believe they should be walking into jobs and earning top dollar. No one wants to graft any more. No one accepts the minimum wage is a starting point, a reflection of their lack of skills and experience. Whether they're young rugby players, lawyers, doctors, finance workers or accountants, the so-called Generation Y– those born between 1978 and 1994 – don't think they have anything to learn. Or at least those who aren't guided by strong parents, working tirelessly against the tide to promote the highest standards and ethics, think they have nothing to learn.

To brand a whole generation as useless would be harsh and unfair. There are some excellent young people, high achievers with dreams, goals, aspirations and abilities that do them credit. But those with balance and grounding are the exception, certainly not the rule, and most of

Generation Y doesn't actually have the patience or dedication to learn. If the gratification isn't instant, they don't want to know.

We can heap blame on our schools – question why so many of them have developed sports academies and poached the best talent. We can berate schools for allowing pupils to chase their rugby dreams at the expense of everything else. We can be horrified when they over-indulge, turn a blind eye and even promote an élitist culture that allows the best players to live their lives by different rules.

Some schools are guilty of churning out children whose egos are so bloated they can't see their own glaring shortcomings. Some schools are complicit in producing poorly prepared graduates who will simply never be able to deliver a World Cup. Complicit, yes. Wholly responsible? No. We must all accept we've played a part in spawning Generation Y.

11
Generation Me

WHEN ROALD DAHL wrote *Charlie and the Chocolate Factory* in 1964, he made some prescient observations. Maybe he simply wanted to create four vile characters, but given how the world has evolved it seems more likely he saw into the future. Dahl's book introduced the reader to Augustus Gloop, the chocolate-obsessed glutton, and the utterly strange Mike Teavee, who did nothing but watch violent television programmes. Veruca Salt was a petulant, spoilt brat who wanted everything and she wanted it now, while Violet Beauregarde was desperate to be famous; her only talent, however, was her ability to chew gum for months at a time.

To those who read the book when it was first published in 1964 these four characters seemed to have sprung from nothing more than the fertile imagination of a hugely talented writer. Even in the 1980s, although they were despicable, Beauregarde and her ilk were laughably so. But now it's not so easy to laugh. Those characters are with us in more than literary form. They are very much alive and well, cropping up in various guises among the youth of today.

New Zealand has an obesity epidemic. There are thousands of Augustus Gloops, all munching their way into the health system. As it was in Willy Wonka's chocolate factory, food is available now in places we never imagined. Supermarket shelves are loaded with junk – products that are cheap to buy, easy to consume and in no way good for us. We have digital TV broadcasting 24 hours of rubbish at which many children sit and gape. There are video games that dazzle and whirr but build children with dextrous thumbs and big tummies. Reality TV was made for Violet Beauregarde. She could have joined all the other wannabes who are short on talent and long on ambition.

And then there's Veruca Salt, poster girl for Generation Y (or Generation Me, as it's sometimes more pertinently labelled), with her insatiable appetite for material goods, always wanting the latest and greatest. As soon as she's given it, of course, she's bored. Generation Me, like Veruca Salt, has developed a culture of entitlement – these young people believe the world is their oyster and there's no need to earn it. It's theirs by right, regardless of whether they either deserve it or can afford it.

So the world created by Dahl is rather like the one in which the All Blacks now operate. It's against this backdrop of obesity, video games, instant gratification and universal sense of entitlement that the selectors must choose 15 men to uphold the history of the jersey. It isn't easy.

It's against this backdrop of obesity, video games, instant gratification and universal sense of entitlement that the selectors must choose 15 men to uphold the history of the jersey.

The values of Generation Me are at odds with the All Blacks. They are also very much opposed to the wider values of rugby. Rugby's culture demands teamwork. It demands hard work. It requires the individual to sacrifice personal ambition for collective achievement. Nothing comes easy on the rugby field. The forwards have to graft and keep grafting until they come out on top. Nothing is won on reputation, or by believing you're entitled to win, or simply because … well, because winning would be nicer than losing.

Rugby is supremely physical. To be fit enough to play, the pain barrier has to be broken. When you're playing, the pain barrier has to be broken again. Rugby is tough, emotionally and physically, and it requires stamina, perseverance, tenacity and dedication.

These are qualities that fewer and fewer young people seem to possess. And this erosion is evident way beyond rugby. The corporate world has felt the full force of Generation Me. The best graduates are in no doubt as to what they're worth, and they're not prepared to wait to earn it. They don't feel an obligation to prove their worth before they ask for the world. In a forgotten age, big law firms and accountancy houses used to interview graduates. Now it's the other way round, although some balance might be restored following the collapse of world markets in 2008. Graduates won't tolerate salaries that reflect their inexperience. Generation Me operates with supreme confidence and they want to be paid big bucks straight away.

Dr Jane Magnusson has observed the change in expectation first-hand. Where once students would have been distraught if they missed an essay deadline, now they barely acknowledge their tardiness. A lecture missed used to be a big deal requiring some serious explanation. Now Dr Magnusson receives informal emails from students, not by way of apology, but demanding that lecture notes be forwarded. The tone is not apologetic; it's casual and assured, testimony to that sense of entitlement.

'Let's look at the real world,' says Dr Magnusson in exasperation. 'Young people don't want to work for the minimum wage. They want to earn what adults are paid. We had to work our way up. Now kids have to be taught to show up on time. If I behaved the way the majority of students behave… It wasn't an option to goof around in class or turn up if you wanted. To not turn in assignments. And we allow it. I was watching this guy on TV, a professor from the States, and he was saying that when he went to school, if he cheated in an exam he would have been kicked out. If you catch a student cheating on an exam now, they get a lawyer.

'They're an entitled generation. We've seen what happens when there are no consequences. Consider obesity – eat what you want, nobody's keeping track of it. I don't know how the Me Generation happened. We used to joke that if you compared the staff and student parking lots, their cars were a lot nicer. The sad thing is that I'm seeing it more and more, even in the academic world. If students come to my office and talk to me about being a psychologist, the first question is, "What can I make?" No one is asking, "What does it take to be a psychologist?" That's sad. In the tough times, if you're not intrinsically motivated then that attitude is going to suck.

'At a sports level, we're losing the people who are willing to go for it all. You play injured, you play without reward, you play without salary, you risk it for the game. You take away that intrinsic motivation, and would players be as motivated to be an All Black these days without the package that comes with it?'

It's hard to shake the suspicion that for most of the professional age there have been too many All Blacks more concerned with the package. There is definitely evidence to support the view that a lot of players don't have the required patience. Greatness doesn't come quickly. The heroes of yesteryear had to earn their status. They had to become All Blacks first, and only by continually playing well did they earn recognition for having been good All Blacks.

The reality now is that many young players aren't prepared to wait. If they haven't cracked the Super 14 after a couple of seasons, there are plenty who run off to Europe where they can pick up decent money and be treated with the respect they feel they deserve. It is all too common now for a player with just a few provincial games behind him to send his video to a European club and be offered a contract. Agents perpetuate the grandiose ideas of Generation Me by supporting them in their need for instant gratification.

Some players just need to be patient, to fix some flaws in their game and continue to plug away at the provincial championship. If they did that, it's likely the professional contract would come and from there, if they applied those same values of perseverance, hard work and self-improvement, All Black selection might follow. But all that is too hard for some. They don't want to work hard because their sense of entitlement tells them they don't have to wait. They can have the money, the fast cars and nice house now – as long as they move overseas.

The All Blacks have felt the impact of Generation Me as much as the corporate world. By 2008, there were more Kiwis playing professionally overseas than were playing in New Zealand. A smaller talent pool obviously makes it harder to produce a winning All Black team.

In the past the All Blacks have always had strength in depth; they could lose a star and wheel another one out in a jiffy. By 2008 it was apparent that depth was being challenged. Even more serious is the type of person they are welcoming into their fold. World Cups can be won by 15 players. South Africa in 2007, England in 2003 and Australia in 1999 pretty much played the same starting XV throughout the tournament. Having strength in depth is nice but not imperative to win a World Cup. Having strong characters is, and that's the danger with Generation Me – they haven't had to struggle for anything. This is a generation whose every whim has been pandered to. And that includes rugby.

THERE HAS been concern in rugby's administrative circles for much of the last decade about the drop-off in playing numbers. The absolute numbers of registered players during the professional era have increased at a moderate rate. But in spite of that there are some worrying trends. The number of teenagers dropping out continues to rise. Rugby is doing an okay job of attracting new players, but not so well at retaining them. The tricky years are the teenage ones.

In 2004 the New Zealand Rugby undertook research to determine first the extent of the teenage drop-out and second, its cause. The statistics were sobering. What the NZRU found was that only about 50 per cent of 13-year-olds would still be playing rugby when they turned 18. They were losing a colossal number of players during that difficult period when young men reach puberty and fall under the influence of hormones, their peer group and, very often, the opposite sex.

No one was expecting figures of that magnitude. The reasons behind the exodus were easier to swallow. The research discovered that more and more teenagers were taking part-time jobs that prevented them from playing on Saturdays. It also found that children were becoming increasingly fearful of being injured and that other sports had become more attractive as a consequence.

Reading between the lines, there was a conclusion to be drawn that playing rugby was increasingly being put in the too-hard basket by Generation Y. It was a sport that demanded too much physically and mentally, and there was the time factor. All that training and playing would get in the way of more interesting pursuits – like shopping or just hanging out and doing very little.

That suspicion was only enhanced when Wellington Rugby decided to conduct similar research in 2007. The capital had experienced a 10 per cent drop in secondary school playing numbers between 2005 and 2007. That was well down on the national figures. According to the New Zealand Secondary School Sports Council, between 2005 and 2007 participation rates for rugby nationally fell from slightly more than 31,000 to 29,845.

As the country's second largest metropolitan area, Wellington was likely to experience many of the conditions flagged in the NZRU report more acutely. In a big city there are more distractions. There is more choice of sporting and leisure pursuits. There is a greater need for young people to earn because money brings independence and greater choice of activities. The Wellington report filled the gaps between the lines in the NZRU report.

Generation Y was hit with both barrels. The report fingered them as a generation of non-committers, who don't seek to improve, give up easily if they aren't top of the class, and are not go-getters. Too few were prepared to invest time at rugby practice. One of the report's conclusions was: 'For all that they grow up fast in technology terms, their emotional growth is much slower than for other generations.' Another was this: '[They] expect to play without reading the instructions because that is their experience in other aspects of their leisure lives.'

This is a generation not prepared to accept the lessons of failure.

The picture painted of modern youth was grim. The numbers dropping out and the report's findings both point to a generation of young people who give up if they don't instantly succeed. They aren't prepared to work hard. This is a generation that demands instant accessibility otherwise they're not interested. This is a generation not prepared to accept the lessons of failure. The concept of trying, trying and trying again is anathema.

Generation X and those before them had a better tuned sense of achievement. If achievement came on a plate it never felt quite as good as when it was hard-won. The struggle was relished, the battle was everything. Not for Generation Y – for them success is the only currency they recognise and if it doesn't come instantly they will just move on in search of something they can conquer with minimum effort.

Interestingly, the Wellington report also hammered rugby bosses for failing to understand Generation Y. Rugby was out of touch with the needs and desires of young people. For nearly 100 years New Zealand boys gravitated towards rugby because that is what young men did. There were fewer alternatives. There was more stigma attached to those who didn't play and no doubt greater peer pressure exerted to ensure people dug out their boots and got on the paddock. Traditions had been established around rugby that remained rigid into the professional era. Those traditions included when teams trained, how they trained and when they played. The game itself, give or take the odd rule change here and there, had remained the same for more than 100 years.

That adherence to tradition, the authors of the report suggested, was a mistake. Some lateral thinking was required. If players were shifting away from rugby, the administrators needed to do something radical to bring them back. There was no point in persevering with the same old, same old, and then acting perplexed when people dropped the sport. The world was changing fast. What young people wanted in the 21st century was very different to what they'd wanted even 10 years earlier. Values, interests and attitudes were different so rugby had to adapt. In other words, rugby was encouraged to pander to Generation Y. The choice was to see teenagers leave in their droves or experiment with some new ideas to keep them interested.

Brent 'Buck' Anderson is the NZRU's head of community rugby. It's his job to foster the grassroots of the game, to grow playing numbers and to help build a sport that is relevant and engages modern youth. He has been hugely successful in his role and much of that success is due to his willingness to adapt traditions. 'Where we've got the most kids playing the game is around 12, 13 and 14,' says Anderson. 'From then on it starts to decline, [most steeply] around 16, 17 and 18 when kids leave school and are probably not joining clubs.

'We are very much trying to get them and then keep them – it's a recruitment then retention strategy. In terms of retention we're trying to make sure there's a really strong link between schools and clubs, so when kids leave school they know where to go and they know some of the people at the clubs – there's familiarity and it's not a big scary world for these kids.

'Wanganui is one province where they are starting to run night rugby for the kids around the 1st XV level and Under 19 so they are not having to play on a Saturday when they're working in part-time activity. That seems to have gone pretty well. There's one club in Auckland – College Rifles – putting in artificial turf and that will allow them to do something similar with hockey, where they can put up floodlights and play 24/7. That will allow further movement from the traditional playing on Saturday afternoon and training Tuesday and Thursday nights. That's one of the things kids want.

'We're trying something called Prozone that's a 10-a-side version of the game and operates on a pay-for-play basis with 25 minutes each half. Kids don't have to join a club as such. They can form a team and play in this type of competition just as a way of getting involved in the game at this transitional age. A lot of the research has shown that if you've still got them at 20 you'll still have them at 25/26. If we can get them through that period [mid-to-late teens], that will help the strength of the clubs.

'This isn't pandering to anyone really. We are just trying to provide different options. It's a totally different world now. One of the things we did in 2003-2004 was to check on how different it was compared with 20 years earlier. When you sit down and look at the changes that have happened – the societal changes and what the kids are interested in – you just couldn't keep doing the same old, same old, and expect it to happen.

'When I was teaching in 1984, the kids had about 12 different sporting options. In 2002 they had something like 34. You've got to cater for their differences – the internet and the use of technology has changed their lives. At 18 they can buy beer over the counter at the supermarket whereas we had to go to the rugby club. How they socialise is totally different – they don't want to go out until 10 or 11 o'clock at night. In our day your social life happened at the rugby club. We've got to be flexible – not pandering – to provide some options to keep them involved.

'We have a development model and it's consistent around the country. Kids know what they're doing; we've made the rules the kids play under match their physical ability at the various skills. For instance, we don't have lineout lifting because they're not strong enough to lift. We've put in place a compulsory coaching course that's all about teaching coaches, who are usually dads or mums, about what skills they can teach the kids so they don't overload them and get them doing stuff they are not capable of doing.

'The situation in primary schools where 80 to 90 per cent of teachers are female means you just cannot expect those people who don't have an affinity with the game, who don't necessarily understand it and are worried about coaching it, to do what you need. We understand that, and that the players are not just going to come. We want them to come – rugby ticks a whole lot of other boxes. It teaches them about sport, commitment, responsibility and fair play, and we have a whole health issue with obesity so kids out running around with a footy ball has got to be a good thing.'

ANDERSON AND the NZRU are between a rock and a hard place. They probably don't see it that way. The choice as they understand it is quite simple – the game will die if they fail to engage Generation Y. The game needs players and the deeper the talent pool is, the more chance the All Blacks have of putting a competitive side out there. That part is agreed. The hidden danger, though, of pandering to Generation Y – and it is pandering – is that it merely endorses their sense of entitlement, reinforces their unshakeable belief that life should be easy and that inconvenience is not for them.

There are certain qualities that are always going to be required to win tests and to win World Cups. The most obvious are commitment, determination, hard work, passion and sheer bloody-mindedness. No side has ever won a World Cup without these qualities.

But if Generation Y is a global problem, why isn't it impacting so heavily upon the other major rugby nations? Why is this more of a problem for New Zealand than England, France or Ireland? The main reason is that rugby authorities in those countries haven't made allowances for Generation Y. There has been no pandering. Rugby is not the national game for the home unions, France, Australia and South Africa.

In England playing numbers have grown rapidly in the last five years and rugby is proving a powerful alternative to football. Professional football in the UK reflects many of the worst aspects of Generation Y. The top end of the game is a magnet for those who want fame, fortune and the shallowest life they can lead. Rugby has been the antidote, the vehicle for those who crave something more rewarding.

Rather than soften the edges of the game, authorities in the UK and France have been able to promote the traditional aspects of rugby and market the sport as one for those with more mental fortitude than their football-playing peers. Essentially those running the game in Europe have made it clear that anyone who subscribes to the loose, can't-be-bothered antics of Generation Y need not bother taking up the game. The code will survive without them.

It's a different story in New Zealand. From their first game, the All Blacks have had an unbreakable work ethic. They have believed passionately in the jersey and been prepared to bleed to ensure victory. The level of commitment to the All Black cause has perhaps been greater than the level of commitment other countries have invested in their respective national rugby teams. The depth of feeling for the All Black jersey has been one of those intangible factors that has given New Zealand the tiniest edge in world rugby.

The quality of the individuals wearing that black jersey has been another factor. And their excellence in rugby skills hasn't been the only difference. New Zealand has a collective work ethic. The pioneering spirit has always allowed people to cherish what hard work can deliver. If the early settlers had given up because something was too hard, the country would never have got where it is now. New Zealanders have always done the hard yards and taken pride in their tenacity, and the All Blacks have been a product of their environment and an embodiment of wider societal values.

The arrival of Generation Y has robbed the All Blacks of one of their most critical intangibles. Margins in test football are tiny. The difference between test teams is infinitesimal and at World Cups, possibly smaller than ever. New Zealand's wider values have been vital to the success of the All Blacks.

Simply put, other rugby playing nations haven't, across the entire populace, been able to emulate New Zealand's work ethic and resourcefulness. England, for instance, has struggled for a long time with a yob culture. The French have fought hard to preserve their work/life balance and tend not to view overtime as something for them – they don't see heroism in going beyond the call of duty and for a time even reduced the 40-hour working week to just 35 hours.

Players come onto the field with a million and one experiences and influences bundled inside them. International players around the world are passionate about their countries, but can any other nation say their players arrived in the test arena throughout the amateur era with the same relentlessly positive experiences as the All Blacks? Did any other country instil in their players such admirable ethics? Did the English bring to the game a similar sense of community and playing for their mates?

The answer is no, and this is the reason why the arrival of Generation Y has hurt the All Blacks more than any other nation. The 1987 All Blacks, like all New Zealand teams before them, carried all the positive, ingrained values they possessed into their rugby. What they learned in life shaped them.

Other countries had teams with strong individuals in that period, and players with excellent values learned from their life experiences. But what makes the All Blacks stand slightly apart is the sheer numbers of good people they have had available to select from. There was almost a guarantee that New Zealanders would reach adulthood with the emotional tools they needed for success intact.

Growing up in New Zealand at any point in the 20th century, it would have been almost impossible to reach your late teens without a work ethic, and a sense of honesty, decency and comradeship. It's a tribute to the entire nation that there are recruitment firms in the City of London who are asked to hire only Kiwis. For the last 30 years thousands of Kiwis have poured offshore and have taken with them all that is good about New Zealand. In the City, being a Kiwi is still regarded as a guarantee that you're a hard worker and a great person to have about the place. But that guarantee is under threat with the arrival of Generation Y.

We can only wonder at just how intensely the current generation feel their sense of entitlement. Have the All Blacks of the professional era been taking the field in the belief they were entitled to win a World Cup? They'd won enough tests, played enough good rugby to believe a World Cup was theirs by right. Their sense of entitlement must have been made stronger by the way the game is bending to suit their needs.

The amateur players had to make sacrifices to pursue their dreams. The farmers had it tough finding people to cover for them when they were training or away for matches. Everyone had it tough balancing their commitments to make time for the sport they loved. Generation Y haven't had to do that. Everything is being shuffled to make it possible for them to play rugby without sacrifice.

The young men of the professional era are very different from the young men of the amateur era. They don't have the same beliefs, ethics or desires and they certainly don't have the same sense of worth. It has been a battle for the All Black coaches in recent years to change mindsets, to foster a better culture and to lower expectations. They have had some success, and the All Black winning record is testament to that.

But World Cups, of course, keep escaping. Could that be because the pressure of World Cups has exposed the cracks in Generation Y? Could it be that when the pressure really, really comes on, when the game comes down to inches, to giving every last ounce of energy, the All Blacks have lost that little extra they once had? Could it be that the influence of Generation Y is too great?

While other countries have been able to attract those young men in search of the antithesis of football and all its excesses and flimsy values, for the survival of the game the All Blacks have had to recruit those who are naturally inclined to give up if things are too much bother. The cracks can be papered over to some extent. The worst excesses of Generation Y can be drummed out. But under the most intense pressure, players revert to their default setting.

The men of 1987 grew up in a world where they had to earn everything. Modern All Blacks grow up surrounded by people who believe they don't have to earn anything. One culture delivered a World Cup; the other has failed three times. That is no coincidence.

12
Style gurus

IT WAS A grim night for New Zealand, dumped out of yet another World Cup – this time earlier than ever before – but there wasn't the slightest hesitation from coach Graham Henry when he was asked just minutes after the final whistle if he had any regrets about the style of rugby employed by the All Blacks.

It was a World Cup chestnut, that question of style. The 1987 All Blacks aside, the other tournaments had been won by teams more proficient without that ball than they were with it. That's possibly a little harsh on the Australian side of 1991, who had some fabulous attacking players, but certainly the 1995, 1999, 2003 and, as it would turn out, the 2007 World Cups were all won with defence-driven rugby.

The South Africans kept flair to a minimum in 2007, as did the Australian and English sides that won respective World Cups in 1999 and 2003. They didn't play a game for romantics to fall in love with. It was solid, structured, territorial rugby where they took few risks, kept the ball safe, performed well in the set-pieces and tackled like demons. Those teams won by exerting pressure. They kept their error counts to a minimum and ground out results. It was effective without ever being entertaining. It was never pretty to watch; it didn't offer much in the way of spectacle, but plenty in the way of drama.

That, though, was the perceived way to win World Cups. They were in a different category from normal tests, or so the experts thought. At a World Cup the pressure on the players would be at its most intense. The hype around the games was enormous and the stakes as high as they would ever be. It was knock-out football and that helped foster an attitude of 'one mistake and you're gone'.

The coaches of those successful World Cup-winning sides all believed that the final stage of the World Cup was not the time or place to be expansive. There was no point in trying to be clever with the ball, in trying to do too much with it. The more passes you made, the more risks you were taking and the more opportunity you were giving opponents to capitalise on your mistakes. The game had to be played conservatively at World Cups, even if a side had been more adventurous prior to the tournament. The game-plan had to be modified, to be toned down in terms of creativity and ramped up in terms of pragmatism. That was something most international coaches were sure about, none more so than Jake White, the man who masterminded South Africa's success in 2007.

White could not be budged from his conviction, no matter how much evidence to the contrary developed in the run-up to the 2007 event. Even in July that year, though he'd seen his side slip to a big defeat in Christchurch against the All Blacks, he was certain the Springboks were still on track to win the World Cup. Whatever had transpired at AMI Stadium was virtually irrelevant, he reckoned. Come September and October in France, it would all be so very different. The South African style of rugby would be successful at that point. The World Cup, and he was adamant on this point, would not be won by adventurous, high-skilled, risk-taking rugby. Which was a problem for New Zealand, as that was the style employed by the All Blacks.

The conviction behind White's views made it imperative to pause and think about what he was saying. There was a weight of evidence to support his argument. Sides playing the way he had outlined had indeed won previous World Cups – except in 1987.

Yet the All Blacks had just hammered South Africa. In fact, the All Blacks had pretty much beaten everyone since late 2004. They hadn't actually lost a game in Europe since November 2002. They had been Tri-Nations champions in 2003, 2005, 2006 and 2007. They had been, almost constantly, the number-one team in the world under the official IRB rankings. Australia had managed to beat them just twice in the nine tests played between the 2003 and 2007 World Cups. South Africa enjoyed three wins. No one from the northern hemisphere had managed to beat the All Blacks since England, in June 2003. Not only that, but no one from Europe had really even come close. No one, not even the most one-eyed Australian or South African, could dispute the global superiority of the All Blacks in tests outside the World Cup between 2003 and 2007.

It was the same in the period after the 1995 World Cup through to the end of 1997; the All Blacks were head and shoulders above the rest of the world. And between 2000 and 2003, they were at least up there with Australia, capable of beating anyone on their day, just not as often or as emphatically as All Black teams from other eras. Throughout that whole period between 1995 and 2007, New Zealand played a style that only varied in detail – the core theme stayed consistent. They played a high-tempo, fluid game that looked to move the ball wide. It was a game that relied on the forwards being able to handle the ball and make good decisions when they had it. They offloaded out of contact, tried to stay on their feet and wanted to keep the pace frenetic so they could use their greater athleticism and aerobic capacity. The backs were all game-breakers, men who could beat their opponents one-on-one, players with flair and imagination and the ability to pass and catch under pressure. The backs were there to score tries, to use their explosive power to express themselves. It was 15-man rugby the All Blacks were after. That was the core philosophy.

It was a style of rugby the rest of the world found almost impossible to deal with – the results achieved by the All Blacks proved that. Yet, it was also a style that had failed to net them a World Cup since 1987.

The All Blacks would sweep everyone aside playing their all-expressive, running rugby and then, come the World Cup, it was a side playing conservative, pressure-inducing football that would lift the William Webb Ellis trophy.

That was why Graham Henry was asked after the All Blacks had lost to France in the 2007 quarter-final whether he had any regrets about the style of rugby the All Blacks had played. There was a growing belief that it took one style of rugby to win the Tri-Nations and another to win World Cups. The four teams who had progressed to the semi-finals of the 2007 event all played the same low-risk way – South Africa, England, France and Argentina.

Should the All Blacks have tried a different route? Should they have perfected a more conservative style in the years leading into the World Cup, maybe lost a few tests as a consequence, but given themselves a greater chance of winning the World Cup? It was a question that could just as easily have been put to John Hart in 1999 or John Mitchell in 2003. When it was put to Henry he was unapologetic: 'Absolutely not,' he said, 'I don't think our players would be engaged by that type of football.'

It was a bold statement. It was as if he was saying that style might be all right for everyone else, but it wouldn't work for us – our players are different, they need something more. They are looking for something more, some deeper emotional fulfilment, from playing international rugby. He was saying rugby was not about winning World Cups in isolation – All Black rugby was more encompassing than that, the responsibilities far greater.

The All Blacks couldn't make a choice to sacrifice their winning record in other tests just to pursue the World Cup dream. It hinted at there being an obligation to not just win every time they played, but for the All Blacks to win by playing in a way that touched the soul of the players and the nation. And it was an answer that raised another question: is there something deep within the psyche of the All Blacks that says style is just as important as substance?

THE ALL BLACKS of 1987 and the rest of their amateur brethren had no such fixation with style. Yes, they tried to play the game in a particular way, to implement the tactics and strategies they thought would deliver victory.

In the case of the 1987 All Blacks, that game plan was not too far removed from the way the All Blacks have played throughout the professional era. The 1987 team was equipped with athletic, mobile forwards like Michael Jones, Alan Whetton and Sean Fitzpatrick. Men who were capable of playing with the ball and who were powerful in the collision, too. In the backs, there were runners everywhere, most notably John Kirwan and John Gallagher, so there was value in spreading the ball wide. It was a mix of brutal forward grunt work and Fancy Dan stuff in the backs.

But – and everyone in the 1987 team is clear on this – if the game was tight with 15 minutes to go, the All Blacks would revert to any style, do anything to make sure they won. At that stage, it wouldn't matter – it was about getting the job done and nothing else. If the win were achieved with a penalty, a drop goal or a try it wouldn't matter. It wouldn't matter if the All Blacks spent the final 10 minutes booting the ball up in the air and chasing after it, or if they scored from a rolling maul that began inside their own half. The means wasn't important. The end was.

'We played very attractive rugby,' says John Drake of the 1987 team. 'But if it had come down to the crunch, we'd have given it to Grant Fox; we would have kicked a penalty, dropped a goal; we didn't care. We were disappointed in the final that we didn't score some more points. But not really disappointed. We just wanted to win.'

They just wanted to win. Well, surely the All Blacks of 2007 just wanted to win? Absolutely they wanted to win. But maybe they got hung up about the means. France went 20-18 ahead with 14 minutes remaining. The drama was intense, the occasion overwhelming. The All Blacks had suffered injuries and their confidence was flagging. France, though, had defended heavily for 66 minutes. They'd made an inordinate number of tackles. They were just about dead on their feet, living off passion and sheer willpower. It was desperate stuff and it was going to go to the wire.

It was apparent to four million New Zealanders and probably millions more watching on TV that the All Blacks just had to get in front to win the game. They didn't need a try; three points would have done it. France had nothing left and were never going to score again. They couldn't get the ball, didn't really want the ball. They had entered closure mode, where all they cared about was defending their line.

The All Blacks had 14 minutes to score three points. They didn't need to carve the French up with a clever backline move. All they had to do was control the ball, work their way close to the posts and then drop a goal. The prospect of being awarded a penalty had faded entirely as referee Wayne Barnes had failed to award one in the previous 26 minutes of the second half, despite numerous French transgressions. It should have been obvious to the All Black coaches and players that they were not going to persuade Barnes to blow his whistle and do them any favours. The drop goal was the only option. That's not being wise after the event, either.

Setting up for a field goal is the lowest-risk ploy, and also the means by which teams can eliminate other factors beyond their control. They didn't need the referee to help them. They didn't need to read the opposition and react to what they were doing. The All Blacks could follow their pattern, decide which route they were going to take and then follow it. The only variable would be the length of time it took them to get close enough to attempt the kick.

World Cup history is littered with famous drop goals. Rob Andrew knocked over a massive one to beat Australia in extra time at the 1995 World Cup. It was the score that allowed England to progress to the semi-final. In that same tournament, as if New Zealanders need to be reminded, Joel Stransky slotted a field goal to win the final. At the following tournament South Africa's Jannie de Beer succeeded with five drop goals in one game to defeat England in the quarter-final, while Stephen Larkham then landed the only field goal of his career in the semi-final, allowing Australia to reach the final. And most famous of all, it was Jonny Wilkinson's drop goal that won the 2003 World Cup for England in the last minute of extra time. The drop goal has been the most successful way for sides to secure victory in the dying stages of World Cup games.

But on that fateful night in Cardiff, the All Blacks appeared convinced they were going to win the game with a try. It almost seemed they were too proud to win with a drop goal – that there was something within their collective psyche that said the All Blacks don't win with drop goals, they win with style, with a sweeping move that leads to a try. For 12 minutes they ignored the drop-goal option, and when they finally realised that the game was all but lost, Luke McAlister attempted one from almost 50 metres out.

The very fact that the All Blacks did eventually attempt one suggests they only saw it as a last-ditch option; the choice of the desperate, a real coffee drinker agreeing to instant only when the craving for caffeine reaches the point of distraction.

The independent review of the World Cup failure of 2007 had this to say about the quarter-final: 'We recognise that in the last 10 minutes of the second half, the All Blacks faced a dilemma. Whether to go for a drop goal without Carter or Evans (injured), or whether to continue to attempt to score through a try or a penalty. The team chose the latter. The rationale was that it had worked for the team before in games in similar situations (examples included Australia in Sydney in 2005, England in London in 2005, South Africa in Durban in 2007). In addition the drop goal had never been executed under pressure – something the coaches acknowledged could have been worked on more as a strategy.

'The coaches did, however, send a message out to the team with

10 minutes to go, to set up for a drop goal. The on-field decision was made to continue with the tactic of attempting to score a try or to get a penalty. When making this decision the players were unaware of a vital piece of information – that the All Blacks had not been given a penalty in the entire second half and were therefore probably unlikely to get one, notwithstanding their pressure, possession and territory.

'The coaches agreed that more emphasis should have been given to execution of a drop goal to score the necessary points to win in a tight finals finish like at Cardiff. That is not a traditional part of the New Zealand game and needs to be developed.'

As a theoretical exercise, it's worth asking whether the 1987 All Blacks would have handled that game in Cardiff the same way. Would they have failed to score three points in 14 minutes? Would they have looked so uncertain? Would they have taken the view that winning was the goal, but that it was important to win with some panache, with a bit of flair and class?

'No chance,' said Drake. 'We had too many players that would have corrected the situation. Right through the team. Joe Stanley, for example, would have said to Grant Fox we don't want it, give it to the forwards to rumble it up. There would have been a lot of talk about it but we would all have known in ourselves that we just had to win – any way we could. We would have cheated to get the win.'

The 2007 All Blacks didn't share that same single-minded devotion to winning any way they could. It never came down to the wire in 1999 or 2003, but neither of those failed All Black sides could say they shared a philosophy with the 1987 team. The question is, why not? What happened to make the All Blacks believe in style over substance at such critical times?

MUCH OF the cultural shift was generated by the arrival of Super 12 and the razzmatazz of professional rugby. In an instant, rugby went from sport to entertainment. The priority of the men running the game in the southern hemisphere was to get bums on seats. This was the brave new world of professionalism and the rules were going to be different. There could no longer be such a heavy reliance on the converted. Those with rugby already in their veins were going to stick with the game no matter what. That was certain. But Super 12 wanted to go after a new audience. It wanted to get away from the dated amateur game where warm beer and cold pies sufficed as hospitality and to craft a more uplifting and modern entertainment experience.

Rugby was no longer going to be a closed shop, a blokes-only experience where it was felt if you hadn't learned the nuances of the game by playing it, you had no business being in the stands watching it. The marketing men of Super 12 were going to consign all that to history. They were going to do sexy. They were going to have cheerleaders. They were going to have music, half-time entertainment, soft drinks, better food and covered seats. They were going to have night-time rugby and put the sport up against the movies and dinner for two. It had to be slick, it had to be stylish, it had to be something people attending would want to come back to. Rugby was going professional and it was going to take a whole new crowd with it.

The vision for Super 12 wasn't going to be fulfilled by just focusing on what was happening off the field. The actual product, so the administrators believed, needed to be sexed up too. The tribal thing wasn't enough on its own.

Rugby was a complex game, too reliant on interpretation by the referee. Very often the game didn't make sense to the casual observer. Sometimes it wasn't great to watch unless you had emotional investment in one of the participating teams. Sometimes it was just too blood and snotters to appeal to anyone other than the die-hards, the very people who would have been out there themselves earlier in the day, bleeding for their own jersey. Super 12 had to engage a wider audience. It was going to be played between February and May, which meant it could be played on top of the ground. There would be, for most of the competition, fast tracks and a dry ball. That was ample reason in itself for teams to employ expansive tactics, to spread the ball wide, to open things up.

In case any side was still reluctant, the administrators came up with the ultimate incentive; they invented the bonus point. Any team that scored four tries would receive an extra championship point. A win would net four points, but a win where four tries were scored would land five points. Over the course of 11 games that could be significant. It meant that there would be an incentive to still throw the ball around late into the game.

And that incentive would apply to both teams as there was also the introduction of the losing bonus point – any side losing by seven points or less would take a point. If they scored four tries and lost by seven points or less, they could take two points.

'What we were out to develop was rugby's answer to one-day cricket,' says David Moffett, the former boss of the New Zealand Rugby Union who was at the helm in 1995. 'We wanted women and young children to come and watch. It was about razzle-dazzle and scoring tries. It was about putting bums on seats and entertaining people and we did that really well. It's mums who decide what sport their kids are going to play. We were hugely successful and we built this phenomenon that attracted huge crowds and we deliberately set out to do that.

'We could control the appointment of the coaches. It would be one of the things we would ask them at the interview. We would ask what style of rugby they believed in and what their strategy for the game was. It was a two-way process. The referees were also very important. There was a conscious decision to encourage the refs to keep the game going. They had to enforce the laws, but try to find a way to use the best law to keep the flow and the continuity. [It was like] one-day cricket [where] they have two versions of the sport. We were asking players to do the same thing.'

A new game was born. The bonus-point culture emerged where teams started to see rugby as an extension of sevens. The razzle-dazzle Moffett was after had arrived. Referees started to wave play on whenever they could. The pace was frenetic; the action was non-stop. The big hits came flying in and the tries flowed. It was easy football to watch. The demographics of the average crowd in New Zealand really did change. More and more women were attracted to Super 12. It was easier to follow as there were fewer stoppages, less baffling rulings to have explained at the breakdown. There was a faster tempo, more skills on show and gritty arm-wrestles became a thing of the past. New Zealand teams took to it instantly. They were brilliant at this type of rugby. They had the athletes, the skills and the vision to adapt to this festival-style sport. They relished playing on hard tracks and they relished being encouraged to be adventurous. The Blues won the first two titles. Then the Crusaders the next three and it has been a competition dominated by New Zealand teams ever since.

But the vision outlined by Moffett had some complications. There was a process of readjustment required, just as in cricket. Being a quality one-day team did not equate to being a quality test side. One game required patience and perseverance, the other was about flashing blades, taking risks and improvisation. They weren't compatible. Habits picked up in the one-day game could be disastrous in the test arena, and it was the same with rugby.

The bonus-point culture of Super 12 flew in the face of test football. Tests were about winning and only winning. There was no requirement to win by a certain amount. It was about the 80 minutes and no more. Yet New Zealand's best players had the notion of adventure very much ingrained after several years of Super 12. It became a natural instinct to push the boundaries regardless of the score. The game could be tight and the leading side might have scored three tries already. With 10 minutes left, what do they do?

In Super 12, they would most likely go for bust – keep flinging the ball about to get the elusive fourth try. That could be critical to their chances of progression. The reward was worth the risk. But in a test this response was all wrong. A test was about closure and this became the lost art of New Zealand rugby. Both the Australian and South African sides seemed to have a better handle on closure than the New Zealanders. Certainly the Australian sides bought into the expansive game that was being encouraged, but they were better at standing back in the final 10 minutes and doing what they had to do to secure the win. Super 12 has corrupted the ability of New Zealand's best players to close down big tests. The bonus-point culture of Super 12, and then Super 14 as it became, has left a gremlin in the minds of too many players.

Is it any wonder after 12 years of Super Rugby that the All Blacks didn't have that closure instinct at Cardiff in 2007?

Is it any wonder after 12 years of Super Rugby that the All Blacks didn't have that closure instinct at Cardiff in 2007? There they were, hammering away at the French line hoping they'd score a try. That was the bonus-point culture at work. Trawl through videos of Super Rugby over the years and see how many New Zealand teams are still desperate to score a try in the last minute, regardless of the score. It is rare indeed for New Zealand Super Rugby sides to drop goals in the dying minutes.

The drop goal is just not in anyone's thinking.

Super Rugby has been both an enhancing and a corrosive agent for New Zealand rugby. At one extreme it has sharpened the explosive skills of the athletes. It has left players better equipped for fast-tempo, mobile rugby. The individual skill of the players is high as a result of the constant exposure they have to running rugby. The All Blacks have been able to harness many of these improvements. The national side has, since the advent of professionalism, tapped into the creativity induced by Super Rugby.

The likes of England, Scotland and even France have all had their difficulties in this period when it comes to expression. They just haven't developed the same expansive skills, haven't encouraged the players to play with such fluidity and freedom. The All Blacks have explored this side of their game to the full.

On the other hand, some of the imperatives of test rugby have been sacrificed on this altar of entertainment. For periods in the last decade or so the All Blacks have not been as authoritative as they once were at the set-piece and the collision. Super Rugby didn't promote the set-piece as anything other than a glorified restart. The collision was high-impact, but not necessarily a contest for the ball. Inevitably, some All Black sides of the professional age have taken the festival skills of Super Rugby to the test arena. That has put them under pressure in some big games and seen them come unstuck.

For the most part though, the All Blacks have maintained enough presence in their tight skills which, combined with their ability to run from everywhere and break the tightest defensive line, has seen them maintain their winning record. The bad habits of Super Rugby have not derailed the juggernaut. Except at World Cups.

World Cups and Super 14 are poles apart. The All Blacks have been punished for not being able to get Super 14 out of their system. Their expansive football is at odds with the perceived way to win World Cups. But it's entirely plausible that the All Blacks could have won any of the 1999, 2003 or 2007 World Cups playing with width and fluidity. They would only have needed to temper things, to have had in their minds that at some stage in the game they might have to flick a switch and stop taking so many risks. If they were in front with 10 minutes to go, they would have to understand there was no need to take risks at that juncture. At that stage, it would be about playing for territory, putting the opposition under pressure by asking them to play their way out of their own half.

They didn't appear to have that knowledge in the system, however. Their commitment to expansive football was total. The idea of adapting, of becoming risk-averse to close the game out, has been lost. It still seems as if somewhere in the back of players' minds they are hunting bonus points in the test arena.

Tri-Nations hasn't helped either, as there are bonus points up for grabs there too, and that's fostered a notion there's something to be taken from defeat. Bonus points have softened the importance of winning. They've created grey areas. But in the World Cup there's only black and white. Only serious psychological analysis could reveal whether buried deep in the subconscious of many All Blacks is the belief that losing is tolerable if a team has played without inhibition in the process. Are players secretly content to lose as long as they entertained and stayed true to their commitment to expansive and adventurous football? Is the art of closure, the ability to shut opponents out of the game, seen by the modern players and management as yet another now redundant skill inherited from the amateur era?

All we have is conjecture, but such theories aren't without merit. The evidence presented by failed World Cup bids can't easily be pushed aside. No one, given the events of 1999, 2003, 2007, and maybe even 1995, can dismiss this thinking as outrageous or claim it's without grounding.

A year on from the World Cup failure in 2007 and the same question was put to Henry as he relaxed in the All Blacks' hotel in Dublin before their Grand Slam test with Ireland. He'd had 12 months to think about things, to ask himself with the benefit of hindsight whether there was some merit in ripping up the blueprint and pursuing a more pragmatic approach.

'I don't think it would press the All Black buttons playing a 10-man game,' he said as emphatically as he'd done that night in Cardiff. 'I don't think the style was wrong; it just didn't win the Rugby World Cup. There have been some periods of New Zealand rugby where we've played a very forward-orientated game. Where the forwards really didn't want to give the ball to the backs. We changed when we got beaten by the Lions, when we got beaten by a side that played an expansive game, and it certainly did New Zealand rugby a lot of good – the game developed immensely after the Lions tour in 1959 and became a 15-man game.

Why is style so important to New Zealanders? Winning is enough for everyone else, but not for New Zealanders.

'I don't think that [10-man rugby] would bring the best out of them and also I think we have a responsibility to play with some style. We've got a fan base in New Zealand that wants to see decent rugby – they don't want to see kick and clap, so I think we have a responsibility to the fan as well. But the major reason is we think it's winning rugby, and we think it's enjoyable rugby and it stimulates the players.'

There it was again, that allusion to New Zealanders being unwilling to accept victory achieved without style. And what about this notion of a responsibility to deliver something that pleases the fans? Every other nation shares that desire to keep its public happy, but their task in that regard is simple – they just have to win.

For England, Ireland and South Africa there is no secondary obligation to deliver victories achieved in a particular manner. All the crowd wants is a test scalp. If that scalp could be taken by playing a brand of rugby that is fast, skilled and compelling, then fantastic. But no one is going to hold out for it, or see a victory ground out as any less satisfying or worthy of celebration than a win achieved with Champagne football. New Zealanders are more demanding of the All Blacks.

Expectations are almost unrealistically high, raising the question, why? Why is style so important to New Zealanders? Winning is enough for everyone else, but not for New Zealanders. They need something more. What does that say about them? What perceptions do New Zealanders have of themselves and of the All Blacks to make them so demanding?

A BITING wind whips across from the Remarkables, picking up colder air on its travels. When it reaches the tourists on the chairlift at Queenstown's Skyline Luge, it turns their hands blue as they grip their seats. Only the mad or truly hardy are out on a day like this. Central Otago is in the grip of winter. It's a day for hot chocolate and warm fires.

Those daft enough to have made the trip up on the gondola know this. They know it because their fingers are numb, their faces ache with the cold and their feet are demanding to return indoors. Everyone who paid for luge tickets knows they've made a mistake. It isn't fun whizzing along in these curious little carts when your hands can barely grip and your ears feel like they might just take off in search of warmer climes. It's totally crazy to even be outside. But even crazier, as everyone on the chairlift can see, is playing rugby in this brutal weather, which is what is happening down below.

The Wakatipu Wanderers are playing Fat Badger Alexandra in the Otago Country Championship. It's some way removed from the professional game in terms of quality. But it concedes nothing in terms of ambition and intent. These are strictly amateur players and on a day cold enough to freeze the fires of hell, both sides are out there doing their best to play expressive football. The ball zips along the backline as best it can. Forwards try to offload in the contact, the game flows – almost. This is rugby played for love of the game. There are a hundred and one other things the 30 men involved could be doing, but they are there in Queenstown doing their best to play rugby the way they believe it should be played.

A week later and the scene in Dargaville is not so different. The weather isn't as extreme, the landscape not quite as dramatic, but the passion in Northland is every bit as intense as it was the previous week at the other end of the country. There are hundreds of children eager to get their hands on the ball. Plenty of dads, too, enjoying their new role as coach, excited at the prospect of nurturing the skills of the next generation. All across the expanse of green there is rugby being played.

In fact, go anywhere in New Zealand on a Saturday morning and there will be rugby. In so many households there will be heightened anticipation of what lies ahead – Saturday is rugby. There will be a frisson of excitement over breakfast. It doesn't matter if you are seven or 27, on a Saturday morning when you swing your legs out of bed there's only one thought to be had – rugby. And the excitement doesn't come from an expectation of standing listlessly by while the first-five boots the leather off the ball, or the forwards stick it up their jumpers and never let the blessed thing out. The excitement comes from the knowledge that rugby is an opportunity to express the gambit of skills and to feel the full range of emotions.

Rugby, for New Zealanders, is all-encompassing. The beauty of the sport is that it demands athleticism, bravery, physicality, flair, creativity, intelligence, speed, vision and tactical nous. For the last 100 years or so, the rest of the world has asked what makes New Zealanders so good at rugby.

There are so many factors, but none more critical than the desire that exists among players from the most junior teams right through to the All Blacks, to play with expression and to play with the ball in hand. For New Zealanders, there is an emotional connection to rugby. That link is made through the joy of expression, of exploiting all the ways there are to beat an opponent. When Graham Henry said he didn't feel the typical style used to win World Cups would engage his players, he was right. Rugby is often referred to as a religion in New Zealand, and in many ways it is. It is a form of worship at least, a means for young and old to gather and pay homage to a sport that pushes all their buttons.

This expressive style of football has delivered a substantial number of victories for the All Blacks and other professional New Zealand teams. Victory, though, for those frozen Wakatipu players and the youngsters in Dargaville wasn't necessarily the number-one priority. Teams across New Zealand could opt to play grinding, kick-and-chase football and bump up their win ratios, but it would bring no satisfaction.

For junior and amateur players across the country, the journey is more important than the destination. Fulfilment comes from playing the game the way it should be played, not from winning alone.

This is the environment in which the best All Blacks are immersed. They have the same memories of Saturday mornings as everyone else. Rugby as expression, rugby as fun, as a means to show who you are and what you can do – that is the culture all across the nation. It is New Zealand's greatest strength and, at World Cups, it has been New Zealand's greatest weakness.

Embedded in the subconscious of most All Blacks is a commitment to play with style, an unshakeable belief that flair and imagination will conquer all. To consider playing any other way is sacrilege. Rugby would mean nothing to New Zealand if it was about slogging it out with big men who didn't have the essence of the sport in their soul.

The rest of the world doesn't understand this conviction. That's because rugby is not a way of life anywhere else. Nowhere else does rugby pervade the fabric of society as it does in New Zealand, nowhere else is it played so instinctively. The desire to run and pass, to take risks, to play with ambition is ingrained. To believe it can suddenly be stamped out in a critical World Cup knockout game is naïve in the extreme. To believe that New Zealanders would be happy to win a World Cup by playing defensive, kick-driven rugby is a failure to grasp the emotional bond the people have with the game. New Zealand would dearly love to win the World Cup, but not at any price. It has to be won by staying true to their vision of how the game should be played.

13
Understanding Pasifika

DEPENDING WHO YOU talk to, the increasing influence of Pacific Island players in New Zealand rugby is either the critical difference or the critical flaw.

The argument that players from a Pacific background are the critical difference is the easier one to make. Since rugby went professional, the athletes have become bigger, faster and stronger. No one disputes that. The athletic growth of the players has radically changed the game. It is now, and has been for the better part of the last decade, a game that is won and lost at the collision point. Momentum is everything in rugby, as is the ability to break tackles and create space. The explosive athlete is the athlete of choice.

Tackling is no longer passive – it's aggressive in the extreme. Defenders have shifted the contact point from the legs to the midriff, where they hope to hit the runner so hard they will dislodge the ball. At the break-down, there is a need to be able to shift bodies and when a forward carries the ball, he's encouraged to find space and if he can't, to make sure he blasts past the first tackler. All that takes explosive power, and it's encouraged in midfield and outside backs as much as it is in the forwards.

A quirk of genetics, fuelled by traditional diets high in protein, has seen the Pacific Islands produce a disproportionate number of explosive athletes. The high-impact, confrontational aspect of rugby also sits well with traditional male culture in the Islands and rugby is the perfect sport for Tongan, Fijian and Samoan men.

The impact Pacific athletes are having on world rugby is staggering.

There are players from the Islands scattered all over the major clubs of Europe. Everyone wants some of that explosive power – that point of difference. There is also a perception that Pacific Islanders are natural ball players who rely more on instinct than on what they learn on the training ground. A tight game can be blown open by the instinctive magic of a Pacific player who sees opportunity that others don't.

The influence of the Pacific athlete is most noticeable in New Zealand rugby. In the last decade the number of professional players of Pacific Island descent holding a professional contract has almost quadrupled. In 2008, of the 140 contracted Super 14 players in New Zealand, 43 had Pasifika heritage. That's almost 31 per cent, yet, according to the last census, Pacific Islanders make up only six per cent of New Zealand's population.

The numbers have grown just as sharply when it comes to the All Blacks. At the 1995 World Cup, Jonah Lomu, Michael Jones, Alama Ieremia and Frank Bunce were the only members of the All Black squad to come from a Pacific background. In 1999 there was a jump from four to six Pacific players in the All Black squad. By 2003 the number had risen to nine and in 2007 there were 11 Pacific players in the 30-man All Black World Cup squad. However, the numbers alone don't quite tell the story.

So much of the All Black game-plan in recent years has been built around the Pacific players. The rugged defence of Jerry Collins and Tana Umaga; the driving power of Keven Mealamu; the work-rate of Rodney So'oialo; the line-breaking ability of Ma'a Nonu; the counter-attacking thrust of Mils Muliaina; the speed and flair of Joe Rokocoko and Sitiveni Sivivatu; the scrummaging bulk of Neemia Tialata – the list goes on and on.

The contribution Pacific players have made to All Black rugby in the professional era has been huge. The contribution they've made to All Black World Cup campaigns has been huge. So often the critical difference between the All Blacks and their opponents has been the inches they've stolen in the collision – the tiny gains they've made by having so many power athletes on the field. The All Blacks have finishing power no other side has been able to match and in the last decade, Christian Cullen and Jeff Wilson aside, the most deadly have been Pasifika – Lomu, Umaga, Rokocoko, Doug Howlett, Sivivatu, Joeli Vidiri and Nonu. The argument that Pacific players have made a huge difference to the ability and impact of the All Blacks is an easy one to make.

However, the second school of thought – that Pacific players are the critical flaw in New Zealand rugby – has some validity too.

First though, it must be stated categorically that there is absolutely no merit in the appalling notion that Pacific players are detrimental to New Zealand rugby because of an inherent lack of decision-making ability.

That some of the fiercest All Black competitors in recent years have been Pacific Islanders doesn't dissuade the racists from their nonsense.

That's racist nonsense. But spend any time in New Zealand rugby circles and you will pick up on this implied flaw in Pacific players. The whispering and nudging is at its worst in the corporate boxes at Eden Park. Auckland, as the largest Polynesian city in the world, has the greatest numbers of Pacific Islanders in its provincial and Super Rugby teams. There have been both Blues and Auckland games in the last few years where all 15 players on the field have been Pasifika. If either of these teams lose, and there are significant numbers of Pacific players on the field, then that may be put forward by some supporters as the key reason for the defeat.

Even if no one spells out what they really mean, the implication is that the preponderance of Pacific players meant there weren't enough strong decision-makers on the field. This is the same racist argument heard in regard to American football: the belief that the quarterback – the equivalent of the first five – should be a white man as he's more suited to the cerebral challenge of the role.

The perpetrators of such abject tosh are able to support their argument by linking the increased Pasifika presence in All Black World Cup squads to the continued failure to improve decision-making under pressure. It's never quite said, publicly at least, as explicitly as that. But hang around rugby circles for long enough and you can't help getting the sense that it's the prevailing view among some fans, possibly even among some coaches and administrators, too.

Those who believe this mush will have a personal experience to trot out backing it up. They can remember a game at school where they were under pressure, or taking a hiding, and the Pacific kids gave up. They have no heart, is the generalisation. They are only good when they're winning.

That some of the fiercest All Black competitors in recent years have been Pacific Islanders doesn't dissuade the racists from their nonsense. Take Michael Jones – was he a man who lacked the composure and vision to make good calls in the heat of battle? Or what about Tana Umaga – how does he fit this theory when he was the best captain the All Blacks have had since Sean Fitzpatrick? Is Keven Mealamu a quitter? Or Rodney So'oialo?

In a lighter moment in Dublin, 2008 the All Black coaches were asked who of the 2007 World Cup squad would be the last man standing if all the players had to partake in cage fighting. There was no hesitation – Mealamu and So'oialo would go the distance. They were hard men whose commitment knew no bounds. The idea of there being an inherent flaw in the psychological make-up of Pacific players has to be kicked a long way into touch. It's offensive and entirely untrue.

However, that is not to say the growing influence of Pasifika players in New Zealand rugby hasn't been without its issues. There may well be a link between World Cup failure and the increased numbers of Pacific players in the All Blacks. But it has nothing to do with any inherent flaw.

ONE AREA where we *can* generalise about Pacific athletes is their genetic heritage. Boys with a Pacific Island background tend to mature physically at an earlier age than their Palagi counterparts. Where a 15-year-old of European descent might well grow significantly into his later teens and fill out considerably, Pacific boys of the same age tend to be physically more mature.

Auckland is the best place to observe this phenomenon. Across the city there are boys wandering around in men's bodies. The difference in size between Pacific and European boys between the ages of 14 to 16 is undeniable. There are many young Pacific Island boys well in excess of 100 kg. At that size, with all the power that implies, they can be lethal on the rugby field. There's not much hope of a skinny white kid, weighing barely 70 kg, hauling down a 100 kg guy who's already fast enough and big enough at 15 to be an All Black test wing.

When you consider the athletic potential of the most promising

Pacific Island teenagers against their Palagi peers, it's almost impossible to go past the former. And, indeed, not many school or age-grade coaches have looked that gift horse in the mouth. At First XV level, particularly in the major metropolitan centres, Pacific players dominate.

In Auckland especially, it's not uncommon to see the bigger, traditional rugby schools field a team made up almost entirely of Pacific athletes. In 2000 the law changed and it was no longer possible for public schools to accept out-of-zone pupils whose fathers had attended the same institution. That meant that Auckland Grammar was going to lose its link with the Pacific community. In the 1950s and 1960s the Tongan hostel – the dwelling where new immigrants lived until they found their feet – was based in St Leonard's Street and in zone. Most Tongan families would move out of zone after they settled but continued to send their sons to Grammar over the years.

The board at Auckland Grammar felt protective about its association with the Tongan community and wanted to preserve it. But really, what the board was worried about was the effect the changed law would have on its First XV. Without access to significant numbers of Pacific Island boys, how would the First XV compete? A special meeting was called and 700 people turned up.

Even at school age the Pacific boys are better equipped to beat tackles, they can offload in the tackle and they can destroy opponents with the power of their defence. It all sounds good, yet there are problems associated with this dominance of the power athlete.

The first problem is player retention – keeping kids from a European background in the sport. If boys, still some way off their physical peak, are asked to play against what are effectively men, the consequences are predictable. It just isn't that much fun. As the New Zealand Rugby Union discovered in 2004, there is a huge teenage drop-out from rugby. Young men, not wishing to lose face in front of their peers, said the main reason they were dropping out was to pursue other interests and to be available for part-time employment. The suspicion remains that the real reason they were giving up was fear of injury. Most metropolitan rugby unions have done their best to alleviate this problem by introducing weight-grade competitions, but it's still a major battle to retain players through their early teens.

Maybe it hasn't been a massive factor in World Cup failures, but there's no doubt that the game in New Zealand is denied two or three potential superstars each year because they gave the game up at 15. There are plenty of examples of European players maturing later, forcing their way into the First XV, and then going on to establish themselves in the professional ranks. But if they give up at 15 they are lost forever. The 65 kg 15-year-old could become the 110 kg juggernaut at 18, but once kids are out of rugby they tend to stay out.

The second problem is the style of rugby that has evolved as a consequence of relying on the power athlete. Because most schools, as discussed, place such importance on the First XV, they tend to select the biggest, fastest and strongest players and as a consequence there has been an erosion of traditional skills. This erosion has nothing to do with the players being Pasifika; it has to do with coaches looking for the best ways to exploit the strength of their teams.

Unlike the situation 20 years ago, most First XVs now are loaded with powerful boys who can carry the ball and beat tackles. Coaches encourage their teams to get the ball into the hands of the most destructive players. It makes sense and is effective. The downside is that this style of football doesn't foster good lifelong habits.

Continually giving the ball to the big men doesn't foster tactical awareness. It doesn't encourage the ball carriers to develop a full portfolio of skills. At schoolboy level they can get away with smashing through tackles. That gets them noticed and sees them advance up the ladder. But by the time many power athletes reach Under-21 or club level, they're up against men just as powerful as they are, and capable of stopping them.

At that point it becomes apparent they haven't really developed alternative skills – that they don't read the game well because they've never had to. They don't offload out of the tackle as well as they should because, until now, they've never been held in the tackle. Many players never learn the necessity of relying on teamwork while they are part of the First XV. The culture is essentially about the individual, about giving the biggest and fastest the greatest number of opportunities to win games single-handed.

School coaches will dismiss this idea out of hand, but there's one irrefutable piece of evidence that proves the decline of traditional values in the school game. Take Daniel Carter, and maybe at a push Stephen Donald, out of the equation and New Zealand is desperately short of quality first fives. In 2009 the Blues couldn't find one and were forced to select Tasesa Lavea, a player they had previously tried and rejected, and Jimmy Gopperth, a player the Hurricanes and Wellington had previously tried and rejected. The Hurricanes were in a similar position; they too had to go with the unknown in Daniel Kirkpatrick and Willie Ripia. New Zealand has increasingly become bereft of quality first fives and Blues coach Pat Lam is in no doubt the problem starts at school.

Those playing first five at a traditional rugby school don't have to learn the tactical ropes the way they used to. They don't necessarily have to develop a traditional kicking game or learn how to move their side around the field. That style of rugby has been made redundant by the number of power athletes, the majority of whom happen to be of Pacific origin.

Simply being big and powerful is not enough at a professional level.

Now, first fives merely have to pick the right runner to feed. They can stand close to the traffic and pop the ball to one of the behemoths who will always be standing on either side. Auckland and the Blues are so distressed by the situation that they even run specialist clinics for promising first fives in the hope of instilling some of the skills so vitally needed in the professional game.

The professional game has been able to pick up many of these promising Pacific athletes who star in the schoolboy game and equip them with a wider range of skills. Simply being big and powerful is not enough at a professional level. It's helpful, but there has to be more to a player's skill set than power. Jerry Collins is possibly the best example of a player who continued to add to his strengths as he played. He was a bruising teenager who starred in national age-grade sides and was an All Black by the time he was 20. His game was all about confrontation and that was what he did best.

When Graham Henry took over as All Black coach in 2004, he wasn't convinced that Collins was offering enough, so he encouraged the Wellington blindside to expand his vision and not always be looking for contact. Collins began to attack space and pass the ball, and he became a more effective player for it.

But there's an inescapable truth that when players are under pressure, they revert to type; they find solace in the things they know they do best. Certainly in 2003 and 2007, when there were significant numbers of power athletes on the field in the critical stages of the respective lost knockout games, there was a sense of individuals reverting to type. The schoolboy system many players had come through led them to believe that, under pressure, it was best to look for the biggest individuals to do something.

Under that same pressure, could it be that many players felt the power of the individual rather than the collective strength of the team was more likely to win the game? Could it be that some of the power athletes, who had spent most of their formative years bashing through smaller defenders, thought they would be able to do just that in the knockout stages of the World Cup?

How many times in Cardiff did the All Black forwards pick and drive? In 2003 the All Blacks seemed to have only one ploy in the second half against Australia – give the ball to Collins and hope he could hammer his way through. It had worked the previous week against South Africa when Collins and Mealamu had carried the ball strongly and to great effect. When the Wallabies knocked those two down, the All Blacks had nothing else and no one really had an alternative strategy. So few of the players had any depth of experience in responding to pressure. In most cases, their past told them that giving the ball to the big guys usually worked.

Most of those power athletes in the All Black World Cup squads of 2003 and 2007 were Pasifika. Reverting to smashing up the middle would have to be considered ineffective decision-making, giving the racists more ammunition.

But again, we have to go back to Lochore and recall that the players are a product of their environment. So many Pacific players have not been helped in their formative years to develop their skills. So many are asked to use their bulk, their explosive frames, to literally smash their way to victory. When schoolboy teams are under pressure, they look to the power athlete to bail them out, to pull off a miracle by running through four people. Despite the effort made in the professional game to develop the skill base of many Pacific players, it's still inevitable that come a critical World Cup encounter, individuals will ignore what they've been told and revert to instinct. That's ineffective decision-making though, less a failing of the individual than of the system that made them.

MORE THAN any other group, Pacific Island players are a victim of New Zealand schools' obsession with rugby. They may seem to be the big winners given their massively disproportionate representation in First XVs across the country. But for many Pacific schoolboys, playing for the First XV turns out to be not only their greatest rugby experience, but their greatest life experience. Life can go downhill fast once they leave school. The adulation, the respect and recognition disappear the moment many Pacific players walk out the school gates.

When Dave Syms warned his colleagues at Palmerston North Boys' High School against the creation of sporting academies, he reminded them that fewer than one per cent of the population will become professional rugby players. He spoke of the danger of putting all the eggs in one basket. Sadly, as we know, many schools have ignored his advice and have allowed school children to pursue their rugby dreams to the detriment of their overall education.

And (although there are no statistics to prove it), just as a disproportionate number of Pacific athletes make it to the professional ranks, so too do a disproportionate number try and fail. In the attempt, the dream of professional success is allowed to override all other facets of their education. It's normal for a teenage boy to hold dreams of playing professionally, to believe he has the goods and that he can neglect his studies because fame and fortune are just around the corner. Plenty of young men are both impetuous and ill-informed. Again, there are no hard facts to back this up but the anecdotal evidence strongly suggests more Pasifika boys than Europeans are setting their sights on professional rugby as a career, and from an earlier age.

That aspiration is only natural. After all, Pacific Island kids look at professional rugby and see so many people from their own or a similar background who've made it – sometimes they're from the same school, from the same street even. That's a powerful incentive, made more powerful by the fact that from an early age, many of these boys are elevated into the First XV. From their mid-teens they are big enough and strong enough to hold down a place in the senior team and enjoy all the associated benefits. It's no surprise if a 16-year-old, who's making representative teams and playing in front of a few thousand people every Saturday, becomes convinced he might make it to the All Blacks. As Mount Albert

Grammar's Dale Burden said, it's not easy keeping expectation in check. It's not easy for New Zealand's educators to keep dreams contained and alternative routes cultivated.

And because it's not easy, are some schools and some teachers guilty of not even trying? Statistically, Maori and Pacific Island boys lag their European peers in academic achievement. Does that create an expectation among teachers that these children are destined to under-perform in the classroom? Are some teachers, even in leading schools, assuming that Pacific kids would be better off chasing their rugby dreams because the reward is worth the risk?

We can have our suspicions, and they are heightened by Burden when he says this: 'One of the issues in Auckland is that it has a growing Polynesian population. And statistically Maori and Pacific Island kids are behind. Very often rugby is the only thing that they tend to do particularly well. Those kids also make up a disproportionate number of the 1A rugby team, and I think there was one point in a recent game where we had only one European kid in the XV. We have 20 per cent [Pacific] kids here at the school, so that isn't reflected in the team. I don't think the fact they play rugby has anything to do with their ability to get academic results.

'The real question is, do these kids make the best effort or are they just jocks? What I would say is they do make the effort because whether they like it or not, the emphasis here, and I can't speak for anywhere else, is that you are not here just to play sport. If you are just here to play sport then you are better off working, earning money doing whatever job you can get and playing for a club.

'You have to have a good report, you have to try your best because if you can't do those things then the secondary school environment doesn't apply – you should be somewhere else. You've got to be involved in meaningful things, otherwise why would you be at school?'

Again, there's an implication from Burden that what happens at Mount Albert doesn't necessarily happen elsewhere. That while the Pacific kids who excel at rugby at Mount Albert are forced into the classroom, maybe they aren't in other institutions. Maybe other teachers take the easy route and hide behind the statistical academic under-performance of Pacific students. If the boys don't progress or achieve much academically, that will merely conform with the expectation. And if Pacific Island boys leave school with no qualifications and then fail to win professional contracts, by then they will no longer be the school's problem.

We can't know for sure what happens at schools across the country – all we know is that significant numbers of Pasifika boys are selected each week for First XVs around the country. In the 1A competition in Auckland the Pacific representation would be in excess of 75 per cent. Yet in any given year, perhaps only – at an absolute maximum – two per cent of those kids will be picked up by the Auckland Rugby Union academy programme.

Those who don't make it… where do they end up? We know, because the statistics tell us, that they are not showing up at universities in any great numbers. We know that very few are going on to enjoy careers as lawyers, doctors, accountants or in other skilled professions. Where these failed rugby protégés do show up in the greatest numbers is in unskilled, low-paid work.

Those are the two sides of the coin for many Pacific schoolboys, and the real heartbreak is that they're left unprepared for either eventuality. On one side lie broken dreams, and on the other a professional rugby career from which many are ill-equipped to leverage the maximum benefits. The chances are higher, because of their socio-economic background and possibly the neglect they've suffered at school, that Pacific players will reach the professional ranks with fewer life skills.

The chances are also higher that they will be isolated, less certain of their self-worth and possibly lacking in self-esteem. There are cultural issues that increase the likelihood of élite Pacific athletes feeling less confident in their ability to make strong decisions. Many Pacific households are dominated by the father (or, in some cases, the mother). It is normal for this dominant parent to make crucial decisions for their sons right up to adulthood and even beyond. In 2008, when Anthony Tuitavake was weighing up whether to stay in New Zealand or take an overseas offer, he left the decision up to his father. He was an All Black, 26 years old, and this was a decision that would have a massive impact on his life. But he was happy to defer to his father, believing he would know best.

None of this should be misconstrued as a suggestion that Pacific athletes can't make good leaders or be strong decision makers. It is merely pointing out that for many it's the norm to have little say in their destiny. That can make it harder for some Pacific players when they reach the All Blacks. They have limited experience in decision-making and have grown up in a culture where they expect to be told what to do.

On the other hand, the All Blacks are trying to foster a culture of players leading themselves, of taking responsibility for their own lives.

The dichotomy here is that, as the game is increasingly becoming the domain of the power athlete, the number of professional players from a Pacific background is only going to rise. The more emphasis placed on explosive power, the more in demand these players will become. The more often they will be selected from an early age, and the more they are going to view rugby as a potential career and hence the more likely it becomes they will be allowed to flag their education.

What the rugby system really can't fix, not even stick a Band Aid on, is the missing education. It's not so easy to instil good values when so many bad ones have been allowed to fester for so long. It's not easy to nurture decision-makers when deferring to others is the instinctive reaction.

Most of the time, the influence of Pacific players in New Zealand does make the critical difference. Most of the time, the All Blacks are not under intense pressure on the field. They have too much talent, too much raw power and too much flair. But at World Cups, the critical difference is very often not a matter of pace and power. As David Kirk believes, the difference is mental; it's the ability to cope with the pressure and make the best use of the pace and power available.

And herein lies the problem for the All Blacks – too many Pacific players have been used for their brawn, and been given next to no help in cultivating their brain. They are taught from their early teens to bash their way to glory – that physical strength will conquer all. New Zealand's continued premature exits from World Cups suggest some kind of major rethink is needed.

14
Under the radar

IT WAS ENOUGH to make Sean Fitzpatrick splutter into his Cloudy Bay. Leave his prawn sandwich sitting half-chewed in a mouth agape. The former All Black captain was in the Twickenham car park, picnicking with his old mate Zinzan Brooke.

The pair had only given the game away the previous year. Age and injury had finally caught up with these old war horses, both of them among the toughest and most savvy customers New Zealand had ever produced. Fitzpatrick and Brooke were not academically gifted but they were street smart. They could dance on their feet, duck a bit, dive a bit and get the job done. They knew how to operate in the jungle of test football. Like most of their All Black colleagues of the late amateur era, they were respected around the world for that ability.

The pair were at Twickenham on 31 October 1999 to watch their former All Black colleagues put right the events of 1995. Of course, the mood of the afternoon had turned decidedly sour as a result of France's second-half revival. There should have been some excited chatter about the looming final, a bit of reminiscing about the old days and a brief catch-up with some of the current squad to slap them on the back and wish them all the best.

Instead, there was disbelief around the tailgate, confused looks and shaking of heads. That turned to astonishment when Josh Kronfeld, openside flanker in the defeated All Black side that day, joined the party. 'He came out to talk to me and Zinzan,' recalls Fitzpatrick, 'and he said, "They were grabbing my testicles and they were still doing it at the end of the game." And I said "What?" '

Fitzpatrick's response wasn't a true expression of his dismay. He was quite horrified that the All Blacks had stood back and allowed the French to indulge in such vile tactics. It would never have happened in his day. 'We would never stand on anyone's head or kick anyone, but we talked about it and when we played the French we would say we weren't putting up with any crap. [We'd say] If they do anything to us... and we'd end up getting them before they got us. That [allowing the 1999 French team to act without retribution] should not have happened. If the French get away with it, they'll do it all day.'

It was a point of principle among the amateur All Blacks that they wouldn't be intimidated by anyone, especially the French, who had always enjoyed a little bit of rugby with their violence. The All Blacks ran a zero-tolerance policy when it came to opposition skulduggery. Those were different times. The referee wasn't expected to be the sole arbiter of justice. He was there to officiate, but a good referee would always be aware there were times when the players needed to be cut a little slack to sort things out for themselves.

Test football is a brutal environment, and physical in the extreme. Players will push the limits and sometimes go beyond them. A hand in the ruck; a sly little jab when the referee can't see; a push, a theatrical dive out of a lineout; a fake injury to slow the game down: these are all ways and means of bending and breaking the rules to frustrate opponents. These are all ways and means of exerting influence on the outcome without the referee having to be involved. Some international teams will take the rule bending a stage further and try eye-gouging, standing on players or, as was the case in the 1999 semi-final, 'bag-grabbing' (as squeezing a player's testicles is known in the trade).

The amateur All Blacks encountered all of this chicanery, and indulged in much of it themselves. They mostly commanded this grey area, this twilight zone where the officials didn't quite dare go. In the amateur days it was vital that a side stood up for itself, and that is precisely what the All Blacks did. They did what they deemed necessary to get the result. They knew a few eggs were going to be broken to get their omelette made. That was very much part of the All Black aura – the knowledge they were tough, resourceful men who were happy to do flick knives and dark alleys if that was where their opponents took them.

The All Blacks were renowned all over the world for their street-wise culture. In fact that may be too kind; they were, in many places, seen as bullies, as remorseless thugs whose Corinthian ethos was buried under a gigantic will to win. Any number of unsavoury acts have been committed by men in black jerseys in the name of getting the job done, of preserving the legend of a team whose passion for the contest runs deeper than that of all others.

Some acts of foul play are a necessary evil.

Colin Meads will never be forgiven by Australians for almost pulling the great Wallaby halfback Ken Catchpole's hamstring clean off the bone. John Ashworth remains a villain in Bridgend for stamping on the face of the brilliant Welsh fullback JPR Williams in 1978, inflicting a horrific injury that required 30 stitches. Jamie Joseph in 1993 stamped on the exposed leg of Kieran Bracken. The English halfback was making his debut and Joseph saw his chance to intimidate. The list could go on and on, but the only point that needs to be grasped is that the All Blacks never backed down; they took the view that everything was fair in love and war.

Fitzpatrick says he can remember an incident from the 1986 test in Nantes that perhaps best typifies the All Black mentality of old. The first scrum went down and there was a crunching noise to his left and, when the two teams came up, there was a slightly irate and indeed volatile Steve McDowell cursing under his breath. The All Black loose-head prop took a few deep breaths and then spoke to his opposite man. 'I remember Steve said to French prop Laurent Seigne, "If you do that again, you're going to be carried off in a stretcher,"' recalls Fitzpatrick. 'He [Seigne] did it again, and he got carried off in a stretcher. The referee said, "What did you do that for?" and Steve said, "I warned him."'

That was it – absolutely no mucking about. No looking at the referee quizzically in the hope he would intervene. McDowell was illegally hit first, so he responded the same way, making sure his retaliation was emphatic. It was the same philosophy as the Chicago police had in their quest to catch Al Capone – if one of their men was put in hospital, they put one of the gangsters into the morgue.

Those of a sensitive disposition might argue that the All Blacks were nothing more than common thugs, and acts of violence on a rugby field can never be justified. But it's best to bin that way of thinking and realise that some acts of foul play are a necessary evil. As former All Black captain Tana Umaga once remarked to a pedantic referee, 'It's not tiddly-winks we're playing.' Some dirty work has to be done in a test. It's imperative there are players in the team who are prepared to go beyond the parameters of fair play and, at times, take the law into their own hands.

The All Blacks were masters at this throughout the amateur era, largely because they didn't isolate the act and evaluate the morality of punching or pushing or whatever it was. Instead, they simply placed everything under the umbrella of resourcefulness. Deciding to kick more to the opposition's left wing after he drops the ball several times, or walloping an aggressive prop off the ball – both acts are about improving the chances of winning the game. Both are tactical decisions – ethics just don't come into it.

Richard Loe, a squad member of the 1987 All Blacks, was certainly one of those men who would step over the line at times. He was recognised as a so-called enforcer, what the corporate world would call a trouble-shooter. Loe did what he felt he had to do to impose himself and to help his team-mates. No one asked him to take on the role of enforcer; it was one of those assumed responsibilities, part of the team culture.

'It's about winning,' says Loe. 'After the 1992 test in Wellington against the World XV, Brendan Venter [South African player in the World XV] came up to [All Black coach] Laurie Mains at the after-match. He said, "That Richard Loe is the dirtiest player. At one point he grabbed me and tried to head-butt me and it wasn't once, it was twice." So Laurie says leave it to me, and marches over. He's looking at me with his back to Venter and he says, "Is it true you tried to head-butt Venter – don't reply, but if it is, meet me in the bar and I'll buy you a drink because I'm shouting."

'I can also remember being in the South of France with the All Blacks one year for a Wednesday game and I was captain. Laurie pulled me aside and said, "I don't care what happens today, just make sure we win. You do what you have to." And then Pinetree [team manager Colin Meads] came along, looked over his shoulder and said, "These are dirty bastards, get stuck in." At some point during the game the referee pulled out a yellow card. I said, "What's that?" And he asked if I'd ever seen one before and I said no. He showed me them both – yellow and red – and told me what they were for, and I said I still didn't know. Of course I knew what

they were for, but you had to do what you had to do, bullshit them…
anything.

'I used to like to think that all the rumour, innuendo and speculation about R. Loe was fine, because at some level the opposition would be worrying about it. There was a very old acknowledged subculture where we said nothing would distract. We play in the same fucking boots, socks, shorts, jersey, none of that shit wrapped around our arms and heads. We did things as a team not as individuals.'

The amateur All Blacks and in particular the 1987 World Cup winners had no sense of inhibition. They had clarity when it came to boundaries – there weren't any really. To hold back against an opponent would have been disastrous. It would have been damaging in the immediate contest, and even more so in terms of diluting the aura and reputation of the All Blacks. The 1987 team weren't thugs. They weren't dirty players. They were tough, aggressive and intimidating, and most important, they were committed to a degree few others could emulate.

That's why Fitzpatrick was aghast to hear Kronfeld complain about French indiscretions. Kronfeld spoke as if he'd been powerless. He was playing the role of victim and that was totally alien to Fitzpatrick. How could that be? How could an All Black side have let the French get away with all that nonsense?

Former All Black captain Andy Dalton was just as bemused by what he saw in London that day. 'We lost the game in 1999 because we let the French bully us. I couldn't believe that when Josh Kronfeld got gouged in the eye they didn't have a mass brawl and sort them out there and then. I couldn't believe that we backed off. Sitting in the stand, that was black and white for me. We needed to fix that. It's a different game now. There are cameras everywhere, but if it came to the crunch I'd probably call the same shot if they were getting away with it. You would sort that out yourself.'

THE PROFESSIONAL All Blacks have operated in an entirely different world to their amateur predecessors. The days of vigilantes like Loe, Meads and McDowell doing their business under the radar are long gone. Like all the other amateur traditions, the subculture of enforcement has been tossed out in the professional game. The modern game has cameras poking into every dark place. The ability of technology to hone in on foul play is quite staggering.

In the All Blacks' first test against the Lions in 2005, a TV camera managed to find evidence of lock Danny Grewcock biting the finger of hooker Keven Mealamu. The incident took place at the bottom of a ruck and Mealamu didn't have a great memory of what point in the game the incident took place. But all the footage was trawled through and, lo and behold, Grewcock's indiscretion had been caught on camera.

It's not just the technology, though, that's putting paid to foul play. Attitudes have changed. The game's administrators are on a mission to clean up the sport. Professionalism means bums have to go on seats and there has been, as David Moffett revealed, a concerted drive to attract women. The old school ways had to go, reckoned the suits. The idea of free-flowing claret and shining black eyes just wouldn't appeal to women.

So now touch judges are empowered to flag foul play and bring it to the attention of the referee. Now referees are critically assessed, and they don't score too well if they stand back and let the players sort things out for themselves. And if the officials on the field should miss anything, there's a citing commissioner watching footage pour out of every camera in search of indiscretions. Should he miss something, both teams have 48 hours after the game to lay a complaint before the commissioner.

It's not just big fish the administrators are after. The yellow and red cards that Loe feigned ignorance of are now an established part of the game. Referees are instructed to use them, particularly the yellow, which results in a player having to leave the field for 10 minutes.

Temporary deprivation of one man can be hugely damaging, as every coach knows. The 2007 All Blacks conceded a try in the quarter-final when Luke McAlister was sin-binned after being adjudged to have obstructed a French player. Brian Lochore and many of the players believe that was the critical turning point in the All Blacks' fortunes. The impact of yellow and red cards extends beyond the immediate 80 minutes as well. Serial offenders who accumulate cards can be suspended, and a red card at a World Cup carries an automatic stand-down of two games. In domestic football there can be a monetary sting, with heavy fines handed out to players suspended for foul play.

Understandably, there's paranoia within coaching circles about play-ers committing indiscretions. Everyone involved in the development of professional players has this puritanical approach to rugby. Discipline is a key feature of the modern game. No one is forgiven – not publicly, at least – for operating outside the law. The culture of enforcement is no longer seen as a necessary evil. It's now just an evil. Everything has to be by the book, which places enormous pressure on referees. They are now the sole arbiter. The professional way is to look quizzically at the referee and plead with him to intervene.

This shouldn't come as a surprise. It is, after all, in keeping with the general demise of resourcefulness and ingenuity in the professional era. It's just one more way in which the players have been relieved of responsibility. It's just one more way in which the professional development system has robbed the All Blacks of an intangible advantage.

And it shouldn't be underestimated how big a role the whole no-nonsense, get-your-retaliation-in-first culture played in enhancing the All Black legacy. Loe can remember playing for the All Blacks against a Welsh club on one tour. 'I always remember Buck Shelford in that game and some guy must have leaned on Buck or something, and Buck whacked him and knocked his teeth clean out of his head. At the after-match Buck stood up and did his thank you speech, and then their captain, with half his teeth missing, did the same and he was just rapt that Buck Shelford had knocked his teeth out. If it had been one of his club mates he would have been bitching and moaning, but it was Buck Shelford, All Black captain.'

That was it. The world knew that not only were the All Blacks an astonishingly gifted rugby side, but that they were hard nuts too – borderline lunatics in some cases. If you tried something on against an All Black, you knew you'd get some back.

Quite what impact that has on the minds of opponents is hard to assess accurately. But as Loe says, he was quite happy for his reputation to be blown out of proportion. Half the battle, maybe more, in rugby is mental and if opponents are spending time worrying about what someone like Loe might get up to, that's very much to the All Blacks' advantage. It has often been said that many international teams used to start 10 points down against the All Blacks as a consequence of the awe in which they held New Zealand.

Much of that mystique has been lost in the professional era. We could put some of it down to familiarity. The All Blacks are no longer an exotic beast. They've been overexposed as a result of their bloated test schedule, and the foibles of many of their players are well known to northern hemisphere opponents. That has done away with some of the fear of playing the All Blacks.

But the sanitisation of the game has been a bigger factor. The All Blacks were expert at intimidating opponents. Their resourcefulness and depth of commitment was allowed free rein in the amateur days. The scrummaging contest takes on a different hue when the opposition prop has to be wary of being carried off on a stretcher. Opposition flankers had to think carefully about whether they were prepared to kill the All Blacks' ball when they knew there would be some severe rucking handed out as a deterrent. The doubt has been removed from opponents' minds, and while it's good for the long-term health of the game that some of the excessive violence has been removed, we have to conclude that the death of the enforcement culture within the All Blacks has hurt them more than it has any other nation at World Cups.

At the 1987 World Cup a minor scuffle broke out in the All Blacks' semi-final against Wales. There were punches being thrown by the Welsh at lock Gary Whetton. It was threatening to boil over when Shelford reached the fracas and clobbered Huw Richards. The big Welsh lock was knocked out cold and that was the end of the fighting. The Welsh backed off. They'd seen how far the All Blacks were prepared to go and they didn't fancy it. Shelford had reacted instinctively – he was doing what he thought was right to protect his team-mate and to show the Welsh that if they wanted to go down that particular road, then the All Blacks were coming with them.

The most remarkable thing about the whole incident was that once Richards was revived, he was promptly sent off for starting the brawl in the first place. It was a lucky break for Shelford that he escaped punishment. But had he been red-carded and forced to miss the final, he would have taken his medicine. His sacrifice would have been worth it. The team had to come first; punching Richards killed much of the niggling that was marring the contest and put the emphasis back on rugby. And once the focus was on rugby, the All Blacks cruised to an easy victory. Which brings it all round to Shelford's punch having a greater purpose.

It is essentially the loss of that culture of self-sacrifice which has tripped the All Blacks up at World Cups. In 1999 Robin Brooke, brother of Zinzan and a lock skilled in the dark arts, left Twickenham mad at himself that he hadn't been the sacrificial lamb. When the French were getting on top and up to no good, he would have quite happily waded in with some of his own forms of retribution and taken the consequences. If he'd been sent off, he would have been fine with it as long as whatever he'd done had dissuaded the French from eye-gouging and bag grabbing. He could have lived with not being part of the team that played the final. It was more important to Brooke for the All Blacks to be in the final than for him to be there with them.

> 'I can't believe that they didn't throw a couple of punches,' says Loe. 'Not hard ones. But got themselves into a good position, hit the big French lock and let them retaliate. Kick the three points and win the game. Someone would have been cited, but so what? It's about winning.'

He didn't do it though, because coach John Hart had drummed into the team the need to keep their discipline, not to be sucked into fighting with the French. It was a flawed call. The French were getting away with anything and everything. Someone on the field had to realise it was best to do something to stop it rather than be defeated and then squeal about it after the game.

It wasn't so different in 2007. The French weren't indulging in underhand tactics. It was, however, clear that referee Wayne Barnes had frozen, that he was totally out of his depth and not in control of the game. The onus was on the All Blacks to decide their own fate, to be responsible for securing the right outcome. Going under the radar should have been an option. 'I can't believe that they didn't throw a couple of punches,' says Loe. 'Not hard ones. But got themselves into a good position, hit the big French lock and let them retaliate. Kick the three points and win the game. Someone would have been cited, but so what? It's about winning. The ability and desire of the modern player to do what's right for the team is nowhere near as strong.'

15
One nation

IT'S AT THIS point that the focus needs to shift to the future. The analysis so far has been focused on the past, trying to make sense of the long-term systemic failings of the rugby development programme in New Zealand. The arrival of professionalism, which turned up on the doorstep unannounced, has done much to advance the athletic ability of the All Blacks but at the cost of their holistic development.

The on-field advances have acted as a kind of heavy-duty paint, covering the flaws that are only exposed at the World Cup. Pressure does that – it works its way into cracks and then blasts open big holes. The New Zealand rugby fraternity has been guilty of ignoring those cracks, or of doing the typical Kiwi thing and assuming that she'll be right. The All Blacks, and by extension, the rest of the country, have paid the price for that approach. Talent alone has not been enough at World Cups. That's a lesson New Zealanders have been painfully slow to learn.

This book isn't an exercise in blame. It's an attempt to find answers, to determine the problems and detail how they've developed and then impacted on the All Blacks at World Cups. That said, there has to be some acknowledgement that the men running professional rugby in New Zealand have been a little arrogant in, until recently, dismissing the importance of building self-reliant, resourceful, innovative individuals.

That arrogance is difficult to understand given the way the All Blacks bombed in both 1999 and 2003. Everyone knew the problems and no one did anything about it until Graham Henry arrived at the end of 2003 and made it a priority to improve the character of the players as much as their passing and kicking. It's unfortunate that this neglect of holistic development has coincided with a wider societal change that has seen educational standards compromised with the benchmarks lowered at the expense of a culture of aspiration.

New Zealand, in the professional age, has become a nanny state, a country paralysed by its fear of causing offence. Political correctness has gone crazy, and New Zealand isn't the country it once was. It's not the egalitarian, look-out-for-your-neighbour place of old. The school of hard knocks is no longer in existence and the All Blacks are now welcoming younger, fitter, faster and stronger men, but men who in some cases may be lacking in self-esteem, self-confidence and the most basic life skills.

The question to be asked now is how well prepared are the All Blacks to remedy their previous failings and win the 2011 World Cup? The tournament will be in their back yard. The public expectation will be huge. The pressure will be unbearable. How much have they learned from 2007, 2003 and 1999? How much headway has been made down the road Brian Lochore started them on in 2004? Do they have the strength of character? Is the leadership model correct? Has the New Zealand Rugby Union got a handle on its World Cup obsession?

There have also been more specific failings related directly to the World Cup. The last three campaigns have seen the All Blacks adopt military-style planning. They haven't yet found the right formula, but will they in 2011? Can they strike the right balance between their playing and their commercial commitments? Can they connect with the nation the way the men of 1987 did? And can the nation provide the appropriate level of support the All Blacks will need?

A WORLD CUP in New Zealand – now there's a thing. Where to start? Home advantage is significant when it comes to World Cups. History shows us that the host nation has predominantly responded well to being based at home. In 1991, the tournament was hosted by the Five Nations, but with the final in London it was fitting that England made it.

In 1995 South Africa hosted and South Africa won. In 1999 Wales hosted and made the quarter-finals, a fair result for a team of only modest ability, while France, who had played their group games and quarter-final in France, made the final. In 2003 Australia hosted, made the final and were just seconds away from winning, while in 2007 France did all the hard work of defeating the All Blacks in the Cardiff quarter-final only to lose to England a week later.

And then of course, there is 1987. The tournament was co-hosted by New Zealand and Australia and the All Blacks won.

So there's a double significance here. There's an advantage to be had playing at home and also the only World Cup the All Blacks have won was in New Zealand. The difficulty for the All Blacks is going to lie in exploiting that home advantage. The All Blacks will come into the tournament under the most colossal pressure. The compounded expectation of failure will be almost unbearable – it will be 24 years since they last won a World Cup.

That alone will make life tough, and the difficulty will be making sure the team isn't buried under the weight of history – that it views the tournament as the ultimate opportunity to give the nation what it wants, and don't dread the occasion. They have to take the positives from playing on grounds they know well and from playing in front of people they know well. And if they are to do that, they have to connect with the tournament and connect with New Zealanders.

They have to harness the World Cup vibe, live in the moment, draw all the positive energy they can and convert it into performance. That might sound a bit new-age and not strictly relevant. But it would be a huge mistake to think so. Tournaments carry their own rhythm, and teams can be swept along on emotion. There is too much evidence of this for it to be dismissed.

Look at Western Samoa in 1991 – they were the team that stole everyone's hearts and, to a man, they all say they felt a connection with the tournament. Everything felt right – the way they trained, the places they stayed, the venues they played. The players felt good about being at the World Cup and their performances backed that up. The more they played, the more the crowds and rugby media warmed to them and they became the darlings of the tournament. They loved being there, everyone loved having them there, and they made the quarter-finals.

The Australians too, enjoyed a positive campaign in 1991 and their ability to win the hearts and minds of their hosts was a critical factor in their success. New Zealanders should know this only too well. The Wallabies played their quarter-final in Dublin and went behind to a spectacular

Irish try with just a few minutes remaining. The Irish thought they had secured the most famous victory, but in the final minute Australia's Michael Lynagh dived over the line to break five million hearts.

It was a little ungracious of the Australians to beat their hosts in such a dramatic manner and they made amends by spending the following week out and about in the city of Dublin, singing the praises of Ireland and all things Irish. It was a masterstroke, as it meant the locals lent their support to the Australians in the semi-final against the All Blacks at Lansdowne Road.

Giving their allegiance to Australia was made easier for the Irish by the All Blacks stomping into town with 'all the gaiety of grave diggers', as one Irish newspaper observed. While the Wallabies were open, friendly and engaging, the All Blacks were surly, aloof and closed off.

Australia fed off the crowd on the day; it was effectively a home game for them, such was their level of support. The All Blacks felt like a team under siege, as if the world was against them, and they played like a team feeling the pressure, like a team that wasn't too happy to be there.

In 1999 the All Blacks again failed to connect with the tournament. They played their pool games in England and then their quarter-final in Edinburgh. Maybe it was the constant moving about, maybe they just didn't like being based in England, but for whatever reason, the All Blacks didn't convince in their first four games. Nor did they really ever endear themselves to the British people or media. They didn't go out of their way to snub their hosts or do anything memorably offensive; they were just a hard team for the neutral to fall for.

They had great players but, except for Jonah Lomu, they never gave off any warmth or revealed much about who they were. Again, it felt as if other teams, particularly the Australians and South Africans, were winning friends and admirers as the tournament went on, but not the All Blacks. It felt as if the Australians and South Africans were happier camps, more relaxed in their surroundings, more certain of who they were and what they were about.

In the week leading up to the semi-final in London, the All Blacks secretly shifted to the South of France for a few days of rest and relaxation. The New Zealand media weren't invited or forewarned of the plan, and it created an uneasy atmosphere between the team and the fourth estate. It also took the All Blacks out of the epicentre of the tournament to somewhere there was no buzz, no sense of occasion, no Rugby World Cup presence at all. That was the idea – the players were being given an opportunity to unwind and de-stress ahead of a crucial game. It was not without merit but, with the benefit of hindsight and the resulting performance at Twickenham, it can be concluded that the move backfired.

It was felt in hindsight that the players should have been in the thick of things that week. They didn't need to be flogged at training or mentally worn down by constant reminders of the importance of the coming game. There could have been a happy balance struck whereby they were exposed to the intensity of the media coverage, and made aware of the presence of thousands of New Zealanders who were in the city for the All Blacks.

It was utterly strange then that in 2003, coach John Mitchell decided to keep the All Blacks based in Melbourne for the duration of the tournament. The All Blacks played two pool games there and also their quarter-final against South Africa. They had made short visits to Brisbane and Sydney for pool games against Tonga and Wales respectively. Five weeks was a long time for the players to be based in one city, and it was a city that had no great rugby heritage.

Sydney and Brisbane are the rugby heartlands of Australia, and these were the two cities where World Cup fever was gripping the hardest. The logic of keeping the players in Melbourne for so long was that they didn't need to worry about travelling and all the hassle that comes with moving hotels, packing kit, finding bags and checking in at airports. With two pool games there and a quarter-final, staying in the city for the early stages was justifiable.

Where the strategy didn't make sense was in the final two weeks of the tournament. Both semi-finals and the final were played in Sydney. The vibe in Sydney was, therefore, intense. You couldn't possibly have been there and remained unaware that the World Cup was on. Melbourne, on the other hand, lost interest in the tournament once its own involvement ended. The inhabitants of Melbourne feel no special affinity with rugby and the All Blacks spent the first part of the semi-final week in anonymity. They were the only team not in Sydney. They were distanced from the tournament and from their own fans.

And what's more, after five weeks in one place the players were bored. They were restless. They felt out of touch with what was happening elsewhere, as if they'd been living under a rock while the rest of the world was having a great time. Mitchell kept them in Melbourne because he felt the lack of distraction, and the anonymity, would help the All Blacks to focus. He was also trying to promote a 'them and us' mentality that he thought would be helped by being out of the limelight. Needless to say, the strategy didn't work. The players felt flat, removed and frustrated at being kept out of the way.

It's harder to fault the 2007 campaign. The 2003 campaign was reviewed in some depth to determine what went right and what went wrong. The All Blacks concluded more effort had to be made to move the players around France and also to engage more openly with their hosts, media and sponsors. The 2003 team had a fractious relationship with the media, encouraged by Mitchell who wanted outside influence to be kept at arms' length. The 2007 squad was harmonious and settled, and warmly welcomed by the French, who loved hosting the All Blacks. There was genuine warmth and affection for them, and various polls as well as anecdotal evidence said that the majority of French people would support the All Blacks once their own team was eliminated.

But circumstances beyond the All Blacks' control had a bearing on their inability to find their rhythm and tap into the energy of the tournament. To gain the hosting rights, the French had promised both Wales and Scotland the right to host two games each. And, with the All Blacks being the biggest draw card, it just so happened that New Zealand had to visit both Edinburgh and Cardiff. It would be drawing a long bow indeed to build this into something significant, but it certainly didn't help the All Blacks that they had to travel to Edinburgh for a pool game.

As beautiful as the Scottish capital is, it was totally removed from the tournament, and to hear stadium announcements at Murrayfield in French first and to have the signs all around the ground in French felt just plain weird. There was no atmosphere in Edinburgh; the city was barely aware the World Cup was on. It took the All Blacks out of the main body of the tournament, and then seeing them play in Wales when France was hosting the tournament had a surreal and anticlimactic feel to it.

That disjointed travel schedule was a momentum stopper, just as much as the weak opponents faced by the All Blacks. They didn't face a serious challenge on their way to topping Group D, and as well as playing one game at the morgue-like Murrayfield against a seriously weakened Scotland team who were saving their best players for their following clash against Italy, they played rugby minnows Romania and Portugal. Both those games were played in carnival-like atmospheres that failed to give the All Blacks any sense of intensity. There they were, cruising their way to the quarter-finals in front of brass bands who provided more compelling entertainment than the procession of All Black tries.

Meanwhile, the French were slugging it out in the group of death that contained Argentina and Ireland. England and South Africa were being battered and bruised by Tonga and Samoa, with the former providing the best story of the tournament, and Australia were pushed by Wales and hit hard by Fiji.

The All Blacks wanted to feel the energy of the tournament but they were dealt a bum hand in that regard. They were sent to the outposts and given no one to play, so they almost felt once again they weren't part of the same tournament as everyone else.

The two tournaments where the All Blacks have made an emotional connection are South Africa in 1995 and New Zealand in 1987. The 1995 World Cup was arguably the best of the lot – it was the first where all the games were played in just one country and it helped immensely that rugby was the national sport of that country.

The All Blacks loved the set-up in South Africa. Travel was kept to a minimum, local interest was huge, the whole country was abuzz with the World Cup, and the All Blacks were the team everyone was talking about. The All Blacks were the stars of the 1995 tournament and Jonah Lomu stopped the world dead in its tracks with his performances. That contentment, and the excitement felt at being the form team, the team everyone wanted to be like, was a major factor in sweeping the All Blacks to the final. They started well in their pool games and then just got better and better – until the final, that is.

In 1987 there wasn't so much hype to feed off. No one really knew what to make of the World Cup. What the 1987 All Blacks did exception-ally well, however, was never to lose sight of who they were representing. They had a clear sense of identity and a direct connection with the wider population.

IT WAS of course a different era. The All Blacks had jobs; they had colleagues to face up to on Monday mornings. They were part of the community, as well known in their localities for being farmers, policemen, electricians and builders as they were for being All Blacks. For the 1987 team, there was no place to hide. After the weekend they had to front up and hear it straight from the people who'd paid money to watch them. They had no distance from their supporters.

'We had to face reality on a Monday morning,' says 1987 flanker Alan Whetton. 'If we lost or if you played badly you got on the large, and maybe I embarrassed myself off the field at a nightclub until one of the boys said time for you to go home. Then you got on a plane the next morning and it was in the paper: "Whetton didn't perform well; he had a poor game."

'And because this reporter had to do his job, you had to accept it. I didn't need anyone to tell me, but he was right I'd played poorly. Reading it meant other people were seeing it, so Monday morning at 7 am on my truck, some would say bad luck. You had to face your public. It was quite humbling. These people hold you in high regard and you were just one of them on Monday morning. You were just one of them. You weren't an All Black. You were still going to the office. There were no excuses.

'People would ask you where you went wrong, so it was quite therapeutic as you were given a chance to talk about it and think, yeah, I have stuffed up, and the light goes on – they say you were a bit slow and you think, yes I was.'

That was normal life around the world for international rugby players of the amateur era, except maybe the All Blacks had to face a more demanding public with rugby being the national game. That connection was bedrock for the 1987 campaign.

But there was more of a link than that. At the end of the pool round, the All Blacks had an extended break before they were due to play Scotland in Christchurch. Rather than keep the boys in the team hotel for that period, coach Brian Lochore decided to take the squad to his home area of Wairarapa Bush and billet the players in local homes. It was a stroke of genius. What better way of reminding the players what being a New Zealander was all about? It was about connecting the team with its supporters, about making the players aware of what they meant to the people they represented. It was also about making sure the players stayed grounded, that they didn't forget that none of them was bigger than the game.

The professional campaigns couldn't have been any further removed. Accusations have been levelled that the All Blacks have been pampered, have maybe overdone the luxury when it comes to the World Cup. It's difficult to agree with those claims. It's now standard practice for the world's leading teams to travel business class and to stay in four- and five-star hotels. If the All Blacks were to fly economy and stay in Travelodges at World Cups, and be dumped out by a country that looked after its players better, New Zealanders wouldn't stand for that.

Do the All Blacks really understand that, for many people, forking out $200 for test tickets is a major expense?

It has to be accepted that to get the best out of the modern athlete you have to give them the best of everything – the best food, the best facilities, the best training, the best hotels. All the peripheral stress has to be removed. Ask the likes of Fiji, Samoa and Tonga who, at each World Cup, can only afford the most basic accommodation and to train at the worst grounds. They crave for that hassle to be removed, for their jobs to be made that much easier – for a little bit of comfort and some help with the laundry. These things might seem minor, but they're a big deal in professional sport – the inches add up.

The most meaningful charge, and one that's harder to defend, is that the All Blacks have lost their emotional bond with their fans. They front up and sign autographs, smile for photos, and meet and greet. But it's in a sterile, behind-the-ropes way, and after an hour or so they can jump on their air-conditioned bus, return to their hotel and forget all about it. The professional All Blacks are entirely removed from the wider populace in a way the 1987 men never were.

Income is a factor. The majority of the players in the 2007 World Cup squad would have been earning well in excess of $250,000 a year with some players earning much, much more. Money is a barrier – it allows those who have it to live a different life. Can a 25-year-old All Black earning $500,000 a year relate to a 35-year-old electrician, a father of three, earning $50,000 a year? Do the All Blacks really understand that, for many people, forking out $200 for test tickets is a major expense? Do they understand the commitment behind such an outlay?

The modern All Black never really gets to know his public. Unlike his amateur predecessor, he tends not to contribute to his community. Except at events that are of interest only to the social pages, All Blacks are rarely sighted in public. They tend to keep out of the way. Their profile is much higher now and they've evolved from players into celebrities, less by choice than because of media hunger to build them up – perhaps so that knocking them down will be that much more spectacular.

The challenge for the 2011 All Blacks is to connect with the nation as well as the 1987 team did. The current team don't have that foundation stone of alternative employment to keep them in touch. They face a much harder task in bonding, but is it too ridiculous to suggest they could follow in the footsteps of the 1987 team and be billeted out somewhere? The All Blacks built in rest and recovery time to both their 1999 and 2007 campaigns.

They could do the same in 2011, except rather than the luxury of the French Riviera they could make do with a less than luxurious farmhouse in Greymouth. We laugh because it sounds far-fetched. But we probably would have laughed too in 1995 if someone had suggested that building better people was going to be just as important as building better players.

The All Blacks ignore these opportunities at their peril. These intangibles have been dismissed before. We were also amused – could scarcely believe it – when on the Sunday after the World Cup final some All Blacks, Richard Loe among them, turned out for their clubs. And on the Monday morning everyone was back to work.

Somehow the right balance has to be struck in 2011. The players need to be plugged into the tournament, suck its energy and use it well. They need to have an emotional connection with their own people to milk their home advantage. But they still need to take care of the sports science, to look after the players and offer them premier facilities. They still need their space to prepare and to recover. They also need the people of New Zealand to do their bit in oiling the wheels of the bonding process.

THE OLD saying is that it takes two to tango. This is entirely true of World Cups and the man organising the 2011 event is concerned about the ability of the New Zealand public to embrace the whole tournament. Chief executive of Rugby New Zealand 2011 Martin Snedden wants to create a festival atmosphere. He wants to fulfil the promise made to the

IRB that New Zealand really is a stadium of four million people.

In pursuit of that goal, various initiatives similar to those used in Australia in 2003 will be encouraged. To build crowds and atmosphere in the venues that are hosting minnows, spectators will be asked to adopt a team, possibly based on whether their house is an odd or even number. Every town and city hosting teams will be encouraged to show the best of New Zealand hospitality – to showcase what remains a great country. But most important of all, what Snedden wants to see is the nation grasping that the tournament is about more than the All Blacks.

The typical New Zealand rugby follower is unrealistically demanding, which makes watching the All Blacks an almost joyless experience.

New Zealanders, whatever they might like to think, are not great supporters. Most Kiwis believe they are. They buy replica shirts. They dress themselves in black, paint their faces and travel the world to watch the All Blacks. That's got to make them good supporters, right?

Wrong. The typical New Zealand rugby follower is unrealistically demanding, which makes watching the All Blacks an almost joyless experience. The relationship between the paying supporter and the All Blacks sits on a permanent knife-edge. It takes just one defeat for everything that went before to be forgotten. There's almost no appreciation within the All Black fan base that their side is beatable on any given day. Some deep-rooted superiority complex kicks in whenever the All Blacks play that leads their supporters to believe victory is inevitable.

If it doesn't happen, there is never an acknowledgement that perhaps the other team was better. No, no, no, it doesn't work like that. As soon as the All Blacks lose, there has to be a post-mortem, a comprehensive analysis of where it all went wrong. The notion that the opposition was a better team gets short shrift. The All Blacks must have underperformed somewhere. They must have failed in either their selection, or their preparation wasn't good enough, or the game-plan wasn't right, or the execution was poor.

On one level the New Zealand rugby public have kept the All Blacks honest for the better part of the last 100 years. When Tana Umaga took over the captaincy in 2004 he said he would never want to see public expectation lowered. It was the constant pressure applied by the nation that made being an All Black the thrill it was, according to Umaga.

There is a fear that if New Zealanders suddenly accept mediocrity, or relish the role of brave loser, then All Black rugby is doomed.

No one is asking New Zealanders to drop their standards. No one thinks they should be uproariously happy if the All Blacks play poorly and crumble to a heavy defeat. The issue is more about expression. It's about learning to live in the moment and take more time to enjoy the achievements of the All Blacks. And to do that, there has to be a realisation that international rugby, and specifically the 2011 World Cup, is an opportunity to be unashamedly proud of New Zealand. It's an opportunity for uninhibited displays of nationalistic fervour. Like Snedden says, the tournament is about far more than just the All Blacks.

On the All Blacks' end-of-year tour to the UK and Ireland in 2008, New Zealanders were shown the perfect example of how to express nationalistic pride. At Murrayfield, the Scots turned the stadium lights off before the game and sang *Flower of Scotland* in the dark. It was spine-tingling. In Dublin, the history of Croke Park was in the All Blacks' faces and spontaneous singing of the *Fields of Athenry* rang around the ground. In Wales, *Land of My Fathers* nearly took the roof off and the Welsh team lived off the emotion for the first 40 minutes.

For the Celts, and indeed for the English, French, South Africans and Australians, tests are an opportunity to showcase their country. To be fiercely proud of the great people, great achievements and little nuances that bring everyone with the same passport together. The Celts in particular emanate a sense of togetherness when they support their international teams. They love to win, but it's not the end of the world if they don't. The occasion counts for just as much. And after the game, they feel they have a duty to continue showcasing the aspects of their countries they love the most – their warmth, generosity and gregariousness as hosts.

New Zealanders, on the other hand, tend to see a test simply as 80 minutes of play. They leave it up to the All Blacks to highlight the qualities of the nation and tend to give little away. The result dictates the mood, and this is what Snedden fears most. He's afraid that if the All Blacks are bundled out early, the tournament will die as the hosts will invest nothing. New Zealanders haven't got a good track record in show-casing the wider country through rugby.

Maybe the crux of the problem lies in the fact that New Zealanders' passion for rugby is eclipsed by their obsession with the All Blacks. Somehow they need to find a way to change that before 2011. The All Blacks want an emotional wave they can surf, and it has to be powered by pride and passion, not expectation and obsession.

There could be as many as 40,000 foreign visitors in New Zealand during the World Cup. The potential economic stimulus is enormous. There is also a great opportunity to win repeat business. New Zealand is a country of wondrous beauty. New Zealand is a country that has pro-duced great achievers, great people. It remains a country with a heart, the sort of place where people stop to ask if they can help when they see someone in strife. It's a country that has plenty to be proud of. If that pride can be expressed, if New Zealand is properly showcased to the wider world, then there's every chance the All Blacks will be swept along. There is every chance the All Blacks will feel more connected with their support and retain a greater sense of just what the black jersey they are wearing means.

It's a big if. Old habits die hard and many New Zealanders strug-gle with the idea of opening up, of doing anything more than nodding staunchly. But All Black assistant coach Wayne Smith believes the tide is turning. On the All Blacks' Grand Slam tour in 2008, he felt there was a growing appreciation among New Zealanders that it was okay to be proud of where you came from. 'Kiwis arrive at Heathrow and all of a sudden the national anthem is important, the haka is important, they lose inhibition and we get fantastic support over here [in the northern hemisphere]. It's different support to what we have at home. It's less in-hibited than at home. I'm the same myself, and my sons. When we came over [to coach Northampton in 2002] you just grabbed hold of every-thing Kiwi. You take such pride in the haka, the black jersey, the black blood running through your veins – it just becomes more intense when you're away from home.

'I think there's a wee bit of staunchness in New Zealand. I can remem-ber at school singing the national anthem every morning. That was what you did and New Zealand-ness was really strong. I think we went away from that. I get the feeling talking to a few teachers that it's coming back and the passion for being a Kiwi is coming back.

'I never learned about Passchendaele at school. I leaned about all sorts of other history that was almost irrelevant. I never learned about the bravery of our people, and that's where your passion comes from, where your sense of belonging comes from. I'm sure there was a burgeoning adolescence of us becoming our own country into adulthood. I see signs of us returning to that. The ANZAC parade is massive now and every Kiwi that comes over to Europe goes to the graves. It's great that the young generation is embracing that. I don't think we're too far away from the people who've lost their inhibitions overseas coming home and keeping it that way when they get back. Auckland is a bit more cosmopolitan as a city and I always feel the atmosphere at Eden Park for an All Black test is really good, and hopefully that's replicated around the country.'

It's not just the players who will be under pressure to perform in 2011; the whole country has to do its bit to prevent 24 barren years becoming 28 barren years.

16

Brand awareness

IT QUICKLY BECAME apparent on the morning of 28 November 2008 that a plan had been hatched to turn New Zealand into one great big adidas shop ahead of the 2011 World Cup. The German manufacturer of the famous three-stripes leisurewear had just signed an extension on its sponsorship deal with the All Blacks. Adidas would be the main sponsor through to 2019. The commitment was major, the financial outlay, although not divulged, was significant. Adidas had made its mind up to become the big player in rugby. The only way to achieve that goal was to stick with the biggest brand of the lot – the All Blacks.

Seen through the sponsors' eyes, 2011 is a massive opportunity. The rugby world will descend upon New Zealand. Many of those who come will fall in love with a land so beautiful it could make you cry. New Zealand is the spiritual home of rugby. The potential to build an unforgettable tourism experience around the World Cup is enormous. The potential to sell All Black jerseys is also enormous and having made such a major commitment, adidas doesn't want to miss its window.

That should make New Zealanders a little nervous. Hubristic marketing by sponsors has been a problem at previous World Cups. But the concern with adidas is not so much focused on what it'll do around the next World Cup itself. At the 2007 World Cup the All Blacks participated in a number of adidas promotional events. At every new venue, a few players would be wheeled out to wave, sign things and talk to the assembled masses. There were other functions to attend as well but no one could really say the demands made of the players were onerous.

Given the money adidas has put into the All Blacks, it has a right to ask for something back; it would be unfair to accuse the company of placing a direct burden on the players. The players can't train all day, every day, and they needed things to distract them. Adidas offered events which did precisely that and, as most players would agree, they didn't go overboard in France. The balance in 2007, as it was at previous World Cups, was about right in terms of the demands sponsors made of players balanced against their preparation needs.

But keeping that balance is going to be increasingly difficult. Maybe it's unfair to even suggest this, but it certainly feels as if the influence of adidas is steadily growing. Both adidas and the New Zealand Rugby Union talk of their partnership in glowing terms. They are at pains to stress there's no tail wagging the dog. It might be fairer to suggest the tail is wagging pretty hard, and it's attached to a dog that's quite happy to be wagged.

The NZRU is happy to be led to any trough that contains money, and it'll drink its fill when it gets there. Adidas is a great door opener, a sponsor that can make things happen. That's why the relationship works – adidas wants its connection with the All Blacks to be globally exposed. It wants the three stripes to be sold in new markets, particularly non-traditional rugby markets. Growing the game is imperative for adidas – it's how it intends to recuperate its investment in the All Blacks.

The NZRU shares this vision. Growing the game works for it too, as does growing the popularity of the All Black brand. Growth leads ultimately to more revenue, which is what both parties are after.

In 2008 the All Blacks played a Bledisloe Cup test in Hong Kong. The fixture was supposedly about promoting rugby in Asia. It was going to inspire thousands of Asian kids to pick up rugby balls and fall in love with the game. What it was really about was making money. It was about exposing the various sponsors to new markets and creating an opportunity to sell more replica shirts.

Neither the NZRU nor the Australian Rugby Union revealed just how much money they made by playing in Hong Kong, but it would have been significant. Informed speculation put the figure at about $3 million each. Later on the same trip, the All Blacks played Munster in Limerick – a game adidas was instrumental in organising, as the German firm also happens to sponsor the Irish side. The NZRU took a match fee and also boosted the All Blacks' popularity in the South of Ireland. Commercially at least, the All Blacks' relationship with adidas is a match made in heaven.

But that in itself is the problem. The All Blacks being commercially successful is now almost the biggest priority for the NZRU. While all communication out of the Wellington headquarters acknowledges that for the money to keep flowing in the All Blacks will have to retain their winning record, there's a sneaking suspicion that many administrators assume this will happen regardless.

What becomes apparent when you look at why the All Blacks have failed to win World Cups is that, in the last 13 years since the game went professional, there have been no one-off, catastrophic administrative decisions undermining the All Blacks' performance.

Instead, the policies followed have gradually eroded the quality of individual being produced for the professional game. There has been a drift away from the amateur model that worked, not a dramatic charge. That's what should be concerning some about the encroachment of adidas and the NZRU's commercial obsession.

In 2008 the All Blacks played 15 tests plus the Munster game. That was a record in a calendar year. At the time of writing, 2009 is shaping up to be much the same, with the NZRU in talks to play another Bledisloe Cup game in neutral territory – probably Tokyo, or possibly Denver, with an extra test against Wales being mentioned and one against the Barbarians XV in London. The NZRU is also hopeful that more mid-week games against European club sides can be arranged to present opportunities for younger, fringe players to be taken away at the end of the year. The money will be rolling in, but the NZRU might not be laughing all the way to the bank.

The All Blacks won a World Cup as a rugby team, not as a brand. They won a World Cup when their culture was based on longstanding rugby traditions, when they were just good New Zealand blokes who played footy like everyone else. There were beer and singalongs, bus trips and late night japes, the same as at the local rugby club. As a team they behaved like rugby players, both on and off the field. As a team they were uninhibited when they felt they had to duck under the radar and sort things out for themselves. As a team they could bond more freely away from the field – a little bit of tomfoolery was very much par for the course.

Maybe it's being unduly harsh on both the NZRU and adidas, but they often appear to forget that the All Blacks are first and foremost a rugby team. There is this undeniable sense that both the NZRU and adidas view the All Blacks as a brand that just happens to be a rugby team. This has seen them undergo a sterilisation process that requires conformity and adherence to brand values at all times.

Is success defined by the number of tests won, or by the number of jerseys sold?

When players get conditioned to that environment, we can only wonder how deeply they suck in the need to protect the brand. A nasty French forward is mucking about in a crucial pool game and needs a belt in the chops. But what about the brand? It wouldn't look good to have pictures splashed around the world of an All Black, in his adidas gear, punching someone.

Then there are questions about evaluating success as a brand. Is success defined by the number of tests won, or by the number of jerseys sold? Is it winning tests, or is it presenting the right corporate image? Is it winning tests, or is it increasing recognition of the All Blacks in overseas markets? It is about all of these things, which dilutes the emphasis placed on winning. The players can lose a test and still receive a slap on the back, still be praised heartily by their employer. Conversely, if they succeed on the field but fail off it, have they done their job? What the NZRU deems to be the All Blacks' top priority has become blurred.

These days the NZRU is just as proud of the fact that the All Blacks rank alongside soccer giants AC Milan in terms of replica jersey sales and brand recognition. Graham Henry's reappointment in 2007 was driven as much by the headway he had made in restoring relationships with key All Black stakeholders as it was by his outstanding record prior to the World Cup. It was a key part of his role in 2004 to improve the image of the All Blacks – the NZRU board was unhappy with the way his predecessor John Mitchell handled that side of his portfolio.

The publication of the NZRU's annual report has taken on greater significance in recent years as well. Now the union is a corporate beast, judged more on profit and loss, on its ability to win new sponsors, handle broadcast deals and keep stakeholders happy than it is on producing a successful All Black team.

So where does the 2011 World Cup fit into all this? Is the goal for the next tournament to win, or to help adidas make a lot of money? Is it for the All Blacks to conduct themselves in an exemplary manner and enhance their attractiveness to global sponsors?

There will be massive disappointment within the NZRU should the All Blacks bomb in the 2011 event. Yet, as hard as that disappointment will be felt, it will be largely offset if the tournament sees a boost in replica jersey sales, attracts a new international sponsor and grows the All Black brand.

The players will feel the pain of failure far more acutely, but the attitude of their employer can't help but rub off on them. The modern All Black can still judge his own career to have been hugely successful if he cuts the right image, is perceived to be upholding the right values, and is deemed a marketable commodity by the corporate backers funding the game. A World Cup medal would be nice, but if it came down to a choice of that against financial security for life, post-rugby endorsement opportunity and a sense of having been a model professional, the latter would be the preference of most modern All Blacks.

The extended adidas deal is only going to emphasise that the All Blacks have many other goals to achieve now as well as winning tests. It has blurred further just exactly what the NZRU sees as the top priority for the All Blacks. The union says it's winning, winning and winning, yet it continues to make it absurdly hard to do so when it asks the All Blacks to play 15 tests in a season.

They say winning is everything, but in 2008 the All Blacks had to play five tests on consecutive weekends – something no professional All Black side has ever had to do outside of World Cups. This need to expose the brand in new markets has dramatically lifted the workload and travel time for test players. The NZRU has followed this strategy even though many of the players who have left to play overseas in recent years have cited time away from home and the oppressive pressure of so many tests in a season as key reasons for leaving.

The NZRU consistently warns that the burden of test football is in danger of burning out the players, yet it constantly tries to shoehorn big games into almost every free weekend. We hear that winning remains the top priority, and yet the NZRU willingly runs the risk of pushing its best players offshore.

WHEN IT comes to the All Blacks, the world really is their oyster. Rugby has gone global with adidas and the NZRU playing a major role in the expansion. The irony of taking the All Blacks all over the world is that the individual players have become aware of their own market value. Having been treated as commodities, key corporate assets, they've realised that they can be traded for significant sums of cash. They have learned there's no real loyalty in the corporate world.

The All Black jersey might remain special; being part of the All Blacks may still be a special experience. But it's special in the same way working for McKinsey's would be special if you were a management consultant, or working for Gordon Ramsay would be special if you were a chef. You'd be working for the best, accruing the experience and benefits of being with the market leader but willing to drop it if a rival came in with an offer that was more appealing.

In the case of the All Blacks, the rivals are the European clubs funded by sugar daddies with deep pockets and driven by egos so big they'd scare a bear. These men want to sign All Blacks because they're recognised as the best, and they put bums on seats. These men are willing to pay colossal salaries to get what they want.

It's also becoming increasingly common now for the big clubs to involve one of their major sponsors in the signing of overseas stars. That could see a sponsor pick up part of an All Blacks' salary in return for promotional work. The attraction of this arrangement is not just the additional cash component, but also the long-term relationship struck with the sponsor that may lead to something once the player moves on or retires.

The NZRU has alerted the players to the fact that they are, essentially, individual brands. The players have become commercially savvy in much the same way as Rod Tidwell, the character played by Cuba Gooding in the hit film *Jerry Maguire*. The players don't quite yell, 'Show me the money,' as Gooding so famously did, but they do weigh up a host of factors in deciding where their futures lie.

As we've seen, it's no longer simply a case of accumulating test caps. Tana Umaga is one of the few All Blacks of the professional age to play out his full career in New Zealand, and even he managed to sneak in a short-term deal with Toulon in the final year of his NZRU contract.

Most big names in the last 10 years have moved offshore to 'enhance their brands' at the tail end of their careers. And in the last few years we've witnessed a marked shift; even players in the prime of their careers have started to see foreign markets as the best place to promote their brand. Luke McAlister left New Zealand at 24, Aaron Mauger was 25 and Carl Hayman was 28, a relative baby in the position he plays.

Dan Carter, one of the greatest players produced in the last 50 years, would have been long gone at the age of 26 had it not been for the innovative deal struck by the NZRU. The national body, fearful it was going to lose such an incredible talent, offered Carter the option of a six-month sabbatical. Carter could skip the 2009 Super 14 to play for a European club – or build the brand offshore – and then return for the Tri-Nations and stay in New Zealand through to the 2011 World Cup. It was a clever deal as it gave the NZRU what it wanted – Carter signed through to the next World Cup – yet it gave the player a break from his normal routine, a massive cash injection as Perpignan were reportedly paying him around $60,000 a game, and it boosted his profile around the world.

The Carter deal changed the landscape dramatically. As innovative as it was, it was also an admission by the NZRU that it was losing the battle to keep its players. It showed the NZRU felt it was time for desperate measures. The lure of the black jersey was at an all-time low. While Carter signed to persevere with his All Black career, he only did so because he was offered the chance to have his cake and eat it too. Without the offshore stint built into his contract, Carter wouldn't have committed to the All Blacks. And that has opened a can of worms.

Carter's colleagues have seen what he has been offered, and most senior All Blacks are interested in striking similar deals. The NZRU can't give them all what they want, though. Carter's absence from the 2009 Super 14 hardly pleased the key stakeholders in that tournament. They had invested in the big stars and they wanted to see them out there. They could tolerate Carter failing to show for one campaign, but there would be a serious backlash if the NZRU suddenly allowed a handful of All Blacks to skip Super 14 each year.

The All Blacks' 2011 World Cup hopes rest heavily on how many senior players the NZRU can persuade to stay. How many players will conclude that extending their NZRU contracts and playing for the All Blacks at the 2011 World Cup will best serve their brands? Dan Carter and

Richie McCaw have already committed their futures to the All Blacks, as has the 2008 player of the year, Andrew Hore, and his rival for the hooking berth, Keven Mealamu.

But there are many critical figures who, at the start of 2009, were uncertain about their plans. Ali Williams, Tony Woodcock, Rodney So'oialo and Mils Muliaina, four of the most capped players in the team, were all weighing up their options. The decision facing them wasn't easy. Williams, Mealamu, So'oialo and Woodcock had been All Blacks since 2002, Muliaina since 2003. All five, particularly So'oialo and Muliaina, had endured consistently heavy workloads for the last six years.

If the All Blacks were going to cram in 15 tests a season before the 2011 World Cup, these players had the impossible task of trying to determine just what kind of physical state they were going to be in when New Zealand played host. They also had to be honest about the robustness of their desire to be there. If they signed extended contracts in early 2009, it's possible they could play another 30 tests at least before the World Cup even kicked off.

All that travel, training, team meetings, pre-match tension and physical commitment – would they still be burning inside to play at a World Cup? Would they still be desperate to lift the All Black World Cup curse or would they be long over test football? It's estimated that a senior All Black spends an average of 180 days away from home in the course of a season. That takes its toll on family life.

Will some players sign on for more, believing that the best thing for their brand is playing at the 2011 World Cup only to regret that choice by 2010? Will some players stay on but reach 2011 so bruised and battered by the demanding schedule that they are of little use by the time the World Cup rolls around?

The more experience and quality the All Blacks have in their squad, the better chance they have of winning the next World Cup. The NZRU's desire to make money in conjunction with their key sponsors, and the commercial awakening of the top players, will seriously challenge the All Blacks' World Cup ambition.

There is, however, one potentially positive aspect to this growing brand awareness – it's at least helping the players to evaluate situations, to take responsibility for their careers, and to make decisions.

17
Better players make better All Blacks

IN THE WAKE of the 2007 World Cup disaster, the All Black management team had to absorb some uncomfortable truths. It wasn't easy to accept that after four years of being hugely successful – four years of believing they'd fixed many of the faults that had tripped up their predecessors at previous World Cups – the All Blacks were in fact just as vulnerable, just as ill-prepared in one vital facet. It turned out that the mantra of the Graham Henry era, 'Better people make better All Blacks,' was in fact not strictly true. Which is why in early 2008 the All Blacks revamped their leadership model to reflect their new belief – that better players make better All Blacks.

When Henry and his colleagues returned from South Africa in August 2004, they concluded that the players needed to take more responsibility in managing the team. They also believed that more energy had to be put into developing their experiences away from the field. Having coached some of the strongest characters during the amateur era, Henry believed that if players were required to make decisions and take ownership of their lives when they weren't playing rugby, those skills would transfer to the test arena. It seemed like a sound enough theory, right up until the All Blacks collapsed in Cardiff.

At that point the leadership model and mantra were both exposed as less robust than they needed to be. In 2005 and 2006 the All Blacks had shown improved mental toughness at critical periods in critical games. In 2005 they were behind against South Africa with four minutes remaining in Dunedin. The Springboks were on top of their game, they had momentum, belief and, of course, the lead. The All Blacks didn't panic. They stayed true to the game-plan and didn't clam up, scoring with four minutes left.

Later that year at Twickenham they were being beaten up by a huge English pack. Again, they believed in what they were doing and closed the game out.

They had to produce one of their bravest performances in years to beat Australia in Brisbane in 2006, and when they fell 12 points behind in the opening game of the 2007 Tri Nations in Durban they continued to spread the ball wide and rip the Boks apart to claim a dramatic and deserved victory.

Yet all of that counted for nothing because, in Cardiff, the decision-making was poor. While it was heartening to see the All Blacks show improved mental strength in critical games, the ultimate goal of the cultural revolution instigated by Henry was to win the World Cup.

There could be no complacency or sense of achievement without the William Webb Ellis trophy. In the wake of the World Cup flop, no one within the All Black management team could sit back and say they just needed to carry on doing the same thing. The model had failed – better people might make better All Blacks, but better people didn't make the All Blacks good enough to win the World Cup.

There had to be a re-think, and not only because the model had failed. Immediately after the World Cup, Anton Oliver, Carl Hayman, Chris Jack, Byron Kelleher, Aaron Mauger, Luke McAlister and Doug Howlett took up overseas contracts. Jack, Oliver, Kelleher, Mauger and Howlett were all in the leadership group. In early 2008, fellow 2007 World Cup squad members, Nick Evans, Chris Masoe, Jerry Collins and Greg Somerville announced they too would be heading offshore, leaving the All Blacks seriously light on experience and quality.

The 2008 All Blacks couldn't be afforded the same level of input and responsibility as the team that played between 2005 and 2007. There were just too many new faces in the squad, too many players who didn't have the experience or confidence to be entrusted with that level of responsibility.

It was decided to tighten the circle of trust – to empower a smaller group of senior players to retain leadership and mentoring roles. It was also decided that, rather than build their leadership skills away from the game, it would make more sense to have them do it on the field.

As All Black manager Darren Shand explains: 'On reflection, we put a lot of energy [from 2004 to 2007] into developing the person with the view that there would be a natural transference because you're increasing the confidence, you're helping them work with others, and those were things that we felt during a game would be important. Now we have to look a lot harder at how we can make that more game-related. We've got to see how we can put them into real game-related situations through the training. Rightly or wrongly, we put the emphasis on developing self-reliance, tried to take guys who were dependent and to make them independent. I think decision-making will always be a part of training, as most of rugby is unstructured and most coaches do set up the way they train to develop decision-making.

'In every campaign I've ever been involved in, you always look at where you're going to draw the line in the sand between democracy and dictatorship. We've got a new and a younger group. We had four years with quite a number of guys who are still here and still believe in that system. If you look at the World Cup campaign, we still did a lot of things right so we have to retain some of that. But at this early stage it's been a lot more management-driven, still with interaction with the key players.

'We've structured it so we have a group [Richie McCaw, Ali Williams, Rodney So'oialo, Dan Carter and Mils Muliaina] who really have a focus on-field – that is, around strategy and game-plan – and a smaller group [Somerville, Mealamu and Conrad Smith] that work with me in managing the environment and the culture. It gives those guys responsibility to drive the new guys and bring them up to the level.'

There were encouraging signs in 2008 that the model was working. The All Blacks lost back-to-back games in the Tri-Nations when captain McCaw was unavailable due to injury. The collective lack of experience was an issue – the drain of talent offshore was finally catching up with the All Blacks and, on paper, they looked a decidedly ordinary team.

When Williams limped off early in the first half against South Africa in Dunedin, the All Black pack could barely muster 100 caps between them. So'oialo, Andrew Hore and Tony Woodcock were the only men who had seen any real action. Anthony Boric at lock was making his first start while Kevin O'Neill, the man who replaced Williams, was debuting off the bench, and John Afoa, Adam Thomson and Jerome Kaino had 15 caps between them.

Lack of experience and an idiotic game-plan were factors the following week in Sydney where the All Blacks delivered one of their worst performances of the professional era. The pressure was really on at that stage. The team had to win or the coaching panel might have been lynched by an angry public. There were factions at home still upset by the re-appointment of Henry, with the latent resentment stoked to boiling point by the loss in Sydney because the Australians were coached by Robbie Deans – the man Henry beat to the All Black job.

Everything was on the line when the All Blacks had to return from Sydney and play the Wallabies at Eden Park a week later. The All Blacks had not lost three tests in a row since 1998, and that was a year of turmoil no one wanted to see repeated.

Under the most intolerable pressure the All Blacks blitzed the Wallabies in a ruthless display of professionalism. The home side were accurate, they were aggressive and they were disciplined. They read the game superbly and crushed the spirit of the Wallabies in a manner no one thought possible. At the core of their performance were the five-strong leadership group.

It was the same again when the All Blacks defeated the Springboks 19-0 in Cape Town, and come the winner-takes-all showdown with Australia in Brisbane, the All Black leadership group displayed remarkable resolve. The All Blacks went behind 12 minutes into the second half and were obviously on the ropes. At the same point in Sydney they'd collapsed.

But there was no repeat. Instead of wilting in the heat and humidity, the leadership group came up with the right answers. The discipline stayed intact. The tempo increased. The intensity rose and the quality of execution stayed high. This was a side that had conviction. This was a side that trusted its instincts and was confident enough to keep making strong decisions when under pressure. No one disappeared. No one decided to take care of their own contract, as Brian Lochore said of the events of Johannesburg and Sydney in 2004.

This was an All Black side that was beatable when compared with its predecessors, and yet here they were closing out games that better sides would have lost. The mental strength was impressive. The leadership of the side under pressure was impressive. But while this gives cause for hope, it shouldn't be seen as reason to believe the problem has been fixed.

The challenge is still massive and with the flow of personnel so fluid, the All Blacks in 2010 could bear little resemblance to the All Blacks of 2008. A leadership model that worked in 2008 might not work in 2011. Shand knows only too well how volatile the environment is. He knows the players coming under his wing seem increasingly younger, and that their opportunities to have developed life skills are even fewer.

'What we are tying to do, because of circumstances around the way players are brought into the rugby environment – i.e. they don't work and have the normal work experiences that we have – is to fast-track their maturation. That's a little bit like putting a needle in a haystack. Everyone's got different learning styles. It's not an exact science. At the knife-edge of what we do, decision-making under pressure is the crucial ingredient – that's the nirvana that you aim for. I don't think they didn't make decisions [in the quarter-final of the 2007 World Cup] – they made decisions. There was leadership. Richie was leading.

'One of the findings of the Independent World Cup Review was a lack of mental skills – that we haven't got that right. The NZRU high-performance unit when we started in 2004 was one person. It's now better resourced. Mental skills is an area that we have to make sure from the high performance, through the unions, the academies and Super 14 that we have resources available so that a lot of those elements are done by the time they get to us. Because this is an area where we've been weak, despite the fact we've got a great record – we can't be too bad because we've still won a hell of a lot of games, more than anyone out there. No international rugby side has got anywhere near the level we have over a long period of time. So we must do some things right.

'Where can you get that little gain? Within our high-performance programme I believe the New Zealand Under-20 team will be better than some franchises [in terms of being mentally prepared]. At that level it's starting to gain momentum.

'I don't know the answer to the question why mental skills have been identified as weak. Societal upbringing is clearly a factor and the professional era does present challenges in giving people opportunities to learn. Perhaps there needs to be an element put back into our competitions that allows the players to have the time to have those everyday experiences where they learn those foundation stones. We are getting kids at a really young age exposed to a high level of competition and sometimes they are not equipped to cope with it, and on some occasions you do have to hold their hand to get them through, whereas [on] others you can't.

'If your end goal is a great performance, some of the things that are done for them are done so that performance isn't compromised. We have to focus on what's important. Take nutrition. We now have players seeking the nutritionist, rather than have him say you are a problem. All of those things are a normal part of professional sporting environments and it's what you put your focus on to get the right goal on the weekend.'

The other critical factor, which is omitted by Shand, is the continued growth of the captain – Richie McCaw. Every effort is being made to fast-track the maturation of those players coming into the All Black system. But when it comes down to critical World Cup games, history shows us that so much depends on the mental strength of just one man – the captain. As much as stronger, self-reliant leaders are needed at the base level, there has to be a charismatic commander at the top. There has to be a guiding light to instil confidence in others and to keep the ship on course in stormy waters. Taine Randell wasn't that man. Reuben Thorne wasn't that man and, in 2007, Richie McCaw wasn't that man. By 2011 however, there is good reason to believe that McCaw might well be that man.

LOOK AT the players who have held aloft the William Webb Ellis trophy. There is something that sets them apart, something that binds them all together.

David Kirk is an intellectual giant, a Rhodes Scholar and a thinker of some depth who has been at the helm of massive corporate entities. Nick Farr-Jones is a Wallaby great, possibly the best captain they've ever had. Francois Pienaar is a man for whom his 1995 Springbok team-mates said they would run through brick walls. John Eales in 1999 was nicknamed 'Nobody', as in 'Nobody is perfect'. Martin Johnson was a scowling, brooding beast of a man who knew how to lead through action and deed, and he was a man who didn't compromise. John Smit survived four years as captain of the Springboks in one of their most turbulent periods – a massive feat of leadership in itself. The evidence is irrefutable – no side has ever won a World Cup without an iconic captain.

No side has ever won a World Cup without an iconic captain.

McCaw, from the moment he wowed Lansdowne Road on his debut in 2001, has been recognised as a player with freakish ability. He hasn't been recognised as a great leader. Until now. Maybe in a similar vein to Sean Fitzpatrick, the captaincy didn't quite sit as comfortably with McCaw as many assumed it would. As Fitzpatrick said, it takes time to grow into the role and feel confident. It's not that McCaw has ever obviously been a bad captain or appeared out of his depth – more that his leadership hasn't seemed to be at quite the same level as his performances.

Maybe that should have been expected. In 2006 McCaw's performance in Brisbane was of such quality that Henry remarked afterwards he didn't think it was possible for anyone to have played any better. In 2008 assistant All Black coach Steve Hansen said, after taking some time to deliberate, that he felt McCaw was the best No 7 ever produced by the All Blacks. It was a huge statement and one that failed to generate much in the way of opposition. Certainly if McCaw is not the best openside flanker ever produced by New Zealand, he is the second best, behind Michael Jones.

The accolades haven't flowed so freely in praise of his captaincy though. In his first season in charge, the All Blacks were operating at the peak of their game. They had a core of players who'd been together for a long time and knew what they were doing. There was experience throughout the side and enough strong characters in the team to allow McCaw to do little more than concentrate on winning the toss and playing well. The team was largely capable of leading itself, and because of its quality and rampant form, there were few occasions where the All Blacks were under pressure. That changed in 2007 when the bulk of the first-choice side was forced to recondition during the early rounds of Super 14. That left many struggling for form and confidence and, inevitably, some of the leadership group became less effective at making critical decisions.

That was apparent in Melbourne when the All Blacks slumped to defeat against the Wallabies. It was a game the All Blacks never should have lost. They were dominating every facet in the first half and had ample opportunity to put Australia away. But their execution was sloppy – some of it no doubt the consequence of having beaten South Africa six days previously in an energy-sapping contest in Durban.

It was more than just tiredness, though, afflicting the All Blacks in the second half. Too many of the leadership group went quiet, just like the bad old days. There was a mental retreat, a return to players looking after themselves and to hell with the collective. The All Blacks stopped making good decisions and they got worse as the pressure mounted.

The blame was laid at McCaw's door. He was the skipper, after all, and like many before him, unable to do much to change the outcome. He wasn't forceful enough with the referee, said some. He was too often, as his job demanded, buried at the bottom of rucks and unable to see what was going on, said others. Another group of critics felt his reputation for playing so close to the laws of the game made it hard for him to have a working relationship with officials. There were grains of truth, just grains mind, in those various interpretations.

There were more fundamental reasons why McCaw wasn't quite fulfilling his leadership potential – and it really was a case of not quite. First, as has already been documented, he was working his way into form during the international season. That was also true of his senior leadership group, which meant there were a lot of players focusing more on their own game than had been the case in recent years.

The constant rotation of players had also diminished some of the understanding that had developed in the previous two seasons. And it had confused the selectors as to the make-up of their best side, and some of the strongest characters – some of the men who'd been hugely influential in 2005 and 2006 – were suddenly unsure of their places. Aaron Mauger and Doug Howlett were two of the most astute leaders in the back division. The former especially brought a calm authority to decision-making and was renowned as a great communicator. He, like Howlett, was pushed to the periphery in 2007 with the selectors preferring younger, less experienced men.

Reuben Thorne was in the squad but rarely on the field, which was mostly true of Greg Somerville, while Keven Mealamu and Chris Jack were both scrapping to make the starting XV having been certainties for much of their test careers. All that meant McCaw was perhaps not as well supported as he should have been and, as has been made clear by the men of 1987 and those before them, the best captains all had competent leaders around them.

Let's not forget what the Independent World Cup Review had to say of the leadership group: 'We consider that on-field leadership and decision-making was a factor in the loss in the quarter-final. Arguably, the team and its leadership group has only occasionally been tested to the same degree over the last four years. The trend, as witnessed in Melbourne earlier in 2007, was for the leaders to revert to type and let McCaw make the calls.'

The fact that McCaw's head was not quite as clear as he would have liked in 2007 can't be dismissed either. He was coming off contract and he wanted to stay with the New Zealand Rugby Union, but negotiations dragged on and on. The NZRU was confident as early as March that they would have things tied up, yet by September McCaw still hadn't committed his future beyond the World Cup.

He has certainty now and with that he has a clear goal – to become an iconic All Black captain, and to lift the William Webb Ellis trophy.

He eventually signed an extension until 2009, the day before the quarter-final and, as he revealed in April 2008, he did so almost out of frustration. He knew he wanted to stay and he knew it was important to have an agreement confirming that. He wasn't happy with the detail but felt he could sign a deal and then come back to it after the World Cup and work on the fine print. Or if he felt he had had enough, he could pull the pin and seek an early release.

It would be doing the professionalism of McCaw a massive injustice to suggest he ran out in Cardiff with anything other than 100 per cent clarity and focus on the job in hand. It's not as if he was in any mental flux over his contract, or allowing negotiations to consume him. But can it be just a coincidence that after re-working his contract in early 2008 and extending it through it to 2011, McCaw's leadership rose to new heights?

At the level at which McCaw operates, the smallest things can make a perceptible difference. The knowledge that he has committed his future to New Zealand through to the next World Cup has given him a sense of contentment and clarity that wasn't quite there in 2007. He has certainty now and with that he has a clear goal – to become an iconic All Black captain, and to lift the William Webb Ellis trophy. He has peace of mind now that his contract is all he wants it to be.

When he was weighing his options in early 2008 – asking himself whether he really did want to go through the rigmarole of negotiating with the NZRU just a few months after putting the last deal to bed – he kept coming back to the same thought: that he wasn't ready to give up playing international rugby. It was still a passion, still something that drove him and still something worth emptying his soul for.

Was he prepared to retire having been recognised as a brilliant player, but an okay captain? Absolutely not, and with his desire fuelled and his mind at peace, he took a giant leap in 2008 towards becoming the new Sean Fitzpatrick. Somehow – maybe it was just perception – he seemed to have a much greater presence on the field. He was standing up to referees, talking to them and, again maybe this was just the perception, marginal calls went in the All Blacks' favour.

As the season progressed, McCaw became bigger and bigger in terms of his influence. He was injured against England in June and without him, the All Blacks crashed badly in Dunedin and Sydney. When McCaw returned to play at Eden Park the following week, they were a different side. Not just because of McCaw's outstanding ability in the No 7 shirt, but because he was on the bridge, chasing victory like Captain Ahab on the hunt for Moby Dick. His leadership group rallied behind him. There was quality decision-making across the team. There was direction. There was focus and there was one man leading the way – McCaw.

The captain was even more impressive in Cape Town. He was the game's shining star, almost as if he had his own gravitational force pulling the ball into his orbit. The All Blacks held the Springboks scoreless – something they'd never done before in the Republic – and Henry had to revise the statement he'd made in Brisbane in 2006, for McCaw had indeed played better in South Africa than he did in Australia.

When the All Blacks won another tight battle to clinch the Tri-Nations in September, there was national agreement that McCaw was moving towards becoming a great All Black captain. His star only shone brighter on the end-of-year tour to the UK and Ireland, and sitting in the All Black team hotel in London before the clash with England that would secure the Grand Slam, he opened up a little.

In the 13 months since Cardiff, McCaw had banished a lot of bad memories. He was so much in control, so comfortable in his post, that it was impossible to remember that everything about the All Black performance that night in Cardiff felt wrong. The endless pick and drive, the refusal to set up for the drop goal, the way referee Wayne Barnes was allowed to strut around like he owned the game.

Impossible because the new McCaw just wouldn't let it happen. As he said in the Royal Kensington Hotel on 26 November 2008: 'I feel like I'm better now than I was 12 to 18 months ago. Experience definitely makes you stronger, you learn to trust your gut instincts a lot more and be more confident in yourself. It also helps that when you try a few things and they come off, you grow in confidence. The first thing you have to do as captain is perform. It depends on the type of leadership you're after, but I believe that if you are performing to a high standard the other stuff, the peripheral stuff, will all follow.

'So if you get into situations and you believe in what you're trying to do, you don't panic, you stay composed. It's not as if you panicked before, it's just you know what works and you get a better feel for what's going on. It's the little things, the subtle little things that can make the difference. I've asked myself why it is that I keep playing the game. And it's because I love training hard all week to test myself against the best. I love the competition and the best part of being captain is that you see how your influence can help other guys perform.'

By 2011, McCaw may well be the first All Black to earn 100 caps. If he avoids injury he will have captained the All Blacks in more tests than anyone – easily beating the 51 internationals that Fitzpatrick managed at the helm. Those statistics alone will earn him iconic status, but there's so much more to McCaw than numbers. He's a leader every bit as worthy as those captains who've lifted the World Cup. He's a leader ready to enter the pantheon, but he knows that to be considered truly great, to remove all possibility of debate, he must be the man standing in the middle of Eden Park on 23 October 2011 clutching the William Webb Ellis trophy.

18
Code crackers

IT WAS AT the Royal Terrace Hotel in Edinburgh where a little spring of optimism started to flow. The Scottish capital had turned on one of its notorious winter mornings where the sky merged with the endless grey stone and never once gave thought to lifting its game. The All Blacks, in their usual oblivious way, traipsed through the hotel in shorts and jandals. It was 5 November 2008 – a date that went down in history because of Britain's love of celebrating failure. There was no sense of failure being embraced at the Royal Terrace Hotel, however.

The All Black starting XV to play Scotland had filed into the upstairs conference room to divulge to the assembled media how they thought the ensuing test would pan out. Holding court was the giant frame of Jamie Mackintosh, the Southland prop who would be making his debut at Murrayfield. Mackintosh had been an All Black-in-waiting since he was 16. He'd been off-the-scale big from his early teens, earning places in national age-grade sides years earlier than his peers.

He was more than just big, though. He was a natural leader, graced with a laconic charm that hid his fierce determination. Articulate, relaxed, clever and funny, Mackintosh gave the impression three days before his debut that he was a senior pro. He wasn't just an All Black-in-waiting; he was an All Black captain-in-waiting. He was the epitome of the new breed of professional player coming through the ranks. He'd been exposed to development programmes for most of his adult life and the benefits were obvious. He was no PlayStation-addicted couch potato. Mackintosh was exactly the sort of character the New Zealand rugby system had been trying to build.

A week later and it was Jimmy Cowan who was flying the flag for the new breed. What made the Southland halfback so intriguing was that he represented both sides of the divide. Earlier in 2008 he'd been in all sorts of trouble. He'd been arrested twice for late-night drunken incidents. By July he was in danger of having his contract terminated. He had a problem with alcohol. There'd been some personal tragedy in his life and he'd turned to booze to help him through it. On the eve of the Tri-Nations, the NZRU had reached a crossroads with Cowan; he either had to accept help and turn his life around, or it had to let him go. He agreed to the former and the NZRU made it a condition of his employment that he abstain from drinking alcohol.

Cowan had fallen as far as he could. In the early days of professionalism, Cowan probably would have just kept falling until he crashed spectacularly. There would have been no offer of help – not because previous regimes were callous, but simply because the mechanism wouldn't have been in place to either recognise the problem or solve it. To see a young player like Cowan come so close to losing his job might not seem like progress. But the improvements in the system were obvious in the way Cowan recovered, the emphatic way he bounced back.

He'd been to his own personal hell earlier in 2008, and by 12 November he was sitting in front of reporters talking about his despair with an honesty and maturity that was impressive and admirable. The questions kept coming and so did his answers. He didn't skip a beat. Nothing was off-limits and the more he talked, the more it became apparent that here was a young man with reserves of character few could match.

From being close to self-destruction in July, he was off the booze by August and very much the first-choice halfback for the All Blacks. He had turned his life around, mainly through his own resolve, but also because he was helped by a system that was no longer riddled with holes and ignorance. His finishing touch came when an Irish reporter asked what it had been like growing up in Mataura. Cowan said it had been good, and the town was more advanced than many thought, what with having a university there. 'A university?' inquired the Irishman. 'Otherwise known as a freezing works,' replied Cowan.

Cowan and Mackintosh were perhaps the best examples of the new breed, but the All Black touring squad of 2008 was filled with impressive young men. There was Richard Kahui, a player of world-class potential who also happens to be articulate, grounded and more than pleasant company. Kieran Read is in much the same mould, and having captained Canterbury to the national provincial title shortly before coming away with the All Blacks, can throw genuine leadership capability into his personal mix. Anthony Boric had been head boy at Rosmini Grammar on Auckland's North Shore and is in possession of a calm demeanour that sets others at ease. Stephen Donald, the back-up first five to Daniel Carter, is another strong character, equipped with all the off-field skills he's ever likely to need.

Predicting the make-up of the All Blacks' 2011 World Cup squad is fraught with danger but, barring injury or dramatic loss of form, Mackintosh, Kahui, Read and Boric are going to be involved. These are the type of men who give reason for optimism. These are the type of characters the All Blacks have lacked since the outset of professionalism. Or at least have lacked in numbers. These are young men with ingrained good values, not players who've come into the All Blacks with little idea and been asked to catch up. These are players who've learned from life, not been sat in a classroom and told to pay attention. These are the players who should give Brian Lochore a sense of relief. When the former All Black captain, coach and selector said his cultural revolution of 2004 came to nothing, these are the men who, by their very professionalism, say that it didn't.

Finally, the system appears to be getting it right more often than it gets it wrong. 'We're seeing guys come through who've had these messages of holistic development from an early age,' says New Zealand Rugby Players' Association boss Rob Nichol. 'If you get to the kids early, then the product you get is so much better, so much better balanced. You're able to get so much more from them, and they're able to get so much out of things. I've noticed that we've come through two generations of players and are on to a third now.

'The first generation came from the old days when they all had jobs and other responsibilities, and they had to take care of themselves and their families before they could even contemplate turning up to play rugby. The next generation – they weren't the lost generation, but they were certainly not well looked after. They knew nothing but rugby. They knew nothing that was happening outside of rugby and to a certain extent we're still working with some of those guys now to make up for the damage that was done.

'Now we're on to this third generation, the era of the academy – the Players' Association evolution, the player development programmes, and this whole focus on the importance of holistic development that has kicked in. We are now almost into a fourth generation, where our programmes are getting to players so much earlier. We could still do a lot more. But the key messages that we deliver to young players are that it's fantastic you have this opportunity to maybe play professional rugby, but it doesn't always swing your way and you need to be doing something else. To be able to be a good player you need to be organised off the field. You need something to motivate you each day and to have an interest. You need to be a good person. It's not good enough to be a good player in a professional team.'

'To be able to be a good player you need to be organised off the field. You need something to motivate you each day and to have an interest.'

SADLY, THE seed of optimism sown in Edinburgh didn't grow into an oak tree. It's a case of two steps forward, one step back with professional players. For every Jamie Mackintosh and Richard Kahui, there is someone who's less tuned into the message of holistic development. No question the professional development is much improved. There are greater numbers of better prepared professionals coming into the élite game. There are fewer cracks for players to fall between off the field. The default graduate is no longer shallow, self-centred and incapable of fielding any criticism. But the system isn't flawless; the production line spits out mainly good eggs but here and there a bad one sneaks through.

This mixed bag makes for a confusing picture. The All Blacks returned from their Grand Slam heroics in December 2008, and much of the feelgood was lost through some unsavoury incidents.

Adam Thomson, a seemingly jovial and laidback kind of guy, was arrested in Havelock North and charged with assaulting his partner. Thomson had perhaps been the All Black find of the season – an honest toiler on the fringes of the Highlanders for most of his career, he jumped into the All Blacks and made everyone wonder how on earth they hadn't noticed him before.

A few weeks later and it emerged that Sione Lauaki, the Chiefs' loose forward who'd been part of the All Black set-up for most of the year, had been arrested in Auckland on New Year's Day. Lauaki was accused of trashing a motel room after an altercation with his partner.

There'd been other incidents during the year. There were those involving Cowan when he was losing his battle with the booze. Just before the Tri-Nations All Black flanker Jerome Kaino was arrested in Auckland for drink driving, and Piri Weepu took diversion after an incident in September when he was picked up by police in Wellington's Courtenay Place banging on the door of a fast-food outlet.

The concern around these incidents is not so much that there's an endemic booze culture within the All Blacks. Let's not forget they're young men and entitled to a social life. The concern is that these incidents show that – even with all the advice in the world, even after receiving guidance and training on how to avoid volatile public situations, and even after having it laid out before them just how detrimental heavy alcohol consumption is to athletic performance – these individuals still managed to get into trouble.

They made poor decisions, and that remains a worry as poor decision-making has blighted so many All Black World Cup campaigns. These lapses hint at an irreparable glitch.

By and large the All Blacks make good decisions on the field. They win most of their games and then, at the World Cup, they've been guilty of making mistakes they never previously have. For the most part, New Zealand's élite players make good decisions off the field. They go out, have a few drinks, enjoy themselves and come home incident free. Then, every now and again, they lapse; they make very poor decisions and tarnish their record.

No matter how hard the coaches work to iron out the on-field flaw, and no matter how hard the professional development managers work to iron out the off-field flaw, it keeps occurring. It makes trusting the All Blacks at the 2011 World Cup a fraught business. In 2008, just when they started showing some real character on the field and some maturity in the way they responded to pressure in the big games, they pricked the bubble of optimism with some seriously ordinary performances off the field.

For every new arrival – like Kahui and Mackintosh – who knocks your socks off, there will be another who has clearly existed for no other reason than to play rugby.

On the strength of Daniel Carter and Richie McCaw alone, the All Blacks have to be fancied to finally break their World Cup drought in 2011. Those two have committed themselves to the All Blacks until then. If the likes of Ali Williams, Tony Woodcock and Rodney So'oialo do the same, then there is the core of an outstanding All Black team. Less experienced men like Ma'a Nonu, Cowan, Kaino, Kahui, Boric and Conrad Smith will have added to their tally of caps by then, and will give the All Blacks confidence and authority. In terms of talent and experience, the All Blacks will have all they need to win the World Cup.

But we still can't say with any certainty whether they will have the depth of character; whether they will have the quality of leadership to continue making good decisions under the fiercest pressure. It seems that no matter how well things are going, there's a compulsion to self-destruct at some point. It's almost as if some players have been pre-programmed to combust at periodic intervals. There's no other explanation. The development system does everything to prevent it, but it's not enough in some cases – boom, without warning, without reason, someone will go out, drink far too much and make a bad decision. It's these random explosions that make everyone wary. If some players can lose the plot off the field, they can all too easily lose it on the field.

The All Blacks have seduced so many into backing them for the World Cup in the past. They dominate, beat anyone and everyone and make us all think they're indestructible. We think on that evidence that their players are superior, that they are without flaw, or have only minor flaws that do little to weaken the team's power.

There's a serious danger of everyone being sucked in again. In 2008 the leadership of the side appeared vastly improved. Both McCaw's captaincy and the contribution of his senior team inspired confidence. The arrival of several new players like Mackintosh and Kahui has been another major boost. And then, of course, there is the way the team played.

The quarter-final loss in Cardiff had a dramatic effect on the confidence of the All Blacks. It was more than just another World Cup defeat. For almost three full seasons they'd been in fifth gear, capable of cruising past the very best teams with minimum effort. The British Lions, Australia, France, Wales and England were all hammered on several occasions. South Africa managed two wins, Australia one – and that was it; three losses in the three years prior to the World Cup. Between 2005 and August 2007, the All Blacks were a dangerously good team. They were good enough to be considered alongside the very best New Zealand had ever produced. And, despite their previous World Cup failings, they were considered by most rugby followers to be a shoo-in to win the William Webb Ellis trophy in 2007.

For such a long time, the gap between the All Blacks and the rest of the world felt too big to bridge.

South Africa's two victories had come in the Republic, a notoriously difficult country for visiting sides to win tests in. And they'd been exactly that – one-off performances in which they'd had the good fortune to catch the All Blacks just that fraction off the pace. Travel, fatigue and injuries had all been factors in those losses, and there was no sense that South Africa were good enough to pull off victory in neutral territory against an All Black side that would be entirely focused and presumably coming very much to the boil in France, 2007.

It felt like too many factors would have to conspire for the All Blacks to lose a World Cup test. It felt like coach Graham Henry had all the bases covered. He had studied the past, worked out exactly where his predecessors had gone wrong and implemented strategies to put armour plating on the soft underbelly of the All Blacks.

The revolution kick-started by Henry and Lochore was a key factor in pushing sceptics into believing in the All Blacks. Surely if – for the first time in the professional age – players were finally being taught how to lead, how to make tough decisions in the heat of battle, they would be able to lay their World Cup ghosts to rest? Where once they had been weak, by 2007 most observers believed they were strong. On their day the All Blacks were untouchable, and they'd spent so long preparing them-selves to make sure that the World Cup *was* their day.

On top of that there was a dearth of obvious challengers. The Boks had won a couple of tests in three years, but they'd never been con-sistent during that period. They didn't convince and nor did Australia – the Wallabies didn't even come close in fact, despite their victory in Melbourne a few months out from the World Cup. Defending champi-ons England were a shambles; France had fallen to record defeats almost every time they'd played the All Blacks in the last few years, and Wales,

Ireland and Scotland were never going to be good enough. Argentina had to be taken seriously, but they didn't have the experience to sustain a challenge to the finishing post.

Everything pointed towards an All Black celebration and yet, once again, the campaign ended in tears. Which is why no one should be fooled by the events of 2008 and the emphatic way the All Blacks bounced back. Remember, after losing the World Cup final in 1995, the All Blacks won the Tri-Nations and test series in South Africa in 1996. They didn't lose a game in 1997.

It was the same after 1999. The All Blacks put the loss at Twickenham behind them to continue on their winning way, slowly improving year by year until they peaked in July and August 2003. That year they pummelled Australia and South Africa by 50 points in consecutive weekends and won the Tri-Nations in such impressive style that it would have taken a seriously brave punter to go against them.

Again, they managed to crawl off the canvas by the end of 2004, putting the horror of the Sydney semi-final behind them. By 2005 they were in peak form, maybe just about holding it through most of 2006, only to imperceptibly let it slide in 2007. The rest of the world now jokes about the All Blacks' uncanny ability to peak at the wrong time – to be playing their best rugby in the middle of the World Cup cycle. Is history repeating itself?

The All Blacks started the 2008 season with so much to prove. So many New Zealanders were left cold by 2007 – not just the crash in Cardiff, but the reconditioning programme during Super 14 and the continued rotation of players even when the All Blacks were at the World Cup. There were many previously passionate supporters who needed to be reconnected with the team, who needed something else to make them feel unambiguously proud to wear black.

With that backdrop, and with so many quality players having departed for fresh challenges, 2008 shaped as one of the toughest in the All Blacks' professional history. They ended the season with 13 wins from 15 tests. They won the Tri-Nations for the fourth consecutive year, retained the Bledisloe Cup and took the Grand Slam on their November tour to Europe. They played with pride, with skill, with creativity, with aggression and, most weeks at least, with the same starting line-up.

No one has any right to believe the All Blacks should have been able to do any more. It was a hugely positive year for the All Blacks, and one in which they did much to reconnect with their adoring public. However, no one should see this comeback as any reason to start believing the pattern will be broken in 2011. What we have surely learned by now is that the three and a half years between World Cups is no accurate guide to what will happen at the event.

Everyone would prefer the All Blacks to come into 2011 on the back of impressive form, with the legacy in good health. Everyone wants to see evidence of the team having fixed some of the perennial issues that surface when it comes under pressure. Everyone wants to see proof that development and leadership structures are working and producing the right kind of people as well as the right kind of athletes.

But as much as New Zealanders want to see the All Blacks dominating and fixing longstanding problems, they simply can't connect the dots yet again and conclude that a brilliant test record will lead to World Cup success. The World Cup is a six-week tournament that comes with its own pressures and its own challenges. The best thing is to ignore it, to abstain from making predictions.

Why not just live in the present and enjoy the victories when they come? Why not see a test victory as simply that – a one-off game where the All Blacks prove they are better than their opponents? The dangers of planning too far ahead have been highlighted all too painfully. To treat the World Cup as a special case hasn't worked. In 1987 the All Blacks took the tournament as it came. There was no planning document, no committee set up to make sure every second of every day was planned and double-planned. There were no sponsors embroidering initials on blankets or digging up dirt from around the country.

The NZRU can take the lead in downplaying the 2011 World Cup, but maybe it's time for all New Zealanders to stand back and ask whether they too are obsessed with the World Cup. Has the nation forgotten how to celebrate test victories? It feels like it. After every test the All Blacks have won in the last six years, time has been spent trying to put the game in context and debate how it sets things up for the World Cup. Tests are no longer seen as 80-minute battles that have no meaning beyond the final whistle. Now they have much greater significance – they offer clues to future performance and highlight areas of concern ahead of the World Cup, even when the blessed thing is still two years away. Why not simply go crazy whenever the All Blacks win a test? Why not take the advice every coach and every player spouts ad nauseam, and 'take things one game at a time'?

Media analyst and 1987 World Cup winner Grant Fox perhaps puts it best: 'I think what eats away at us about our legacy is that it creates an expectation of being the best. Mostly, between World Cups we've been the best side and I think we're looking at winning the World Cup to ratify that. I would hate to go through having a less than 50 per cent ratio between World Cups and winning the World Cup. It would be nice to have both. I desperately want another group of All Blacks to experience winning a World Cup. There's no way I want to be thought of as being part of a special group who were the only All Blacks team to win the World Cup.

'The Australian attitude is so different to ours – just move on. Maybe it's because rugby is the national obsession. That's fine. It would be all over if we lost the passion. I think we need to analyse and offer constructive criticism, but we should never get personal and I think post-World Cup it has. We beat ourselves up on this. We really do.'

Epilogue

HAVING WANTED IT for so long, New Zealanders might not know how to feel if the All Blacks win the World Cup in 2011. The cork will go pop but what gushes out is not so easy to predict.

There's a fair chance it will be relief and nothing else – certainly at first. The nation will be tightly wound. There will be the double stress of hosting and having the eyes of the world on little old New Zealand, and of course all that worry about how the All Blacks will fare. The nerves will be jangling through each play-off round.

Given what happened in Cardiff, no one will make the mistake of taking progress to the semi-finals for granted. It will be unbearable, and when emotion runs that deep, it doesn't tend to turn quickly to elation with the right outcome.

It may take days, weeks – possibly even months – before there's any mass outpouring of joy. Before everyone sits back and realises they have good reason to feel more than relief; to feel that it's okay to actually celebrate, to cheer, to head out into the street and embrace your neighbour, to wave a flag, to sing the national anthem; to phone family members overseas and declare your unashamed pride in what's been achieved; to take the family out for dinner and order lamb and drink Marlborough's best Sauvignon Blanc; to phone up talkback radio, give them your real name and admit that it feels good, bloody good in fact, to wake up in the morning knowing the All Blacks have won another World Cup.

New Zealanders owe it to themselves to take the smooth with the rough. They've done the hard bit – the breast beating, the gnashing of teeth, the witch hunts, the sulking; they've been taunted by the rugby brotherhood, even the Poms – the masters of uninspiring rugby and the team everyone loves to hate – who've been able to gloat and wave their 2003 World Cup victory in New Zealand's face.

The suffering has been intense. It has been prolonged and has chewed away at the nation for far too long. The pain has been real, the inquests into the repeated failures torturous. Each World Cup defeat has been felt in the soul. The wounds have not been superficial.

Can New Zealanders really end all that in 2011, just shrug and move on? Would that be cathartic? Would that be the right way to end 24 years of waiting? Is relief really going to be all that can be mustered?

Hopefully not, because that wouldn't be healthy. It wouldn't be right to have obsessed about this phenomenon for so long and then pretend it was never really that big a deal anyway. We all know it's been a very big deal. The continued failure has been discussed around water coolers across New Zealand; lunches have gone on too long in search of answers; blokes have stared into their beer and pleaded with their mates to tell them why.

And it hasn't been confined to New Zealand: these same scenarios have played out in Sydney, Brisbane, Edinburgh and London – anywhere Kiwis are living in numbers.

This has been a truly fascinating study, trying to determine why the All Blacks haven't been able to win a World Cup since 1987. But enough is enough. All good things have to come to an end and this is a story that needs to be put to bed. It's kind of scary to think what might happen if the All Blacks fail again in 2011. There are times when it feels like New Zealanders have actually come to enjoy the pain of defeat – that this four-yearly baring of the soul has become an eagerly anticipated ritual, an event in itself.

Only very occasionally, though, does it feel like a useful part of the landscape. The rest of the time it feels a little too real, a little too close to the surface for comfort. Normal life will only resume when the All Blacks actually do what they're supposed to do and win the blessed thing.

To be asked to hold on for another four years could break this country's spirit; it could lead to riots – well, probably not, but there might be an angry edge to the grieving. Another collapse could see everyone – convinced that the All Blacks will never again win the World Cup – lose all hope. Everyone might just stop thinking about the World Cup, write it off as an event for other nations. The New Zealand Rugby Union's obsession might die an instant death. If it doesn't, they will be in serious danger of going stark raving mad – 28 years of waiting can do that.

For the sake of New Zealand's mental health, it would be best if the All Blacks cruised through to the final of the next World Cup playing expansive, creative rugby and then blitzed the final with a flawless, perfect performance. The victory should be met with nothing but euphoria. Grown men should hug and kiss; Graham Henry, if he is still coach, should be awarded a knighthood right then and there, and give one to Richie McCaw too; hell, the assistant coaches can have them, the bag man, the guy who drives the team bus to Eden Park – it's going to be a time to be generous. It will be a time to be proud, to be vocal, to be emotional. It will be the time the All Blacks deliver. It has to be – New Zealand might not be able to deal with anything else.